Information Security: Principles and Practices

Second Edition

Mark S. Merkow
Jim Breithaupt

800 East 96th Street, Indianapolis, Indiana 46240 USA

Information Security: Principles and Practices, Second Edition

Copyright © 2014 by Pearson Education, Inc.

ISBN-13: 978-0-7897-5325-0
ISBN-10: 0-7897-5325-1

Library of Congress Control Number: 2014937271

Printed in the United States of America

Second Printing: July 2015

Trademarks

Warning and Disclaimer

Special Sales

For information about buying this title in bulk quantities, or for special sales opportunities (which may include electronic versions; custom cover designs; and content particular to your business, training goals, marketing focus, or branding interests), please contact our corporate sales department at corpsales@pearsoned.com or (800) 382-3419.

For government sales inquiries, please contact governmentsales@pearsoned.com.

For questions about sales outside the U.S., please contact international@pearsoned.com.

Associate Publisher
Dave Dusthimer

Acquisitions Editor
Betsy Brown

Development Editor
Jeff Riley

Managing Editor
Sandra Schroeder

Senior Project Editor
Tonya Simpson

Copy Editor
Krista Hansing Editorial Services, Inc.

Indexer
Publishing Works

Proofreader
Paula Lowell

Technical Editors
Tatyana Zidarov
Chris Crayton

Publishing Coordinator
Vanessa Evans

Cover Designer
Alan Clements

Compositor
Trina Wurst

Contents at a Glance

Preface xiii

1 Why Study Information Security? 2

2 Information Security Principles of Success 18

3 Certification Programs and the Common Body of Knowledge 36

4 Governance and Risk Management 54

5 Security Architecture and Design 80

6 Business Continuity Planning and Disaster Recovery Planning 110

7 Law, Investigations, and Ethics 126

8 Physical Security Control 146

9 Operations Security 166

10 Access Control Systems and Methodology 182

11 Cryptography 200

12 Telecommunications, Network, and Internet Security 224

13 Software Development Security 260

14 Securing the Future 280

A Common Body of Knowledge 292

B Security Policy and Standards Taxonomy 302

C Sample Policies 306

D HIPAA Security Rule Standards 320

Index 324

Table of Contents

Preface xiii

Chapter 1: Why Study Information Security? 2

Introduction. 2

The Growing Importance of IT Security and New Career Opportunities 3

    An Increase in Demand by Government and Private Industry. 4

Becoming an Information Security Specialist 4

    Schools Are Responding to Demands. 6

    The Importance of a Multidisciplinary Approach 7

Contextualizing Information Security 7

    Information Security Careers Meet the Needs of Business. 8

Summary. 11

Test Your Skills. 11

Chapter 2: Information Security Principles of Success 18

Introduction. 18

Principle 1: There Is No Such Thing As Absolute Security 19

Principle 2: The Three Security Goals Are Confidentiality, Integrity,
and Availability 20

    Integrity Models. 21

    Availability Models. 21

Principle 3: Defense in Depth as Strategy 22

Principle 4: When Left on Their Own, People Tend to Make the Worst
Security Decisions 24

Principle 5: Computer Security Depends on Two Types of Requirements:
Functional and Assurance. 24

Principle 6: Security Through Obscurity Is Not an Answer. 25

Principle 7: Security = Risk Management 25

Principle 8: The Three Types of Security Controls Are Preventative,
Detective, and Responsive 27

Principle 9: Complexity Is the Enemy of Security 29

Principle 10: Fear, Uncertainty, and Doubt Do Not Work in Selling Security . 29

Principle 11: People, Process, and Technology Are All Needed to
Adequately Secure a System or Facility. 29

Principle 12: Open Disclosure of Vulnerabilities Is Good for Security! 30

Summary. 31

Test Your Skills. 31

Chapter 3: Certification Programs and the Common Body of Knowledge   **36**

Introduction. 36

Certification and Information Security 37

International Information Systems Security Certifications Consortium (ISC)^2 . . 38

The Information Security Common Body of Knowledge. 39

    Information Security Governance and Risk Management. 39

    Security Architecture and Design 40

    Business Continuity and Disaster Recovery Planning 40

    Legal Regulations, Investigations, and Compliance. 41

    Physical (Environmental) Security 41

    Operations Security. 42

    Access Control 42

    Cryptography. 42

    Telecommunications and Network Security 43

    Software Development Security 43

Other Certificate Programs in the IT Security Industry 44

    Certified Information Systems Auditor 44

    Certified Information Security Manager. 44

    Certified in Risk and Information Systems Control 44

    Global Information Assurance Certifications. 44

    (ISC)^2 Specialization Certificates 45

    CCFP: Certified Cyber Forensics Professional. 45

    HCISPP: HealthCare Information Security and Privacy Practitioner. . . . 45

    Vendor-Specific and Other Certification Programs 46

Summary. 47

Test Your Skills. 47

Chapter 4: Governance and Risk Management   **54**

Introduction. 54

Security Policies Set the Stage for Success 55

Understanding the Four Types of Policies. 57

Programme-Level Policies 57

Programme-Framework Policies 59

Issue-Specific Policies 60

System-Specific Policies 61

Developing and Managing Security Policies 62

Security Objectives 62

Operational Security 62

Policy Implementation. 63

Providing Policy Support Documents. 64

Regulations 64

Standards and Baselines 66

Guidelines 67

Procedures. 67

Suggested Standards Taxonomy 67

Asset and Data Classification. 67

Separation of Duties 68

Employment Hiring Practices. 69

Risk Analysis and Management. 70

Education, Training, and Awareness 72

Who Is Responsible for Security?. 73

Summary. 74

Test Your Skills 74

Chapter 5: Security Architecture and Design   **80**

Introduction. 80

Defining the Trusted Computing Base 81

Rings of Trust. 81

Protection Mechanisms in a TCB 84

System Security Assurance Concepts. 86

Goals of Security Testing 86

Formal Security Testing Models. 87

The Trusted Computer Security Evaluation Criteria 87

Division D: Minimal Protection 88

Division C: Discretionary Protection 88

Division B: Mandatory Protection 88

Division A: Verified Protection 90

The Trusted Network Interpretation of the TCSEC. 91

The Information Technology Security Evaluation Criteria 91

Comparing ITSEC to TCSEC 91

ITSEC Assurance Classes 92

The Canadian Trusted Computer Product Evaluation Criteria 93

The Federal Criteria for Information Technology Security 93

The Common Criteria 94

Protection Profile Organization. 95

Security Functional Requirements. 96

Evaluation Assurance Levels 98

The Common Evaluation Methodology 100

Confidentiality and Integrity Models 101

Bell-LaPadula Model. 101

Biba Integrity Model 102

Advanced Models 102

Summary. 104

Test Your Skills. 104

Chapter 6: Business Continuity Planning and Disaster Recovery Planning   110

Introduction. 110

Overview of the Business Continuity Plan and Disaster Recovery Plan 111

Why the BCP Is So Important 112

Types of Disruptive Events 113

Defining the Scope of the BCP 114

Creating the Business Impact Analysis. 114

Disaster Recovery Planning. 115

Identifying Recovery Strategies 116

Understanding Shared-Site Agreements. 116

Using Alternate Sites 116

Making Additional Arrangements. 117

Testing the DRP. 118

Summary. 120

Test Your Skills. 120

Chapter 7: Law, Investigations, and Ethics   **126**

Introduction. 126

Types of Computer Crime 127

How Cybercriminals Commit Crimes 128

The Computer and the Law. 129

Legislative Branch of the Legal System 130

Administrative Branch of the Legal System 130

Judicial Branch of the Legal System 130

Intellectual Property Law 131

Patent Law. 131

Trademarks 132

Trade Secrets. 132

Privacy and the Law. 133

International Privacy Issues 133

Privacy Laws in the United States 134

Computer Forensics. 135

The Information Security Professional's Code of Ethics. 136

Other Ethics Standards 137

Computer Ethics Institute. 138

Internet Activities Board: Ethics and the Internet. 138

Code of Fair Information Practices 139

Summary. 140

Test Your Skills. 140

Chapter 8: Physical Security Control   **146**

Introduction. 146

Understanding the Physical Security Domain 147

Physical Security Threats 148

Providing Physical Security 149

Summary. 160

Test Your Skills. 160

Chapter 9: Operations Security   **166**

   Introduction. 166

   Operations Security Principles 167

   Operations Security Process Controls 168

   Operations Security Controls in Action 170

      Software Support 171

      Configuration and Change Management 171

      Backups. 172

      Media Controls 172

      Documentation 174

      Maintenance 174

      Interdependencies. 175

   Summary. 177

   Test Your Skills. 177

Chapter 10: Access Control Systems and Methodology   **182**

   Introduction. 182

   Terms and Concepts 183

      Identification 183

      Authentication 183

      Least Privilege (Need to Know) 183

      Information Owner. 184

      Discretionary Access Control. 184

      Access Control Lists 184

      User Provisioning 194

      Mandatory Access Control. 185

      Role-Based Access Control 185

   Principles of Authentication. 186

      The Problems with Passwords. 186

      Multifactor Authentication. 188

   Biometrics. 189

   Single Sign-On 190

      Kerberos. 191

      Federated Identities 192

Remote User Access and Authentication. 192

    Remote Access Dial-In User Service. 193

    Virtual Private Networks 193

Summary. 194

Test Your Skills. 194

Chapter 11: Cryptography   **200**

Introduction. 200

Applying Cryptography to Information Systems 201

Basic Terms and Concepts 201

Strength of Cryptosystems 203

    Cryptosystems Answer the Needs of Today's E-Commerce. 205

    The Role of Keys in Cryptosystems. 206

Putting the Pieces to Work 209

    Digesting Data. 209

    Digital Certificates 212

Examining Digital Cryptography 214

    Hashing Functions. 214

    Block Ciphers 214

    Implementations of PPK Cryptography. 215

Summary. 218

Test Your Skills. 218

Chapter 12: Telecommunications, Network, and Internet Security   **224**

Introduction. 224

An Overview of Network and Telecommunications Security 225

Network Security in Context 226

The Open Systems Interconnection Reference Model 226

    The Protocol Stack 226

    The OSI Reference Model and TCP/IP 229

    The OSI Model and Security 231

Data Network Types. 233

    Local Area Networks. 233

    Wide Area Networks 233

    Internet. 233

Intranet 234

Extranet 234

Protecting TCP/IP Networks 234

Basic Security Infrastructures 235

Routers. 236

Firewalls 237

Intrusion Detection Systems 245

Intrusion Prevention Systems. 248

Virtual Private Networks. 249

IPSec 249

Encapsulating Security Protocol 251

Security Association 251

Internet Security Association and Key Management Protocol 252

Security Policies 252

IPSec Key Management 253

Applied VPNs. 253

Cloud Computing. 254

Summary. 255

Test Your Skills. 255

Chapter 13: Software Development Security   **260**

Introduction. 260

The Practice of Software Engineering 261

Software Development Life Cycles. 261

Don't Bolt Security On—Build It In 263

Catch Problems Sooner Rather Than Later 264

Requirements Gathering and Analysis 265

Systems Design and Detailed Design 266

Design Reviews 267

Development (Coding) Phase. 268

Testing 270

Deployment 270

Security Training 272

Measuring the Secure Development Program. 272

    Open Software Assurance Maturity Model (OpenSAMM) 272

    Building Security in Maturity Model (BSIMM) 272

Summary. 273

Test Your Skills. 273

Chapter 14: Securing the Future   **280**

Introduction. 280

Operation Eligible Receiver 281

Carders, Account Takeover, and Identity Theft 282

    Some Definitions. 282

    ZeuS Banking Trojan. 282

    Phishing and Spear Phishing 283

    Other Trends in Internet (In)Security 284

    The Year (Decade?) of the Breach 284

The Rosy Future for InfoSec Specialists 285

Summary. 286

Test Your Skills. 286

Appendix A: Common Body of Knowledge   **292**

Access Control. 292

Telecommunications and Network Security 293

Information Security Governance and Risk Management 294

Software Development Security 295

Cryptography 296

Security Architecture and Design 297

Operations Security 298

Business Continuity and Disaster Recovery Planning. 299

Legal Regulations, Investigations, and Compliance 300

Physical (Environmental) Security. 301

Appendix B: Security Policy and Standards Taxonomy   **302**

Appendix C: Sample Policies   **306**

Sample Computer Acceptable Use Policy. 306

    1.0.0 Acceptable Use Policy 306

Sample Email Use Policy 310

    1.0.0 Email Use Policy 310

Sample Password Policy 312

    1.0.0 Password Policy 312

Sample Wireless (WiFi) Use Policy 317

    1.0.0 Wireless Communication Policy 317

Appendix D: HIPAA Security Rule Standards   **320**

HIPAA Security Standards 320

Administrative Procedures 321

Physical Safeguards 321

Technical Security Services 322

Technical Security Mechanisms 322

Index   **324**

Preface

When teaching a complex and ever-changing discipline such as information security, students are best served by beginning with a high-level understanding of the subject before they tackle the details. A solid grasp of the objectives, terminology, principles, and frameworks will help them understand how to place issues in a proper context for determining working solutions. That is the goal of this text: to introduce students to the most important topics of information security and pique their interest to learn more.

The body of knowledge (as it is called in the IT security industry) is vast, deep, and, at times, baffling. Solutions are not always straightforward because the problems they address are rarely intuitive. No cookbook or universal recipe for IT security success exists. Ideally, protecting computer systems from attacks and unauthorized access means anticipating problems and devising strategies to address how people, processes, and technologies interact. The goal, although not always realistic, is to prevent these problems from happening instead of simply reacting to them as so many organizations do today.

This is rarely easy.

This book navigates the ocean of information technology (IT) security issues while keeping the technical jargon to a minimum. Chapters are ordered to follow the major "domains" of the Common Body of Knowledge, to help prepare students for a more detailed examination of the topics, if that is their desire.

If you decide to enter the field of information security, you'll find this book helpful in charting your course in joining the ranks of professionals and specialists in information security.

About the Authors

Mark Merkow, CISSP, CISM, CSSLP, is a technical director for a Fortune 100 financial services firm, where he works on implementing and operating a software security practice for the enterprise. He has more than 35 years of IT experience, including 20 years in IT security. Mark has worked in a variety of roles, including applications development, systems analysis and design, security engineering, and security management. Mark holds a master's degree in decision and info systems from Arizona State University (ASU), a master's of education in Distance Learning from ASU, and a bachelor's degree in Computer Info Systems from ASU.

Jim Breithaupt is a data integrity manager for a major bank, where he manages risk for a large data mart. He has more than 30 years of data processing experience and has co-authored several other books on information systems and information security, along with Mark Merkow.

Acknowledgments

From Mark Merkow:

To begin, I'm deeply grateful to my friend and co-author, Jim, who has an amazing ability to turn the obscure into the transparent. Without Jim, there would be no book.

Thanks to my wife, Amy Merkow, as always, for her positive attitude, full support, and unwavering belief in the written word.

I also want to thank our far-scattered children, Josh Merkow, Jasmine Merkow, Brandon Bohlman, and Caitlyn Bohlman, for their support throughout the writing process.

Tremendous thanks goes to Betsy Brown, Tonya Simpson, and the entire staff at Pearson, along with Jeff Riley at Box Twelve Communications, for their commitment to excellence, efficiency, and positive attitude, all of which make working with them a total pleasure.

Special thanks goes to my agent, Carole Jelen at Waterside Productions, for the remarkable effort that goes into book contracting and publication.

From Jim Breithaupt:

First, I would like to thank Mark Merkow for being the guiding light of every writing project he has asked me to share with him. If it weren't for Mark's extensive knowledge of data processing and his enthusiasm for our endeavors, this book, like all the others, would never have come to fruition. I would also like to acknowledge Margaret and my children, Faye and Bo, who are my joy and inspiration. Finally, I'd like to give a tip of the hat to Carole Jelen with Waterside Productions for her assistance, and to the fine technical reviewers and editors at Pearson for helping make this book possible.

We Want to Hear from You!

As the reader of this book, *you* are our most important critic and commentator. We value your opinion and want to know what we're doing right, what we could do better, what areas you'd like to see us publish in, and any other words of wisdom you're willing to pass our way.

We welcome your comments. You can email or write to let us know what you did or didn't like about this book—as well as what we can do to make our books better.

Please note that we cannot help you with technical problems related to the topic of this book.

When you write, please be sure to include this book's title and author as well as your name and email address. We will carefully review your comments and share them with the author and editors who worked on the book.

Email: feedback@pearsonitcertification.com

Mail: Pearson IT Certification
         ATTN: Reader Feedback
         800 East 96th Street
         Indianapolis, IN 46240 USA

Reader Services

Visit our website and register this book at www.pearsonitcertification.com/register for convenient access to any updates, downloads, or errata that might be available for this book.

Chapter 1

Why Study Information Security?

Chapter Objectives

After reading this chapter and completing the exercises, you will be able to do the following:

- Recognize the growing importance of information security specialists to the information technology (IT) infrastructure and see how this can translate into a rewarding career
- Develop a strategy for pursuing a career in information security
- Comprehend information security in the context of the mission of a business

Introduction

With the rapid advances in networked computer technology during the last few decades and the unprecedented growth of the Internet, the public has become increasingly aware of the threats to personal privacy and security through computer crime. Identity theft, pirated bank accounts, forgery—the list of electronic crimes is as unlimited as the imaginations of those who use technology in harmful and dangerous ways. As much as consumers and businesses like the convenience of the Internet and open computer networks, this ease of access also makes people vulnerable to technically savvy but unscrupulous thieves. To protect computers, networks, and the information they store, organizations are increasingly turning to information security specialists.

An information security specialist is more than a technician who prevents hackers from attacking a website. In fact, you might be surprised to learn that the discipline is actually as much a solid grounding in business management as it is an understanding of cryptography and firewalls, two of the tools security specialists use to protect information systems. In this book, we examine both practical and theoretical skills, but we begin by trying to answer the first question most students starting out in the field ask: Why study information security?

The Growing Importance of IT Security and New Career Opportunities

According to Chief Information Officers (www.cio.com), a website devoted to issues affecting CIOs and other information officers, information security is the process of protecting the confidentiality, integrity, and availability (CIA) of data from accidental or intentional misuse. This discipline is a combination of technical and nontechnical approaches designed to reduce the risk to information systems that have increasingly open system architectures. This means that as organizations open more parts of their systems to customers, business partners, and employees, they also open themselves to greater risk of attack from computer hackers. A bank that offers its customers an online, interactive website to manage checking accounts and credit cards opens itself to the threats of forged emails that appear to come from the bank (phishing) but are actually a clever attack to harvest the user IDs and passwords needed to access the site. After these are acquired, bank customers are surprised to learn that their accounts have been cleaned out, and they can't quite figure out why or know what to do about it.

Other attacks in recent years have included viruses, worm outbreaks, denial of service (DoS), and Trojan horse programs that prevent internal users from accessing the systems they need to perform their jobs. Security professionals then must find the source of the problem, eradicate it, and repair the damage it left behind.

Large corporations use the Internet to transmit data back and forth with business suppliers, referred to as business-to-business, or B2B, processing. A manufacturing company might transmit shipping information to a third-party website where business partners can view the status of their orders. An internal company Internet, or intranet, typically gives its employees the capability to access coverage information from a health provider. Increased services to both vendors and employees create worlds of possibilities in satisfying customer needs, but they also create risks where none existed before: risks to the confidentiality, integrity, and availability of confidential or sensitive data.

The goal of this text is not to make you an expert in the technical details of information systems security. Instead, you will gain a solid foundation in the *fundamental principles of information security* and learn where to go to find out more about a specific topic, perhaps in pursuit of a career in information security.

As custodians of this vast amount of information stored in corporate and public databases, information managers have created new positions within their organizations to address information security–related issues. Realizing that information security is the admission price for being in business, these managers have added to their already overwhelming duties the obligation to protect the confidentiality, integrity, and availability of personal information—terms that you will know by heart by the end of this text. Although concern for the well-being of society can be a powerful motivator for information security managers, increasing governmental regulation such as privacy legislation and the fear of unwanted publicity over a hacked site often are what drive these managers to action. No one, from the personal computer user on a laptop to the CIO of a major corporation, can afford to ignore the importance of information security.

But why should a concern over information security translate into a possible career in information security?

An Increase in Demand by Government and Private Industry

The U.S. Department of Labor predicts that the occupational outlook for computer and information systems managers will grow much faster than the average for all occupations. From 2012 to 2022, the number of information security analysts in the workforce alone is anticipated to grow from 75,000 to 102,000, or 36 percent (source: www.bls.gov/emp/ep_table_103.htm).

FYI: Corporate IT Security Jobs Pay

The 2013 Computerworld Salary Survey shows that information security specialists with one to five years of experience saw salary increases from $81,907 in 2012 to $84,243 in 2013 (including salary and bonuses; source: www.computerworld.com/s/salary-survey/tool/result).

Additionally, the specialized training of information security professionals coupled with the growing importance of security in general could result in even higher demand for expertly trained individuals. The U.S. Bureau of Labor Statistics predicts the following:

> The security of computer networks will continue to increase in importance as more business is conducted over the Internet. The security of the Nation's entire electronic infrastructure has come under renewed focus in light of recent threats. Organizations need to understand how their systems are vulnerable and how to protect their infrastructure and Internet sites from hackers, viruses, and other acts of cyber-terrorism. The emergence of "cyber-security" as a key issue facing most organizations should lead to strong growth for computer managers. Firms will increasingly hire cyber-security experts to fill key leadership roles in their information technology departments, because the integrity of their computing environment is of the utmost concern. As a result, there will be a high demand for managers proficient in computer security issues (source: www.collegegrad.com/careers/manag30.shtml).

Becoming an Information Security Specialist

A specialty in information security does not come easily. Serious students must be prepared for a challenging slate of classes in security architecture, laws and ethics, access control, disaster recovery planning, and other coursework that might not be an obvious prerequisite.

One major educational institution, Carnegie Mellon (www.cmu.edu), established the Information Network Institute (INI) in 1989 as a leading research and education center in the field of information networking.

The INI offers five graduate degree programs in the areas of information networking, information technology, and information security. The degree in information security prepares students to carry out these tasks:

- Identify the information security risks an organization faces

- Associate these risks with problems related to technology and human beings

- Identify and evaluate the technology tools available to minimize risk, reduce system vulnerabilities, and maintain computer services

- Oversee the development of a secure information security (IS) infrastructure

- Keep abreast of IS policies, laws, and market forces, and perform impact analysis for an organization

- Maintain professional growth in IS disciplines

Although the path to becoming an information security specialist is not rigidly defined, most experts in the field believe that the following steps are becoming increasingly important to a professional interested in entering the information security (InfoSec) world:

- Get the right certifications, most notably the Certified Information Systems Security Professional (CISSP) certification. However, other certifications such as the Global Information Assurance Certification (GIAC) from the SANS Institute, are increasingly sought-after by large IT organizations. GIAC offers 26 specialized security certifications ranging from the GIAC Security Essentials Certification (GSEC), which provides a foundation in basic security principles, to the more advanced GIAC Certified Forensic Analyst (GCFA), who specializes in advanced incident handling scenarios (you can learn more about such certificates at www.giac.org).

- Beginners or those early in their careers in IT Security might consider the Systems Security Certified Practitioner (SSCP) from (ISC)². The SSCP is considered the Baby Brother to the CISSP and covers 7 of the 10 CISSP Domains and has reduced requirements for experience and/or education (source: https://www.isc2.org/sscp/default.aspx).

- Consider earning a graduate degree in information security, preferably one that combines technical with business training, connecting the Denial of Service (DoS) attack with the Denial of Revenue (DNR) fallout.

- Increase your disaster recovery and risk management skills, as not all security threats are detected before they happen. The individual who understands how to keep an operation running after an attack is that much more valuable to an organization.

- Build a home laboratory using the freeware and shareware readily available to individual users. The proliferation of once-private domain software allows students to learn on their own as well as in the classroom.

- Give something back to the information security community by working with professional organizations and certification groups to develop best practices and enhance the Common Body of Knowledge.

- Get on a project working with strategic partners, something that will give you valuable experience working with vendors, business customers, and Internet service providers (ISPs) and broad exposure to the far-reaching issues of information security.

- Consider an internship in IS if you're still in school—good advice in any discipline.

- Take a second look at government jobs. Although some students may consider working for a government agency a less lucrative proposition than working in private industry, the fact is that the graying of the workforce is leading to a dearth of experienced and qualified personnel.

Schools Are Responding to Demands

Homeland security is a hot topic not only in corporate America. Higher education is also responding to the need with new and robust certificate programs, degrees, and special-interest courses.

Hundreds of community colleges, four-year universities, technical institutes, and postgraduate programs are offering degrees and certificates in emergency preparedness, counterterrorism, and security. Students study topics ranging from political science and psychology, to engineering and biotechnology so they can prepare for possible disasters, cyber and physical.

Many companies have added homeland security sectors and Critical Infrastructure Protection (CIP) programs to their organizations, and individuals educated in the field are in demand.

One program the Department of Homeland Security supports is Naval Postgraduate School for Homeland Defense and Security (www.chds.us). The school educates high-ranking emergency management and public safety officials about policy analysis, advanced strategy, and information technology. Some of the certificate programs and concentrations related to InfoSec majors include the following:

- At Ohio State University, students can get a degree in political science, sociology, or computer science with a concentration in homeland security, in which they focus on such areas as network security and bioterrorism.

- At George Washington University in Washington, D.C., students can earn certificates in crisis and disaster management, telecommunications, and national security. The certificates are offered through the school's Homeland Security Policy Institute.

- Northeastern University in Boston offers programs in the law enforcement aspect of homeland security through its College of Criminal Justice. The university also received a grant from the National Institute of Justice to educate students about al-Qaeda banking and the gray market, the practice of transferring money from abroad to other countries, possibly to finance illicit activities.

- Monroe Community College in Rochester, New York, has a $26 million Homeland Security Management Institute complete with a crime scene simulator, forensics lab, hazardous materials training area, and aircraft simulator. It also offers training that educates community members on what to do if disaster strikes.

The Importance of a Multidisciplinary Approach

A multidisciplinary approach describes the breadth of people's knowledge and experience across a wide variety of interests—scientific, liberal arts, business, communications, and so on. Those who are able to maintain a wide view of the world (or a business situation) tend to excel when working in information security.

Lee Kushner and Mike Murray of *Search Security Magazine* wrote an article describing information security as a popular career choice among information technology (IT) professionals. Because of the variety of skills needed, people with many different backgrounds are attracted to the field, and what used to be a cottage industry is becoming mainstream. With these changes in the industry, career management, career development, and career planning are vital to future success.

To have a successful information security career, one must have the skills of a technologist but be able to think like a business leader; this involves understanding how security benefits the organization's business goals and knowing how to network and make connections beyond just IT (source: http://searchsecurity.techtarget.com/tip/An-introduction-to-Information-Security-Career-Advisor).

What is the benefit of melding hard-core computer courses with nontechnology studies? The answer is perspective. Computer code is binary, but the real world isn't. Exposure to nontechnical areas gives InfoSec professionals a greater ability to address and solve the complex problems encountered in IT/IS environments. For instance, a computer science student could write a term paper on the history of cryptography and illustrate it with examples of the different encryption techniques intelligence agents have used throughout the ages. A programming class project could focus on the importance of good business practices and human resource management. In other words, information security specialists need to have a holistic view of the world around them and avoid a strictly technical orientation.

The bottom line? A wide range of educational experiences is a good foundation for an InfoSec career.

Contextualizing Information Security

As the world's computers become more interconnected, and as more people and companies rely on the global village to communicate and transact, systems become more exposed to successful break-in attempts. As noted by Bruce Schneier, Principal of Counterpane Internet Security Inc. and foremost expert and authority on computer security, "The only secure computer is one that is turned off, locked in a safe, and buried 20 feet down in a secret location—and I'm not completely confident of that one, either" (Schneier 1995).

Disconnected and buried computers don't serve anyone well, and eventually someone will connect one of these to the Internet. Understanding the risks in making these connections is comparable to launching an effective defense against a well-armed and well-prepared enemy. To defend yourself adequately, you need to prepare for anything the offense throws at you. This preparation begins with a comprehensive understanding of the security umbrella, as Figure 1.1 illustrates.

FIGURE 1.1   An umbrella of information security.

As you see in Figure 1.1, InfoSec is a discipline that's difficult to put your arms around. Each topic within the umbrella can easily fill an entire book, and many would require an encyclopedia for a more complete understanding. Information security draws upon the best practices and experiences from multiple domains, but it always begins with the nontechnical, human-centric aspects of a security posture. An organization's security posture defines its tolerance for risk and outlines how it plans to protect information and resources within its charge. This posture is documented in standards, guidelines, and procedures that must exist long before a single program is written or a computer is installed.

Information Security Careers Meet the Needs of Business

Companies are not spending millions of dollars in information security just for the sake of security. IT security is needed to protect the business both from itself and from outsiders who would cause it harm.

To support business operations, regardless of the industry, a number of common positions and career opportunities are needed to prevent and respond to business needs.

- Security administrators work alongside system administrators and database administrators to ensure that an appropriate separation of duties can prevent abuse of privilege when new computer systems are implemented and users begin to access these systems. The security administrators help to establish new user accounts, ensure that auditing mechanisms are present and operating as needed, ensure that communications between systems are securely implemented, and assist in troubleshooting problems and responding to incidents that could compromise confidentiality, integrity, or availability of the systems.

- Access coordinators are delegated the authority on behalf of a system owner to establish and maintain the user base that is permitted to access and use the system in the normal course of their job duties.

- Security architects and network engineers design and implement network infrastructures that are built with security in mind. Skills needed here include understanding firewall designs, designing and developing intrusion detection/prevention systems and processes, and determining how to configure servers, desktop computers, and mobile devices to comply with security policies.

- Security consultants work with project-development teams to perform risk analysis of new systems by balancing the needs of business with the threats that stem from opening up access to data or managing new information that could compromise the business if it fell into the wrong hands. Security consultants are usually internal personnel who are assigned to project-development teams and remain with the project from inception to implementation.

- Security testers are the white-hat hackers paid to test the security of newly acquired and newly developed or redeveloped systems. Testers who can mimic the activities of outside hackers are hired to find software problems and bugs before the system is made available. Their work reduces the likelihood that the system will be compromised when it's in day-to-day operating mode.

- Policymakers and standards developers are the people who look to outside regulators and executive management to set the tone and establish the specific rules of the road when interacting with or managing information systems. Policymakers formally encode the policies or management intentions in how information will be secured.

- Compliance officers check to see that employees remain in compliance with security policies and standards as they use information systems in their daily work. Compliance officers usually work with outside regulators when audits are conducted and are often charged with employee security training and awareness programs to help maintain compliance.

- Incident response team members are alerted when an intrusion or security incident occurs. They decide how to stop the attack or limit the damage as they collect and analyze forensics data while interacting with law enforcement personnel and executive management.

■ Governance and vendor managers are needed to ensure that outsourced functions are operating within security policies and standards. The IT industry continues to rely on off-shore developers, managed security services, and outsourced computer operations, so the growth of governance personnel is assured.

For a view of a typical structure and context of where IT security fits within a typical large corporation, see Figure 1.2.

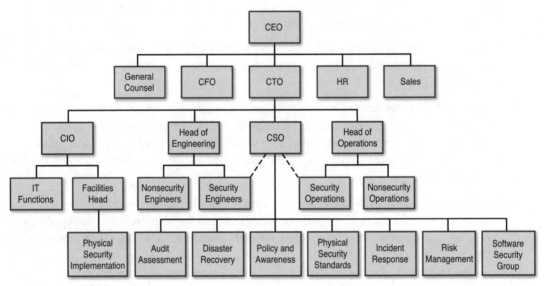

FIGURE 1.2   A typical information security organization structure.

> **Note**
>
> The job of security compliance/governance professional is listed as the seventh hottest job in the Forecast 2014 issue of *Computerworld Magazine*. Twenty-one percent of respondents to the *Computerworld* annual forecast survey indicated they would be hiring for this skill in the next 12 months (source: www.computerworld.com/s/article/9242548/8_hot_IT_skills_for_2014).

Studying InfoSec is challenging and often overwhelming to beginners. It's easy to get lost or confused when studying security because students must understand many areas. Instead of approaching the discipline with a focus on one or two major areas, students are better served by understanding InfoSec in context, as you'll begin to see in Chapter 2, "Information Security Principles of Success." This is best accomplished by understanding the principles, foundations, and durable, rarely changing "truths." With a principles-based view of InfoSec, you'll be able to analyze a security need in the right frame of reference or context so you can balance the needs of permitting access against the risk of allowing such access.

Summary

Technology experts are recognizing the increasing importance of a rigorous information security discipline. This need is based on the expanding use of technology, primarily the Internet, and the risks posed to networked systems, many of which are not secure and remain vulnerable to attacks from within and outside an organization.

This realization has led to a growing demand for professionals trained in information security. This is reflected in the growing job prospects for those seeking a career in information security, which look better than average for the year 2014 and beyond. The explosive growth of e-commerce and the pervasive personal and business uses of the Internet have created a growing demand for information security specialists.

Homeland security, critical infrastructure protection, and cyberterrorism have raised the stakes in the global village and underscored the need for constant vigilance and preventative, detective, and corrective controls. Threats must be countered sufficiently to enable companies to conduct business in a safe, secure, and embracing environment that focuses on meeting business and personal needs.

The fundamentals of information security are mostly commonsense principles, approaches, and concepts that work together like a symphony to provide the harmonious mix of risk and reward that modern business demands.

Test Your Skills

MULTIPLE-CHOICE QUESTIONS

1. Information security is primarily a discipline to manage the behavior of _____.

    A. Technology

    B. People

    C. Processes

    D. Organizations

2. Careers in information security are booming because of which of the following factors?

    A. Threats of cyberterrorism

    B. Government regulations

    C. Growth of the Internet

    D. All of the above

3. Which of the following best represents the three objectives of information security?

   A. Confidentiality, integrity, and availability

   B. Resilience, privacy, and safety

   C. Confidentiality, secrecy, and privacy

   D. Safety, access control, and secrecy

4. A program for information security should include which of the following elements?

   A. Security policies and procedures

   B. Intentional attacks only

   C. Unintentional attacks only

   D. None of the above

5. The growing demand for InfoSec specialists is occurring predominantly in which of the following types of organizations?

   A. Government

   B. Corporations

   C. Not-for-profit foundations

   D. All of the above

6. Which college curriculum is more appropriate for a career in information security?

   A. Business administration

   B. Computer information sciences

   C. Both A and B

   D. None of the above

7. What is meant by the phrase "the umbrella of information security"?

   A. When it rains, it pours.

   B. IS incorporates many different pursuits and disciplines.

   C. Just as it is bad luck to open an umbrella indoors, it is bad luck not to have an information security policy.

   D. IS policies, like umbrellas, should never be loaned to others because they are easily lost or misused.

8. The formal study of information security has accelerated primarily for what reason?

   A. Common breaches of computer systems

   B. The formation of the U.S. Department of Homeland Security

   C. Object-oriented programming

   D. Increasingly interconnected global networks

9. Which of the following would make an individual seeking a career in information security more marketable?

   A. CISSP certification

   B. GIAC certification

   C. Evaluating virus-protection software on a home computer

   D. All of the above

10. Which of the following statements is true of a career in information security?

    A. A career in information security has a better job growth outlook than other areas within IT.

    B. A career in information security is limited by the programming languages the candidate knows.

    C. A career in information security will eventually disappear with improvements in IS tools.

    D. A career in information security is a highly complex but narrow discipline.

11. Which of the following statements is true of a sound information security policy?

    A. A sound information security policy is worth any price.

    B. A sound information security policy is a balance between the cost of protecting information and the value of the information being protected.

    C. A sound information security policy belongs exclusively to the IT department.

    D. A sound information security policy results in unique practices and policies specific to the owning IT department.

12. Which of the following topics are part of an information security practice?

    A. Laws and ethical practices

    B. Access controls

    C. Security architecture

    D. All of the above

13. Which of the following roles helps development teams meet security requirements?

    A. Policymakers

    B. Compliance officers

    C. Security consultants

    D. Security architects

14. Who is responsible for ensuring that systems are auditable and protected from excessive privileges?

    A. Compliance officers

    B. Access coordinators

    C. Security administrators

    D. Policymakers

15. Which of the following roles is responsible for ensuring that third-party suppliers and outsourced functions remain in security compliance?

    A. Compliance officers

    B. Vendor managers

    C. Security architects

    D. Access coordinators

EXERCISES

EXERCISE 1.1: Looking at Salary Growth Among Information Security Careers

1. Visit *InformationWeek Magazine* online at http://reports.informationweek.com/search, and search for Security Salary Survey reports.

2. Compare the growth in salaries since the year 2011 in careers related to InfoSec. Record and graph the data in an Excel worksheet.

3. Identify the year-over-year increases in wages from 2011 to 2013.

EXERCISE 1.2: Searching for College Programs in IS

1. Search the Internet for certificate and degree programs in information security.

2. Search the Internet for certificate and degree programs in information assurance, and review some of the results.

3. Search the Internet for certificate and degree programs in network security, and review some of the results.

4. Search the Internet for certificate and degree programs in physical security, and review some of the results.

5. Identify common elements among these programs and, conversely, determine what makes each one unique.

EXERCISE 1.3: Comparing National Security Agency Education in Information Assurance Programs

1. Visit the National Security Agency Centers of Academic Excellence home page, at www.nsa.gov/ia/academic_outreach/nat_cae/index.shtml.

2. Review the criteria for measuring educational institutions that participate in the program.

3. Review the list of participating institutions, and select a college or university in your region or state.

4. Determine what components or aspects of the curriculum from that institution are common with the curriculum outlined in this chapter.

EXERCISE 1.4: Researching Local Organizations for Information Security

1. Search the Internet for local chapters of the following organizations, and answer these questions:

   InfraGARD

   (ISC)^2

   ISACA

2. Who do these organizations want to attract?

3. Which organization interests you the most? Why?

EXERCISE 1.5: Researching Education for Certifying in Information Security

1. Visit the Training Camp (www.trainingcamp.com/global).

2. Look for certification programs in information security.

3. Review the courses these programs offer.

4. Determine how these course offerings compare with state university programs in information security.

PROJECTS

PROJECT 1.1: Identifying the Multidisciplinary Approach

Based on what you have learned so far about information security, what do you think is meant by "information security in a business context"? Think about other seemingly unrelated coursework you are taking and examine ways in which it can help build a foundation for a background in information security.

PROJECT 1.2: **Getting Some Practical Advice**

Select a local business or organization with a sizeable IT department (more than 100 IT employees), and identify the person in charge of information security. Interview the individual and ask for practical advice about the kind of training and experience the IT security manager is looking for in candidates.

PROJECT 1.3: **Charting Your Course**

What area of information security seems most interesting to you at this point? What motivates you to investigate this area further for career opportunities?

Chapter 2

Information Security Principles of Success

Chapter Objectives

After reading this chapter and completing the exercises, you will be able to do the following:

- Build an awareness of 12 generally accepted basic principles of information security to help you determine how these basic principles apply to real-life situations
- Distinguish among the three main security goals
- Learn how to design and apply the principle of defense in depth
- Comprehend human vulnerabilities in security systems to better design solutions to counter them
- Explain the difference between functional requirements and assurance requirements
- Comprehend the fallacy of security through obscurity to avoid using it as a measure of security
- Comprehend the importance of risk-analysis and risk-management tools and techniques for balancing the needs of business
- Determine which side of the open disclosure debate you would take

Introduction

Many of the topics information technology students study in school carry directly from the classroom to the workplace. For example, new programming and systems analysis and design skills can often be applied on new systems-development projects as companies espouse cloud computing and mobile infrastructures that access internal systems.

Security is a little different. Although their technical skills are certainly important, the best security specialists combine their practical knowledge of computers and networks with general theories about security, technology, and human nature. These concepts, some borrowed from other fields, such as military defense, often take years of (sometimes painful) professional experience to learn. With a conceptual and principled view of information security, you can analyze a security need in the right frame of reference or context so you can balance the needs of permitting access against the risk of allowing such access. No two systems or situations are identical, and no cookbooks can specify how to solve certain security problems. Instead, you must rely on principle-based analysis and decision making.

This chapter introduces these key information security principles, concepts, and durable "truths."

Principle 1: There Is No Such Thing As Absolute Security

In 2003, the art collection of the Whitworth Gallery in Manchester, England, included three famous paintings by Van Gogh, Picasso, and Gauguin. Valued at more than $7 million, the paintings were protected by closed-circuit television (CCTV), a series of alarm systems, and 24-hour rolling patrols. Yet in late April 2003, thieves broke into the museum, evaded the layered security system, and made off with the three masterpieces. Several days later, investigators discovered the paintings in a nearby public restroom along with a note from the thieves saying, "The intention was not to steal, only to highlight the woeful security."

The burglars' lesson translates to the information security arena and illustrates the first principle of information security (IS): Given enough time, tools, skills, and inclination, a malicious person can break through any security measure. This principle applies to the physical world as well and is best illustrated with an analogy of safes or vaults that businesses commonly use to protect their assets. Safes are rated according to their resistance to attacks using a scale that describes how long it could take a burglar to open them. They are divided into categories based on the level of protection they can deliver and the testing they undergo. Four common classes of safe ratings are B-Rate, C-Rate, UL TL-15, and UL TL-30:

- **B-Rate:** B-Rate is a catchall rating for any box with a lock on it. This rating describes the thickness of the steel used to make the lockbox. No actual testing is performed to gain this rating.

- **C-Rate:** This is defined as a variably thick steel box with a 1-inch-thick door and a lock. No tests are conducted to provide this rating, either.

- **UL TL-15:** Safes with an Underwriters Laboratory (UL) TL-15 rating have passed standardized tests as defined in UL Standard 687 using tools and an expert group of safe-testing engineers. The UL TL-15 label requires that the safe be constructed of 1-inch solid steel or equivalent. The label means that the safe has been tested for a net working time of 15 minutes using "common hand tools, drills, punches hammers, and pressure applying devices." *Net working time* means that when the tool comes off the safe, the clock stops. Engineers exercise more than 50 different types of attacks that have proven effective for safecracking.

- **UL TL-30:** UL TL-30 testing is essentially the same as the TL-15 testing, except for the net working time. Testers get 30 minutes and a few more tools to help them gain access. Testing engineers usually have a safe's manufacturing blueprints and can disassemble the safe before the test begins to see how it works.

FYI: Confidentiality by Another Name

Confidentiality is sometimes referred to as the principle of least privilege, meaning that users should be given only enough privilege to perform their duties, and no more. Some other synonyms for confidentiality you might encounter include *privacy*, *secrecy*, and *discretion*.

As you learn in Chapter 5, "Security Architecture and Design," security testing of hardware and software systems employs many of the same concepts of safe testing, using computers and custom-developed testing software instead of tools and torches. The outcomes of this testing are the same, though: As with software, no safe is burglar proof; security measures simply buy time. Of course, buying time is a powerful tool. Resisting attacks long enough provides the opportunity to catch the attacker in the act and to quickly recover from the incident. This leads to the second principle.

FYI: Confidentiality Models

Confidentiality models are primarily intended to ensure that no unauthorized access to information is permitted and that accidental disclosure of sensitive information is not possible. Common confidentiality controls are user IDs and passwords.

Principle 2: The Three Security Goals Are Confidentiality, Integrity, and Availability

All information security measures try to address at least one of three goals:

- Protect the confidentiality of data
- Preserve the integrity of data
- Promote the availability of data for authorized use

These goals form the confidentiality, integrity, availability (CIA) triad, the basis of all security programs (see Figure 2.1). Information security professionals who create policies and procedures (often referred to as governance models) must consider each goal when creating a plan to protect a computer system.

FIGURE 2.1 The CIA triad.

FYI: CIA Triad

The principle of information security protection of confidentiality, integrity, and availability cannot be overemphasized: This is central to all studies and practices in IS. You'll often see the term *CIA triad* to illustrate the overall goals for IS throughout the research, guidance, and practices you encounter.

Integrity Models

Integrity models keep data pure and trustworthy by protecting system data from intentional or accidental changes. Integrity models have three goals:

- Prevent unauthorized users from making modifications to data or programs
- Prevent authorized users from making improper or unauthorized modifications
- Maintain internal and external consistency of data and programs

An example of integrity checks is balancing a batch of transactions to make sure that all the information is present and accurately accounted for.

Availability Models

Availability models keep data and resources available for authorized use, especially during emergencies or disasters. Information security professionals usually address three common challenges to availability:

- Denial of service (DoS) due to intentional attacks or because of undiscovered flaws in implementation (for example, a program written by a programmer who is unaware of a flaw that could crash the program if a certain unexpected input is encountered)

- Loss of information system capabilities because of natural disasters (fires, floods, storms, or earthquakes) or human actions (bombs or strikes)

- Equipment failures during normal use

Some activities that preserve confidentiality, integrity, and/or availability are granting access only to authorized personnel, applying encryption to information that will be sent over the Internet or stored on digital media, periodically testing computer system security to uncover new vulnerabilities, building software defensively, and developing a disaster recovery plan to ensure that the business can continue to exist in the event of a disaster or loss of access by personnel.

Principle 3: Defense in Depth as Strategy

A bank would never leave its assets inside an unguarded safe alone. Typically, access to the safe requires passing through layers of protection that might include human guards and locked doors with special access controls. Furthermore, the room where the safe resides could be monitored by closed-circuit television, motion sensors, and alarm systems that can quickly detect unusual activity. The sound of an alarm might trigger the doors to automatically lock, the police to be notified, or the room to fill with tear gas.

Layered security, as in the previous example, is known as defense in depth. This security is implemented in overlapping layers that provide the three elements needed to secure assets: prevention, detection, and response. Defense in depth also seeks to offset the weaknesses of one security layer by the strengths of two or more layers.

In the information security world, defense in depth requires layering security devices in a series that protects, detects, and responds to attacks on systems. For example, a typical Internet-attached network designed with security in mind includes routers, firewalls, and intrusion detection systems (IDS) to protect the network from would-be intruders; employs traffic analyzers and real-time human monitors who watch for anomalies as the network is being used to detect any breach in the layers of protection; and relies on automated mechanisms to turn off access or remove the system from the network in response to the detection of an intruder.

Finally, the security of each of these mechanisms must be thoroughly tested before deployment to ensure that the integrated system is suitable for normal operations. After all, a chain is only as good as its weakest link.

In Practice

Phishing for Dollars

Phishing is another good example of how easily intelligent people can be duped into breaching security. Phishing is a dangerous Internet scam, and is becoming increasingly dangerous as targets are selected using data available from social media and enable a malicious person to build a profile of the target to better convince him the scam is real. A phishing scam typically operates as follows:

- The victim receives an official-looking email message purporting to come from a trusted source, such as an online banking site, PayPal, eBay, or other service where money is exchanged, moved, or managed.

- The email tells the user that his or her account needs updating immediately or will be suspended within a certain number of days.

- The email contains a URL (link) and instructs the user to click on the link to access the account and update the information. The link text appears as though it will take the user to the expected site. However, the link is actually a link to the attacker's site, which is made to look exactly like the site the user expects to see.

- At the spoofed site, the user enters his or her credentials (ID and password) and clicks Submit.

- The site returns an innocuous message, such as "We're sorry—we're unable to process your transaction at this time," and the user is none the wiser.

- At this point, the victim's credentials are stored on the attacker's site or sent via email to the perpetrator, where they can be used to log in to the *real* banking or exchange site and empty the account before the user knows what happened.

Phishing and resultant ID theft and monetary losses are on the increase and will begin to slow only after the cycle is broken through awareness and education. Protect yourself by taking the following steps:

- Look for telltale signs of fraud: Instead of addressing you by name, a phishing email addresses you as "User" or by your email address; a legitimate message from legitimate companies uses your name as they know it.

- Do not click on links embedded in unsolicited finance-related email messages. A link might look legitimate, but when you click on it, you could be redirected to the site of a phisher. If you believe that your account is in jeopardy, type in the known URL of the site in a new browser window and look for messages from the provider after you're logged in.

- Check with your provider for messages related to phishing scams that the company is aware of. Your bank or other financial services provider wants to make sure you don't fall victim and will often take significant measures to educate users on how to prevent problems.

Principle 4: When Left on Their Own, People Tend to Make the Worst Security Decisions

The primary reason identity theft, viruses, worms, and stolen passwords are so common is that people are easily duped into giving up the secrets technologies use to secure systems. Organizers of Infosecurity Europe, Britain's biggest information technology security exhibition, sent researchers to London's Waterloo Station to ask commuters to hand over their office computer passwords in exchange for a free pen. Three-quarters of respondents revealed the information immediately, and an additional 15 percent did so after some gentle probing. Study after study like this one shows how little it takes to convince someone to give up their credentials in exchange for trivial or worthless goods.

Principle 5: Computer Security Depends on Two Types of Requirements: Functional and Assurance

Functional requirements describe what a system *should* do. Assurance requirements describe how functional requirements should be implemented and tested. Both sets of requirements are needed to answer the following questions:

- Does the system do the right things (behave as promised)?
- Does the system do the right things in the right way?

These are the same questions that others in noncomputer industries face with verification and validation. Verification is the process of confirming that one or more predetermined requirements or specifications are met. Validation then determines the correctness or quality of the mechanisms used to meet the needs. In other words, you can develop software that addresses a need, but it might contain flaws that could compromise data when placed in the hands of a malicious user.

Consider car safety testing as an example. Verification testing for seat belt functions might include conducting stress tests on the fabric, testing the locking mechanisms, and making certain the belt will fit the intended application, thus completing the functional tests. Validation, or assurance testing, might then include crashing the car with crash-test dummies inside to "prove" that the seat belt is indeed safe when used under normal conditions and that it can survive under harsh conditions.

With software, you need both verification and validation answers to gain confidence in products before launching them into a wild, hostile environment such as the Internet. Most of today's commercial off-the-shelf (COTS) software and systems stop at the first step, verification, without bothering to test for obvious security vulnerabilities in the final product. Developers of software generally lack the wherewithal and motivation needed to try to break their own software. More often, developers test that the software meets the specifications in each function that is present but usually do not try to find ways to circumvent the software and make it fail. You learn more about security testing of software in Chapter 5.

Principle 6: Security Through Obscurity Is Not an Answer

Many people in the information security industry believe that if malicious attackers don't know how software is secured, security is better. Although this might seem logical, it's actually untrue. Security through obscurity means that hiding the details of the security mechanisms is sufficient to secure the system alone. An example of security through obscurity might involve closely guarding the written specifications for security functions and preventing all but the most trusted people from seeing it. Obscuring security leads to a false sense of security, which is often more dangerous than not addressing security at all.

If the security of a system is maintained by keeping the implementation of the system a secret, the entire system collapses when the first person discovers how the security mechanism works—and someone is always determined to discover these secrets. The better bet is to make sure no one mechanism is responsible for the security of the entire system. Again, this is defense in depth in everything related to protecting data and resources.

In Chapter 11, "Cryptography," you'll see how this principle applies and why it makes no sense to keep an algorithm for cryptography secret when the security of the system should rely on the cryptographic keys used to protect data or authenticate a user. You can also see this in action with the open-source movement: Anyone can gain access to program (source) code, analyze it for security problems, and then share with the community improvements that eliminate vulnerabilities and/or improve the overall security through simplification (see Principle 9).

Principle 7: Security = Risk Management

It's critical to understand that spending more on securing an asset than the intrinsic value of the asset is a waste of resources. For example, buying a $500 safe to protect $200 worth of jewelry makes no practical sense. The same is true when protecting electronic assets. All security work is a careful balance between the level of risk and the expected reward of expending a given amount of resources. Security is concerned not with eliminating all threats within a system or facility, but with eliminating known threats and minimizing losses if an attacker succeeds in exploiting a vulnerability. Risk analysis and risk management are central themes to securing information systems. When risks are well understood, three outcomes are possible:

- The risks are mitigated (countered).
- Insurance is acquired against the losses that would occur if a system were compromised.
- The risks are accepted and the consequences are managed.

Risk assessment and risk analysis are concerned with placing an economic value on assets to best determine appropriate countermeasures that protect them from losses.

The simplest form of determining the degree of a risk involves looking at two factors:

- What is the consequence of a loss?
- What is the likelihood that this loss will occur?

Figure 2.2 illustrates a matrix you can use to determine the degree of a risk based on these factors.

Likelihood	**Consequences**				
	1. Insignificant	2. Minor	3. Moderate	4. Major	6. Catastrophic
A (almost certain)	High	High	Extreme	Extreme	Extreme
B (likely)	Moderate	High	High	Extreme	Extreme
C (moderate)	Low	Moderate	High	Extreme	Extreme
D (unlikely)	Low	Low	Moderate	High	Extreme
E (rare)	Low	Low	Moderate	High	High

FIGURE 2.2   Consequences/likelihood matrix for risk analysis.

After determining a risk rating, one of the following actions could be required:

- **Extreme risk:** Immediate action is required.
- **High risk:** Senior management's attention is needed.
- **Moderate risk:** Management responsibility must be specified.
- **Low risk:** Management is handled by routine procedures.

In the real world, risk management is more complicated than simply making a human judgment call based on intuition or previous experience with a similar situation. Recall that every system has unique security issues and considerations, so it's imperative to understand the specific nature of data the system will maintain, what hardware and software will be used to deploy the system, and the security skills of the development teams. Determining the likelihood of a risk coming to life requires understanding a few more terms and concepts:

- Vulnerability
- Exploit
- Attacker

Vulnerability refers to a known problem within a system or program. A common example in InfoSec is called the buffer overflow or buffer overrun vulnerability. Programmers tend to be trusting and not worry about who will attack their programs, but instead worry about who will use their programs legitimately. One feature of most programs is the capability for a user to "input" information or requests. The program instructions (source code) then contain an "area" in memory (buffer) for these inputs and act upon them when told to do so. Sometimes the programmer doesn't check to see if the input is proper or innocuous. A malicious user, however, might take advantage of this weakness and overload the input area with more information than it can handle, crashing or disabling the program. This is called buffer overflow, and it can permit a malicious user to gain control over the system. This common vulnerability with software must be addressed when developing systems. Chapter 13, "Software Development Security," covers this in greater detail.

An exploit is a program or "cookbook" on how to take advantage of a specific vulnerability. It might be a program that a hacker can download over the Internet and then use to search for systems that contain the vulnerability it's designed to exploit. It might also be a series of documented steps on how to exploit the vulnerability after an attacker finds a system that contains it.

An attacker, then, is the link between a vulnerability and an exploit. The attacker has two characteristics: skill and will. Attackers either are skilled in the art of attacking systems or have access to tools that do the work for them. They have the will to perform attacks on systems they do not own and usually care little about the consequences of their actions.

In applying these concepts to risk analysis, the IS practitioner must anticipate who might want to attack the system, how capable the attacker might be, how available the exploits to a vulnerability are, and which systems have the vulnerability present.

Risk analysis and risk management are specialized areas of study and practice, and the IS professionals who concentrate in these areas must be skilled and current in their techniques. You can find more on risk management in Chapter 4, "Governance and Risk Management."

Principle 8: The Three Types of Security Controls Are Preventative, Detective, and Responsive

Controls (such as documented processes) and countermeasures (such as firewalls) must be implemented as one or more of these previous types, or the controls are not there for the purposes of security. Shown in another triad, the principle of defense in depth dictates that a security mechanism serve a purpose by preventing a compromise, detecting that a compromise or compromise attempt is underway, or responding to a compromise while it's happening or after it has been discovered.

Referring to the example of the bank vault in Principle 3, access to a bank's safe or vault requires passing through layers of protection that might include human guards and locked doors with special access controls (prevention). In the room where the safe resides, closed-circuit televisions, motion sensors, and alarm systems quickly detect any unusual activity (detection). The sound of an alarm could trigger the doors to automatically lock, the police to be notified, or the room to fill with tear gas (response).

These controls are the basic toolkit for the security practitioner who mixes and matches them to carry out the objectives of confidentiality, integrity, and/or availability by using people, processes, or technology (see Principle 11) to bring them to life.

In Practice

How People, Process, and Technology Work in Harmony

To illustrate how people, process, and technology work together to secure systems, let's take a look a how the security department grants access to users for performing their duties. The process, called user access request, is initiated when a new user is brought into the company or switches department or role within the company. The user access request form is initially completed by the user and approved by the manager.

When the user access request is approved, it's routed to information security access coordinators to process using the documented procedures for granting access. After access is granted and the process for sharing the user's ID and password is followed, the system's technical access control system takes over. It protects the system from unauthorized access by requiring a user ID and password, and it prevents password guessing from an unauthorized person by limiting the number of attempts to three before locking the account from further access attempts.

In Practice

To Disclose or Not to Disclose—That Is the Question!

Having specific knowledge of a security vulnerability gives administrators the knowledge to properly defend their systems from related exploits. The ethical question is, how should that valuable information be disseminated to the good guys while keeping it away from the bad guys? The simple truth is, you can't really do this. Hackers tend to communicate among themselves far better than professional security practitioners ever could. Hackers know about most vulnerabilities long before the general public gets wind of them. By the time the general public is made aware, the hacker community has already developed a workable exploit and disseminated it far and wide to take advantage of the flaw before it can be patched or closed down.

Because of this, open disclosure benefits the general public far more than is acknowledged by the critics who claim that it gives the bad guys the same information.

Here's the bottom line: If you uncover an obvious problem, raise your hand and let someone who can do something about it know. If you see something, say something. You'll sleep better at night!

Principle 9: Complexity Is the Enemy of Security

The more complex a system gets, the harder it is to secure. With too many "moving parts" or interfaces between programs and other systems, the system or interfaces become difficult to secure while still permitting them to operate as intended. You learn in Chapter 5 how complexity can easily get in the way of comprehensive testing of security mechanisms.

Principle 10: Fear, Uncertainty, and Doubt Do Not Work in Selling Security

At one time, "scaring" management into spending resources on security to avoid the unthinkable was effective. The tactic of fear, uncertainty, and doubt (FUD) no longer works: Information security and IT management is too mature. Now IS managers must justify all investments in security using techniques of the trade. Although this makes the job of information security practitioners more difficult, it also makes them more valuable because of management's need to understand what is being protected and why. When spending resources can be justified with good, solid business rationale, security requests are rarely denied.

Principle 11: People, Process, and Technology Are All Needed to Adequately Secure a System or Facility

As described in Principle 3, "Defense in Depth as Strategy," the information security practitioner needs a series of countermeasures and controls to implement an effective security system. One such control might be dual control, a practice borrowed from the military. The U.S. Department of Defense uses a dual control protocol to secure the nation's nuclear arsenal. This means that at least two on-site people must agree to launch a nuclear weapon. If one person were in control, he or she could make an error in judgment or act maliciously for whatever reason. But with dual control, one person acts as a countermeasure to the other: Chances are less likely that both people will make an error in judgment or act maliciously. Likewise, no one person in an organization should have the ability to control or close down a security activity. This is commonly referred to as separation of duties.

Process controls are implemented to ensure that different people can perform the same operations exactly in the same way each time. Processes are documented as procedures on how to carry out an activity related to security. The process of configuring a server operating system for secure operations is documented as one or more procedures that security administrators use and can be verified as done correctly.

Just as the information security professional might establish process controls to make sure that a single person cannot gain complete control over a system, you should never place all your faith in technology. Technology can fail, and without people to notice and fix technical problems, computer systems would stall permanently. An example of this type of waste is installing an expensive firewall system (a network perimeter security device that blocks traffic) and then turning around and opening all the ports that are intended to block certain traffic from entering the network.

People, process, and technology controls are essential elements of several areas of practice in information technology (IT) security, including operations security, applications development security, physical security, and cryptography. These three pillars of security are often depicted as a three-legged stool (see Figure 2.3).

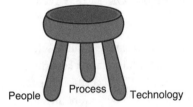

People   Process   Technology

FIGURE 2.3   The people, process, and technology triad.

Principle 12: Open Disclosure of Vulnerabilities Is Good for Security!

A raging and often heated debate within the security community and software developing centers concerns whether to let users know about a problem before a fix or patch can be developed and distributed. Principle 6 tells us that security through obscurity is not an answer: Keeping a given vulnerability secret from users and from the software developer can only lead to a false sense of security. Users have a right to know about defects in the products they purchase, just as they have a right to know about automobile recalls because of defects. The need to know trumps the need to keep secrets, to give users the right to protect themselves.

Summary

To be most effective, computer security specialists not only must know the technical side of their jobs, but also must understand the principles behind information security. No two situations that security professionals review are identical, and there are no recipes or cookbooks on universal security measures. Because each situation calls for a distinct judgment to address the specific risks inherent in information systems, principles-based decision making is imperative. An old saying goes, "If you only have a hammer, every problem looks like a nail." This approach simply does not serve today's businesses, which are always striving to balance risk and reward of access to electronic records. The goal is to help you create a toolkit and develop the skills to use these tools like a master craftsman. Learn these principles and take them to heart, and you'll start out much further along than your peers who won't take the time to bother learning them!

As you explore the rest of the Common Body of Knowledge (CBK) domains, try to relate the practices you find to one or more of these. For example, Chapter 8, "Physical Security Control," covers physical security, which addresses how to limit access to physical spaces and hardware to authorized personnel. This helps prevent breaches in confidentiality, integrity, and availability, and implements the principle of defense in depth. As you will find, these principles are mixed and matched to describe why certain security functions and operations exist in the real world of IT.

Test Your Skills

MULTIPLE CHOICE QUESTIONS

1. Which of the following represents the three goals of information security?

    A. Confidentiality, integrity, and availability

    B. Prevention, detection, and response

    C. People controls, process controls, and technology controls

    D. Network security, PC security, and mainframe security

2. Which of the following terms best describes the assurance that data has not been changed unintentionally due to an accident or malice?

    A. Availability

    B. Confidentiality

    C. Integrity

    D. Auditability

3. Related to information security, confidentiality is the opposite of which of the following?

   A. Closure

   B. Disclosure

   C. Disaster

   D. Disposal

4. The CIA triad is often represented by which of the following?

   A. Triangle

   B. Diagonal

   C. Ellipse

   D. Circle

5. Defense in depth is needed to ensure that which three mandatory activities are present in a security system?

   A. Prevention, response, and prosecution

   B. Response, collection of evidence, and prosecution

   C. Prevention, detection, and response

   D. Prevention, response, and management

6. Which of the following statements is true?

   A. The weakest link in any security system is the technology element.

   B. The weakest link in any security system is the process element.

   C. The weakest link in any security system is the human element.

   D. Both B and C

7. Which of the following best represents the two types of IT security requirements?

   A. Functional and logical

   B. Logical and physical

   C. Functional and assurance

   D. Functional and physical

8. Security functional requirements describe which of the following?

   A. What a security system should do by design

   B. What controls a security system must implement

   C. Quality assurance description and testing approach

   D. How to implement the system

9. Which of the following statements is true?

   A. Security assurance requirements describe how to test the system.

   B. Security assurance requirements describe how to program the system.

   C. Security assurance requirements describe to what degree the testing of the system is conducted.

   D. Security assurance requirements describe implementation considerations.

10. Which of the following terms best describes the probability that a threat to an information system will materialize?

   A. Threat

   B. Vulnerability

   C. Hole

   D. Risk

11. Which of the following terms best describes the absence or weakness in a system that may possibly be exploited?

   A. Vulnerability

   B. Threat

   C. Risk

   D. Exposure

12. Which of the following statements is true?

   A. Controls are implemented to eliminate risk and eliminate the potential for loss.

   B. Controls are implemented to mitigate risk and reduce the potential for loss.

   C. Controls are implemented to eliminate risk and reduce the potential for loss.

   D. Controls are implemented to mitigate risk and eliminate the potential for loss.

13. Which of the following terms best describes a cookbook on how to take advantage of a vulnerability?

   A. Risk

   B. Exploit

   C. Threat

   D. Program

14. Which of the following represents the three types of security controls?

   A. People, functions, and technology

   B. People, process, and technology

   C. Technology, roles, and separation of duties

   D. Separation of duties, processes, and people

15. Which of the following statements is true?

   A. Process controls for IT security include assignment of roles for least privilege.

   B. Process controls for IT security include separation of duties.

   C. Process controls for IT security include documented procedures.

   D. All of the above

EXERCISES

EXERCISE 2.1: Understanding the Importance of Information Confidentiality

Why is confidentiality important to corporate information? What kinds of abuses can you think of in the absence of controls on confidentiality? What criminal activities could be reduced or eliminated if confidentiality controls were effectively implemented?

EXERCISE 2.2: Evaluating Real-World Defense in Depth

Find some analogies to the principle of defense in depth in the physical world, and make some diagrams of the mechanism you locate. Consider how a bank implements defense in depth and how corporations protect themselves from intruders entering their buildings.

EXERCISE 2.3: Avoiding Security Through Obscurity

Why is security through obscurity a bad idea for the overall security of a system?

EXERCISE 2.4: Identifying a Phishing Scam

Go to www.opendns.com/phishing-quiz/ and take the "Think You Can Outsmart Internet Scammers?" quiz. How well did you perform at identifying phishing scams?

EXERCISE 2.5: Evaluating Risk Management

Every day, you make risk-management decisions in your daily life. Should you get in the car and drive to the store? Should you jaywalk or cross at the light? Should you get on that airplane? Think about the risk-management decisions you make when using your PC:

1. What kinds of judgments do you make before downloading a piece of software?

2. What kinds of judgments do you make before writing an email to your boss?

3. What mental steps do you go through before taking some action?

PROJECTS

PROJECT 2.1: Understanding Email-Borne Viruses

1. Visit one or more of the antivirus software developer sites (Symantec, MacAfee, Computer Associates, Trend Micro, and so forth), and see if you can identify which viruses and worms require a user to click on an email attachment to replicate.

2. Trace the sophistication of the virus writers over time, and try to determine how they circumvent any improvements in user awareness of and education toward preventing viruses from spreading.

PROJECT 2.2: Researching Hackers

Open disclosure of software vulnerabilities is often associated with gray-hat hackers, described as security researchers who aren't particular about who learns about their findings. Research the three types of hackers (white hat, gray hat, and black hat), and try to determine their typical positions on full disclosure of software problems before patches or new versions of the software are made available in the marketplace. Use Google or your favorite Internet search engine with a query of "Open Disclosure of Software Vulnerabilities" to help you formulate your answers.

PROJECT 2.3: Comparing Physical and Virtual Risk-Management Techniques

1. How is risk management for physical systems similar to risk management for computer systems?

2. How are the two different?

3. What skill sets are required for each type?

Chapter | **3**

Certification Programs and the Common Body of Knowledge

Chapter Objectives

After reading this chapter and completing the exercises, you will be able to do the following:

- Analyze the Certified Information Systems Security Professional (CISSP) certificate program as the gold standard in information technology (IT) security certification
- Define and describe the role of the International Information Systems Security Certifications Consortium
- Distinguish the contents of the 10 domains of the Common Body of Knowledge
- Distinguish the CISSP from other security certification programs in the industry

Introduction

This chapter outlines the more prominent information security certifications available to individuals interested in becoming security professionals or ones already in the field who are interested in advancing their careers. To help you in those efforts, we begin with the most prominent and most demanded certification available to professionals and practitioners: the Certified Information Systems Security Professional (CISSP) and the Systems Security Certified Practitioner (SSCP) certificates, administered by The International Information Systems Security Certifications Consortium (IISSCC, or [ISC]²).

The CISSP and SSCP are based on formal testing of content knowledge and practical experience found in the security professional's Common Body of Knowledge (CBK). The CBK is a compilation and distillation of all security information collected internationally that is relevant to information security professionals. CISSPs are information assurance professionals who define the architecture, design, management and/or controls that ensure the security of business environments. The CISSP was the first certification in the field of information security to meet the stringent requirements of the ISO/IEC Standard 17024.

This book uses the CBK and its 10 domains as the organizing framework to introduce the field of information security (commonly referred to as InfoSec) and to help students decide what area(s) of InfoSec they might want to pursue.

When you get an idea of the structure of the CBK, you can find other industry certification programs that are complementary to the CISSP and SSCP.

Certification and Information Security

Information security professionals invest corporate resources in information assets such as technology, architecture, and processes. Industry standards, ethics, and certification of information systems (IS) professionals and practitioners are critical to ensuring that a high standard of security is achieved. Certification benefits both the employer and the employee.

Benefits of (ISC)² certification to employers include the following:

- **Global recognition:** (ISC)² certifications are recognized internationally, allowing employers to evaluate candidates on a level playing field throughout the world. The credentials also provide increased credibility for your organization when working with vendors and contractors.

- **Common language:** Vendor-specific credentials can be limiting when new technologies are introduced. Conversely, (ISC)² credential holders speak a universal language, circumventing ambiguity with industry-accepted terms and practices.

- **Experience:** Credentialed professionals have often gained years of experience in the industry and have met a prescribed educational standard.

- **Continuing professional education:** Certificate holders must continue their education every year to maintain their certification. This ensures that employers are hiring only individuals who are most prepared to handle the onslaught of ever-changing information security challenges with new and innovative alternatives to the status quo.

- **Certification mandate:** More organizations are requiring certified information security personnel. Service providers and subcontractors are also choosing certified staff with superior credentials.

The benefits of (ISC)² certification to professionals include the following:

- Confirmed working knowledge of information security; tested and verifiable proof of proficiency in your field

- Higher salary and promotion potential

- Entry into one of the largest communities of recognized information security professionals in the world

- Access to unparalleled global resources, peer networking, mentoring, and a wealth of ongoing information security opportunities

Oversight and governance of the professional certification process are needed to help maintain its relevance and currency and to aid professionals in networking with other professionals for collaboration in problem solving and job seeking. To meet that need, the (ISC)² organization was created.

International Information Systems Security Certifications Consortium (ISC)²

The (ISC)² is a global, not-for-profit organization dedicated to these goals:

- Maintaining a Common Body of Knowledge for information security

- Certifying industry professionals and practitioners according to the international IS standard

- Administering training and certification examinations

- Ensuring that credentials are maintained, primarily through continuing education

Governments, corporations, centers of higher learning, and other organizations worldwide demand a common platform to use in administering and mastering the dynamic nature of information security. (ISC)² helps fulfill these needs. Thousands of IS professionals in more than 60 countries worldwide have attained certification in one of the two primary designations administered by the (ISC)²:

- Certified Information Systems Security Professional (CISSP)

- Systems Security Certified Practitioner (SSCP)

Both credentials indicate that certified individuals have demonstrated experience in the field of information security, passed a rigorous examination (6 hours, 250 questions), subscribed to a code of ethics, and will maintain certification with continuing education requirements. The CISSP is intended for people in managerial positions or for senior personnel who have oversight for multiple areas of information security. The SSCP is intended for people who specialize in areas of security operations. It's possible to attain both certificates, beginning with the SSCP and then, with further exposure to other areas of InfoSec and advanced experience, gaining the CISSP.

In 2004, the International Standards Organization (ISO) gave its stamp of approval to the CISSP security certification for IT professionals. The American National Standards Institute (ANSI), the U.S. representative to the Geneva-based ISO, announced that the standards bodies are granting certificate accreditation to the CISSP credential. Roy Swift, an ANSI program director, said the CISSP is the first IT certification to be accredited under ISO/IEC 17024, the standard that is a global benchmark for workers in various professions.

> **FYI: ISO/IEC 17024**
>
> The ISO/IEC 17024:2003, "Conformity Assessment—General Requirements for Bodies Operating Certification of Persons," standard outlines the requirements for bodies operating a certification of persons program. It was developed with the objective of achieving and promoting a globally accepted benchmark for organizations offering certifications programs. Certifying people is one means of providing assurance that the certified person meets the requirements of the certification scheme. Confidence in the respective certification schemes is achieved by means of a globally accepted process of assessment, subsequent surveillance, and periodic reassessments of the competence of certified persons.
>
> You can find out more about ISO/IEC 17024 at www.iso.org/iso/home/store/catalogue_ics/catalogue_detail_ics.htm?csnumber=52993.

The Information Security Common Body of Knowledge

The CBK is a compilation and distillation of all security information collected internationally that is relevant to information security professionals. The (ISC)² was formed, in part, to aggregate, standardize, and maintain this information because no industry standards previously existed.

The (ISC)² works to ensure that accomplished and experienced IS professionals with CISSP certification have a working knowledge of all 10 domains of the CBK, as the (ISC)² website describes (www.isc2.org). Note that you will not find material in this book that covers all the information in the CBK. To do so would require a much more comprehensive text. Instead, you will gain a good understanding of the underlying principles for each of the 10 domains and the topics needed to make an informed decision on whether information security is right for you as a career choice and which areas of concentration you may find most appealing.

Many books cover specialized areas of InfoSec, and you might want to acquire some for a more complete examination of the domains. The goal here is not to prepare you for industry certification exams, but rather to give you sufficient detail to make an informed choice for a possible career in information security.

The following pages describe the 10 domains of the CBK.

Information Security Governance and Risk Management

The Governance and Risk Management domain (see Chapter 4, "Governance and Risk Management,") emphasizes the importance of a comprehensive security plan that includes security policies and procedures for protecting data and how it is administered. Topics include

- Understanding and aligning security functions with the goals, mission, and objectives of the organization

- Understanding and applying security governance

- Understanding and applying concepts of confidentiality, integrity, and availability

- Developing and implementing security policies

- Managing the information life cycle (classification, categorization, and ownership)

- Managing third-party governance (on-site assessments, document exchange and review, process and policy reviews)

- Understanding and applying risk management concepts

- Managing personnel security

- Developing and managing security education, training, and awareness

- Managing the security function (budgets, metrics, and so on)

Security Architecture and Design

The Security Architecture and Design domain (see Chapter 5, "Security Architecture and Design"), one of the more technical areas of study within the CBK, discusses concepts, principles, structures, and standards used to design, implement, monitor, and secure operating systems, equipment, networks, applications, and other controls to enforce various levels of confidentiality, integrity, and availability. Specific topics cover

- Understanding the fundamental concepts of security models (confidentiality models, integrity models, and multilevel models)

- Identifying the components of information systems security evaluation models (such as Common Criteria)

- Understanding security capabilities of information systems (memory protection, trusted platform modules, and so on)

- Pinpointing the vulnerabilities of security architectures

- Recognizing software and system vulnerabilities and threats

- Understanding countermeasure principles (such as defense in depth)

Business Continuity and Disaster Recovery Planning

Business Continuity Planning (BCP), along with the Business Impact Assessment (BIA) and the Disaster Recovery Plan (DRP), is the core of this domain. The following topics are included in this domain:

- Understanding business continuity requirements

- Conducting business impact analysis

- Developing a recovery strategy

- Understanding the disaster recovery process

- Exercising, assessing, and maintaining the plans

Chapter 6, "Business Continuity Planning and Disaster Recovery Planning," covers this domain.

Legal Regulations, Investigations, and Compliance

This domain covers the different targets of computer crimes, bodies of law, and the different types of laws and regulations as they apply to computer security. Other topics included in this domain are

- Understanding legal issues that pertain to information security internationally

- Adopting professional ethics

- Understanding and supporting investigations

- Understanding forensic procedures

- Following compliance requirements and procedures

- Ensuring security in contractual agreements and procurement processes (such as cloud computing, outsourcing, and vendor governance)

Chapter 7, "Law, Investigations, and Ethics," covers this domain.

Physical (Environmental) Security

Topics covered in this domain include securing the physical site using policies and procedures coupled with the appropriate alarm and intrusion detection systems, monitoring systems, and so forth. Topics include

- Understanding site and facility design considerations

- Supporting the implementation and operation of perimeter security (physical access controls and monitoring, keys, locks, safes, and so on)

- Supporting the implementation and operation of facilities security (badges, smart cards, PINs, and so on)

- Supporting the protection and securing of equipment

- Understanding personnel privacy and safety (duress, travel, and so on)

Chapter 8, "Physical Security Control," covers this domain.

Operations Security

This domain covers the kind of operational procedures and tools that eliminate or reduce the capability to exploit critical information. It includes defining the controls over media, hardware, and operators with special systems privileges. Specific topics include

- Understanding security operations concepts (need-to-know, separation of duties, and so on)
- Employing resource protection
- Managing incident response
- Implementing preventable measures against attacks
- Implementing and supporting patch and vulnerability management
- Understanding change and configuration management
- Understanding system resilience and fault-tolerant requirements

Chapter 9, "Operations Security," covers this domain.

Access Control

Who may access the system, and what can they do after they are signed on? That is the focus of this CBK domain. Specific topics include

- Understanding identification, authentication, authorization, and logging and monitoring techniques and technologies
- Understanding access control attacks
- Assessing effectiveness of access controls
- Understanding the identity and access provisioning life cycle

Chapter 10, "Access Control Systems and Methodology," covers this domain.

Cryptography

This domain contains the stuff of espionage and spy novels. It involves encrypting data so that authorized individuals may view the sensitive data and unauthorized individuals may not. Cryptography is a highly complex topic. The InfoSec specialist needs to understand the function but not necessarily the mechanics of cryptography. Topics in the Cryptography domain include

- Identifying the application and use of cryptography
- Comprehending the cryptographic life cycle
- Understanding encryption concepts

- Identifying key management processes

- Using digital signatures

- Identifying nonrepudiation

- Recognizing the methods of cryptanalytic attacks

- Using cryptography to maintain network security

- Using cryptography to maintain application security

- Understanding the public key infrastructure (PKI)

- Identifying certificate-related issues

- Understanding information-hiding alternatives

Chapter 11, "Cryptography," covers this domain.

Telecommunications and Network Security

This domain covers another technical segment of the CBK. Topics include not just network topologies, but also their weaknesses and defenses. Many of the operational tools, such as firewalls, fall into this domain, along with the following subject areas:

- Understanding secure network architecture and design

- Securing network components

- Establishing secure communications channels (VPN, SSL, and so on)

- Understanding network attacks (denial of service, spoofing, and so on)

Chapter 12, "Telecommunications, Network, and Internet Security," covers this domain.

Software Development Security

Application development in a networked environment (see Chapter 13, "Software Development Security") focuses on sound and secure application development techniques. This domain requires a good understanding of the controls needed for the software development life cycle (SDLC), and how they're applied during each phase. Topics covered in this domain include

- Understanding and applying security in the SDLC

- Understanding the environment and security controls

- Assessing the effectiveness of software security

Chapters 4–13 are devoted to these 10 domains in a sufficient level of detail to help you to decide whether a career in InfoSec is for you.

Other Certificate Programs in the IT Security Industry

Although the CISSP and SSCP are the gold standards for IT security, many other certification programs also exist. Some of these programs are complementary to the CISSP, and others demonstrate a proficiency in specific areas within information security. The following section discusses a few of these programs.

Certified Information Systems Auditor

Once the exclusive domain of IT auditors, the Certified Information Systems Auditor (CISA) has become a sought-after certification for senior-level personnel and management. The subject areas of the CISA have moderate overlap with the CISSP, but the CISA focuses more on business procedures than technology. The Information Systems Audit and Control Association and Foundation (ISACA; www.isaca.org), founded in 1969, administers the CISA certification. The CISA certification itself has been around since 1978. More than 106,000 professionals have earned the CISA designation since its inception.

Certified Information Security Manager

In 2003, ISACA deployed the Certified Information Security Manager (CISM) certification. This certification recognizes the knowledge and experience of an IT security manager. The CISM is ISACA's next-generation credential and is specifically geared toward experienced information security managers and people with information security management responsibilities. The CISM is designed to provide executive management with assurance that those earning the designation have the required knowledge and ability to provide effective security management and consulting. It is business oriented and focuses on information risk management while addressing management, design, and technical security issues at a conceptual level. Although its central focus is security management, all those in the IS profession with security experience can find value in CISM.

Certified in Risk and Information Systems Control

The CRISC, another certificate from ISACA, is a rigorous assessment to evaluate the risk management proficiency of IT professionals and other employees within an enterprise or financial institute. CRISC holders can help enterprises understand business risk and have the technical knowledge to implement appropriate information system controls.

Global Information Assurance Certifications

The SANS Institute (www.sans.org) has also jumped on the certification bandwagon with its suite of 26 certifications under the Global Information Assurance Certification (GIAC) program. GIAC certifications are intended primarily for practitioners or hands-on personnel such as system administrators, network engineers, software developers, and the people who manage them. You can find information on all the GIAC certifications at www.giac.org/certifications/categories.

(ISC)² Specialization Certificates

After the original conception of the CISSP, and with the continuous evolution of information security, (ISC)² discovered a need to develop credentials to address the specific needs and requests from their members. Three CISSP concentrations are available in these functional areas:

- Architecture (CISSP-ISSAP)

- Engineering (CISSP-ISSEP)

- Management (CISSP-ISSMP)

Other additional certificates from (ISC)² include

- The Certified Secure Software Lifecycle Professional (CSSLP) helps to validate a candidate's application security competency within the software development life cycle (SDLC). Certificate holders have proven proficiency in these areas:

    - Developing an application security program in an organization

    - Reducing production costs, application vulnerabilities, and delivery delays

    - Enhancing the credibility of the software development organization

    - Reducing loss of revenue and reputation due to a breach resulting from insecure software

CCFP: Certified Cyber Forensics Professional

The evolving field of cyber forensics requires professionals who understand far more than just hard drive or intrusion analysis. The field requires certified professionals who demonstrate competence across a globally recognized common body of knowledge that includes established forensics disciplines, as well as newer challenges such as mobile forensics, cloud forensics, anti-forensics, and more. The CCFP credential indicates expertise in forensics techniques and procedures, standards of practice, and legal and ethical principles to ensure accurate, complete and reliable digital evidence admissible to a court of law. It also indicates the ability to apply forensics to other information security disciplines, such as e-discovery, malware analysis, and incident response.

HCISPP: HealthCare Information Security and Privacy Practitioner

The HCISPP credential is designed to ensure that practitioners have the foundational knowledge, skills, and abilities to protect and keep vital healthcare information secure. The HCISPP is intended for individuals who implement, manage, or assess security and privacy controls that address the unique data protection needs of healthcare information.

Vendor-Specific and Other Certification Programs

Vendor-neutral certification programs such as those described previously differ in focus and objectives from vendor-specific certification programs. In the IT security industry, dozens of vendor-specific certificates are available for practitioners. A few of these programs are listed next. For a comprehensive list of what's available in the industry, visit www.certmag.com.

Cisco Security Tracks and Certificates

The Cisco Certified Network Professional Security (CCNP Security) certification program is aligned specifically to the job role of the Cisco Network Security Engineer responsible for security in routers, switches, networking devices, and appliances, as well as choosing, deploying, supporting, and troubleshooting firewalls, VPNs, and IDS/IPS solutions for their networking environments. The following exams are required to attain the CCNP Security certificate:

- 642-637 SECURE: Securing Networks with Cisco Routers and Switches

- 642-618 FIREWALL: Deploying Cisco ASA Firewall Solutions

- 642-648 VPN: Deploying Cisco ASA VPN Solutions

- 642-627 IPS: Implementing Cisco Intrusion Prevention

For more information about the CCNP Security certificate, visit www.cisco.com/web/learning/certifications/professional/ccnp_security/index.html.

Certificate of Cloud Security Knowledge

The Cloud Security Alliance (CSA) has developed a widely adopted catalogue of security best practices, "Security Guidance for Critical Areas of Focus in Cloud Computing, V2.1." In addition, the European Network and Information Security Agency (ENISA) whitepaper "Cloud Computing: Benefits, Risks and Recommendations for Information Security" is an important contribution to the cloud security body of knowledge. The Certificate of Cloud Security Knowledge (CCSK) provides evidence that an individual has successfully completed an examination covering the key concepts of the CSA guidance and ENISA whitepaper. For more information, visit ccsk.cloudsecurityalliance.org/.

Certified Ethical Hacker

The goal of the ethical hacker is to help the organization take preemptive measures against malicious attacks by attacking the system itself, all while staying within legal limits. This philosophy stems from the proven practice of trying to catch a thief, by thinking like a thief. If hacking involves creativity and thinking out-of-the-box, then vulnerability testing and security audits will not ensure the security proofing of an organization. The Certified Ethical Hacker (CEH) Program certifies individuals in the specific network security discipline of ethical hacking from a vendor-neutral perspective. For more information, visit www.eccouncil.org/CEH.htm.

For a comprehensive directory of security certification programs, visit csoonline.com/article/485071/the-security-certification-directory#informationsecurity.

Summary

The International Information Systems Security Certification Consortium maintains the ever-evolving Common Body of Knowledge through ongoing reviews of references and best practices to ensure its relevance and effectiveness.

The information security CBK consists of 10 domains that cover all the areas of InfoSec that practitioners and managers are encouraged to know to excel in their careers and provide their employers with industry best practices that have proved successful.

The benefits of certification and immersion into the CBK are clear to both employers and professionals who commit to life-long learning and to the betterment of themselves and their careers. The role of the security professional is expanding, fueled by growing demands from the IT industry and national governments that are experiencing a growing threat to computing systems and operations.

Test Your Skills

MULTIPLE-CHOICE QUESTIONS

1. (ISC)^2 was formed for which of the following purposes?

    A. Maintaining a Common Body of Knowledge for information security

    B. Certifying industry professionals and practitioners in an international IS standard

    C. Ensuring that credentials are maintained, primarily through continuing education

    D. All of the above

2. Which of the following statements best describes the information security Common Body of Knowledge?

    A. The information security Common Body of Knowledge is a compilation and distillation of all security information collected internationally of relevance to information security professionals.

    B. The information security Common Body of Knowledge is a volume of books published by the (ISC)^2.

    C. The information security Common Body of Knowledge is a reference list of books and other publications put together by practitioners in information security.

    D. The information security Common Body of Knowledge is an encyclopedia of information security principles, best practices, and regulations.

3. How many domains are contained within the CBK?

   A. 5 domains

   B. 10 domains

   C. 7 domains

   D. 3 domains

4. The Information Security Governance and Risk Management domain includes which of the following?

   A. Identification of security products

   B. Documented policies, standards, procedures, and guidelines

   C. Management of risk to corporate assets

   D. B and C only

5. The Security Architecture and Design domain includes which of the following?

   A. Concepts and principles for secure operations

   B. Concepts and principles for secure programs

   C. Concepts and principles for secure designs of computing resources

   D. Concepts and principles for secure application development

6. The Access Control domain includes which of the following?

   A. A collection of mechanisms to create secure architectures for asset protection

   B. Instructions on how to install perimeter door security

   C. A methodology for applications development

   D. A methodology for secure data center operations

7. The Software Development Security domain includes which of the following?

   A. An outline for the software development environment to address security concerns

   B. A recipe book for developers to follow in building secure application software

   C. A language guide on programming security functions

   D. Quality assurance testing of custom-developed software

8. The Operations Security domain includes which of the following?

   A. Mechanisms for secure access to a data center

   B. Identification of controls over hardware, media, and personnel

   C. Help-desk support for security incidents

   D. Consulting on IT projects

9. The Physical (Environmental) Security domain includes which of the following?

    A. A code of conduct for employees

    B. Perimeter security controls and protection mechanisms

    C. Data center controls and specifications for physically secure operations

    D. B and C

10. The Cryptography domain includes which of the following?

    A. Principles, means, and methods to disguise information to ensure confidentiality, integrity, and authenticity

    B. Tools and techniques to intercept competitive secrets

    C. Procedures on how to protect Internet communications

    D. Procedures on how to discover cryptographic keys

11. The Telecommunications and Network Security domain includes which of the following?

    A. Technology, principles, and best practices to secure telephone networks

    B. Technology, principles, and best practices to secure corporate networks

    C. Technology, principles, and best practices to secure Internet-attached networks

    D. All of the above

12. The Business Continuity and Disaster Recovery Planning domain includes which of the following?

    A. Plans for recovering business operations in the event of loss of access by personnel

    B. Management practices to determine software security risks

    C. Documented plans for interacting with law enforcement

    D. Maintenance of current versions of all software in use by the organization

13. The Law, Regulations, Investigations, and Compliance domain includes which of the following?

    A. Teams of lawyers to determine the legality of security decisions

    B. Private law enforcement personnel

    C. Methods to investigate computer crime incidents

    D. A council to determine the ethical behavior of security personnel

14. People more interested in certifying themselves as security experts in a business context should consider preparing for which of the following certifications?

    A. GIAC

    B. CISA

    C. ISSAP

    D. SSCP

15. People more interested in certifying themselves as security technical practitioners should consider preparing for which of the following certifications?

   A. CISM and GIAC

   B. GIAC and CEH

   C. CISSP and CISM

   D. SSCP and CISA

16. The growth in the security profession is driven by which of the following?

   A. New technology

   B. Growth of the Internet

   C. Demands by industry and government for scarce resources

   D. Overseas hackers

EXERCISES

EXERCISE 3.1: Assessing the Benefits Gained Through Industry Certification

1. List some of the certificate programs that would interest you if you choose a profession in information security.

2. Name three advantages certified professionals have over noncertified professionals when applying for a job.

3. Explain how an employer could use information about certifications to evaluate potential employees.

EXERCISE 3.2: Preparing for Certification Tests

1. Search your favorite online bookstore for books in print that help prepare professionals to sit for the CISSP and CISM certificates.

2. Aside from the organization of the books, what can you find in common among them?

3. Do you believe that drills from exam test banks are a good method for the beginner to prepare for certifications? Why or why not?

EXERCISE 3.3: Understanding Hot Topics in Information Security

1. List some of the current topics and issues in information security that you think concern IT and business managers.

2. Visit the Search Security website (www.searchsecurity.com) to see how your list maps to hot topics found on the website.

3. As a practitioner, how would you respond to these concerns when company management looks to you for information and recommendations?

EXERCISE 3.4: Researching Growth in Internal Security Departments

1. Describe the composition and size of the security department at your place of employment or at your school. You might need to talk to the IT professionals within your organization to develop this description and to address the following steps.

2. Explain whether the department has grown in size during the past few years. If it has grown, how much has it grown and for what reasons? (Has the organization grown? Or is there more work for the security professionals to do?)

3. Explain whether the managers feel that recruiting qualified employees has been difficult. What sort of experience or certifications do the managers look for in potential employees?

EXERCISE 3.5: Understanding ISO_/IEC 27002 and CBK Domains

1. Research the ISO_/IEC 27002 International Standard, Code of Practice for Information Security Management (www.iso27001security.com/html/27002.html).

2. Determine how its organization is similar to the CISSP CBK. List the similarities.

3. List the area(s) that are different and how they are different.

PROJECTS

PROJECT 3.1: Comparing Certificate Programs

1. Consider security industry certification such as the SSCP and CISSP versus security vendor certifications such as those from Cisco Systems (www.cisco.com). Why do you think someone might pursue vendor certification instead of industry certification?

2. In any situations, would having both types of certifications be beneficial? If so, describe the situations.

3. What certifications would make good combinations for certain domain areas?

4. Which certificates do you think would be more valuable to hiring managers?

5. Which certificates do you think employers are demanding for security personnel?

PROJECT 3.2: **Understanding Concentration (ISC)² Certifications**

In addition to the CISSP and SSCP, the (ISC)² offers concentration certifications for management (ISSMP), security architecture (ISSAP), and engineering (ISSEP)

1. Research these concentrations at the (ISC)² website (www.isc2.org).

2. Explain why professionals might want to attain one or more of them beyond the CISSP credential.

3. Do you see additional personal value beyond the CISSP for these certificates? If so, list the values you see. If not, explain why.

4. Explain why employers might seek personnel who hold these certificates.

PROJECT 3.3: **Understanding Information Privacy and Information Security**

Information privacy and information security are two sides of the same coin. You can't have privacy without security.

1. Using an Internet search engine, distinguish between issues related to privacy and issues related to security.

2. What overlapping issues do you find?

3. Why are U.S. lawmakers seemingly more concerned with privacy controls and protections than requiring U.S. companies to maintain effective IT security programs?

4. What are some of the controls being mandated through legislation?

5. Do you believe these controls are (or will be or can be) effective? Why or why not?

Chapter 4

Governance and Risk Management

Chapter Objectives

After reading this chapter and completing the exercises, you will be able to do the following:

- Choose the appropriate type of policies to document a security programme
- Distinguish among the roles of standards, regulations, baselines, procedures, and guidelines
- Organize a typical standards and policies library
- Classify assets according to standard principles
- Incorporate the separation of duties principle when creating a security policy
- Outline the minimum pre-employment hiring practices for organizations
- Analyze and manage risk
- Outline the elements of employee security education, awareness, and training
- List the eight types of people responsible for security in an information technology (IT) setting

Introduction

This chapter describes the first domain of the Certified Information Systems Security Professional (CISSP) Common Body of Knowledge (CBK): Governance and Risk Management. This domain appears first because it establishes the framework and foundation for all the other domains to build upon.

Governance and risk management is a broad set of executive support and management activities that define an IT security programme. (*Note:* This spelling is used to distinguish a management programme from a computer program.) A programme, unlike a project, is an ongoing management activity that is constantly funded and intended for the preservation and advancement of the organization.

As with any programme, an IT security programme begins with statements of management's intent. These goals are translated into security policies (statements of management intent) and then used to drive the details of how the programme will run, who will be responsible for day-to-day work, how training and awareness will be conducted, and how compliance to policies will be handled.

Other areas addressed within the Information Security Governance and Risk Management practices domain are activities related to information classification, risk management concepts and techniques, and security roles and responsibilities to ensure ongoing organizational security consciousness.

Security Policies Set the Stage for Success

Policies are the most crucial element in a corporate information security infrastructure and must be considered long before security technology is acquired and deployed. Security industry expert Marcus Ranum explains: "If you haven't got a security policy, you haven't got a firewall. Instead, you've got a thing that's sort of doing something, but you don't know what it's trying to do because no one has told you what it should do" (Ranum, 2003). Implementing security technology with no predetermined rules about what it should do results in accidental protection, at best—even a broken clock is right twice a day!

Effective policies can rectify many of the weaknesses from failures to understand the business direction and security mission, and can help prevent or eliminate many of the faults and errors caused by a lack of security guidance.

An organization faces many technology and strategic choices when deciding how to protect its computer assets. Some choices are made based on trade-offs, but others involve conflicting trade-offs, questions about an organization's strategic direction, and other factors that can't be easily quantified. Technology providers are at times overly anxious to push product out the door, and unwitting managers might choose to buy technology without determining what problem(s) it might solve. Once established, policies become the basis for protecting both information and technology resources and for guiding employee behavior. However, they are not sufficient on their own. Familiarity with these types of policies is required to aid people within a company in addressing computer security issues that are important to the organization as a whole. Effective policies ultimately result in the development and implementation of better computer security and better protection of systems and information.

Policies may be published on paper or electronically via a corporate intranet. Tools to automate the mechanics of policy creation, management, maintenance, and dissemination are commercially available. (For more information about these tools, visit NetIQ for the VigilEnt Policy Center at www.netiq.com.)

Figure 4.1 illustrates a typical structure of a corporate policy and standards library. The top of the hierarchy (the charter) is a document, often issued by executive management, to establish and operate an information security programme. The Policy level is then linked to that document to show continuity and completeness for the documentation that establishes the operating requirements and activities related to information security.

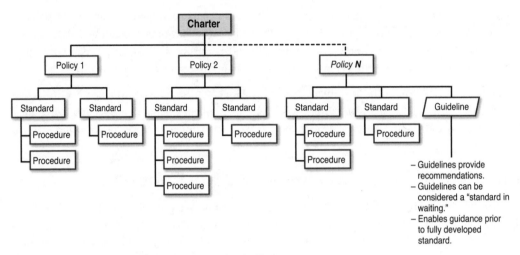

FIGURE 4.1   A typical policies and standards library structure.

An effective policy contains the following information:

- Title

- Purpose

- Authorizing individual

- Author/sponsor

- Reference to other policies

- Scope

- Measurement expectations

- Exception process

- Accountability

- Compliance management and measurements description

- Effective/expiration dates

- Definitions

This structure is a best practice within the industry for comprehensive coverage of the topics found in security policies. As people gain experience and exposure to policies, a common structure helps them quickly locate the information they seek.

Understanding the Four Types of Policies

According to the National Institute of Standards and Technology (NIST) Computer Systems Laboratory (CSL), a division of the U.S. Department of Commerce, computer security policies come in four types. Policies and the follow-up documents in the library start at a very high level of understanding and become more specific (granular) at the lower levels.

- Programme-level policy is used for creating a management-sponsored computer security program. A programme-level policy, at the highest level, might prescribe the need for information security and can delegate the creation and management of the program to a role within the IT department. Think of this as the mission statement for the IT security program.

- Programme-framework policy establishes the overall approach to computer security (as a computer security framework). A framework policy adds detail to the program by describing the elements and organization of the program and department that will carry out the security mission.

- Issue-specific policy addresses specific issues of concern to the organization. These issues could be regulatory in nature—for example, the Payment Card Industry (PCI) data security standard, Sarbanes-Oxley (SOX), or the Gramm-Leach-Bliley Act (GLBA), to name a few.

- System-specific policy focuses on policy issues that management has decided for a specific system.

You can find a complete IT security policy and standards library taxonomy found in Appendix B, "Security Policy and Standards Taxonomy." You also can find specific types of policy and standards examples Appendix C, "Sample Policies."

The following sections describe each policy type in greater detail.

Programme-Level Policies

Management needs a programme-level policy to help establish a security programme, assign programme-management responsibilities, state an organization-wide computer security purpose and objectives, and establish a basis for policy compliance.

The head of the organization or other senior officials, such as the organization's top management officers, typically issue programme-level policy. A programme-level policy, sometimes called an information security charter, establishes the computer security program and its basic framework. This high-level policy defines the purpose of the programme and its scope within the organization, assigns responsibilities for direct programme implementation (to the computer security organization) and responsibilities to related offices, and addresses compliance issues.

The components of programme-level policy follow:

- The purpose clearly states the purpose of the programme. This includes defining the goals of the computer security programme and its management structure. Security-related needs, such as confidentiality, integrity, and availability, might form the basis of organizational goals established in policy. For instance, organizations responsible for maintaining large mission-critical databases might stress a reduction in errors, data loss, or data corruption. In an organization responsible for maintaining confidential personal data (as in most e-commerce systems), the goals might emphasize stronger protection against unauthorized disclosure. A programme-management structure should be organized to best address the goals of the programme and respond to the particular operating and risk environment of the organization. Important issues for the structure of the central computer security programme include management and coordination of security-related resources, interaction with diverse communities, and the capability to relay issues of concern to upper management. The policy could also establish operational security offices for major systems, particularly those at high risk or those most critical to organizational operations.

- The scope specifies which resources (including facilities, hardware, and software), information, and personnel the programme covers. Often the programme covers all systems and agency personnel, but this is not always the case. In some instances, a policy might name specific assets, such as major sites and large systems. Sometimes tough management decisions arise when defining the scope of a program, such as determining the extent to which the programme applies to contractors and outside organizations using or connected to the organization's systems. Scope should also consider home-based employees (telecommuters), mobile employees who access company resources from remote locations, employees using wireless technology, and employees who "bring their own devices" to the workplace (commonly referred to as BYOD, or bring your own device).

- Responsibilities address the responsibilities of the officials and offices throughout the organization, including the role of line managers, applications owners, users, and the information processing or IT organization. The policy statement distinguishes between the responsibilities of computer services providers and the responsibilities of the managers of applications using the computer services. It can also establish the basis for employee accountability. Overall, the programme-level assignment of responsibilities covers activities and personnel that will be vital to the implementation and continuity of the computer security policy.

- Compliance authorizes and delineates the use of specified penalties and disciplinary actions for individuals who fail to comply with the organization's computer security policies. Because the security policy is a high-level document, penalties for various infractions are normally not detailed therein. However, the policy might authorize the creation of compliance structures that include violations and specific penalties. Infractions and associated penalties are usually defined in issue- and system-specific policies.

When establishing compliance structures, an organization must consider that employee violations of policy can be unintentional. For example, nonconformance can be due to a lack of knowledge or training. Each policy and standard should contain a section on compliance management and metrics to help management educate employees on their responsibilities and provide a measurement tool to help determine the document's effectiveness. The web-based policy- and standards-management systems (mentioned earlier) offer facilities to "push" a new or revised standard or policy to the audience that needs to be aware of changes and then provide awareness training (if needed), quizzes to gauge user understanding of the changes, and a mechanism to record a user's decision to comply with the new standard or request intervention from the security department.

Programme-Framework Policies

Programme-framework policies provide an organization-wide direction for broad areas of programme implementation. These policies might be issued to ensure that everyone complies with acceptable use rules (e-mail, Internet, cellphones and other wireless devices, and so on), or that everyone correctly addresses disaster planning and risk analysis issues. Managers or departments with sufficient authority to direct all organization components on computer security issues create programme-framework policies. This may be the organization's management official or the head of the computer security programme (such as the chief information officer or, more commonly, the chief information security office).

Programme-framework policies define the organization's security programme elements that form the foundation for the computer security programme. The programme-framework policy reflects information technology management's decisions about priorities for protection, resource allocation, and assignment of responsibilities.

The areas the programme-framework policy addresses vary within each organization, as does the way in which the policy is expressed. Some organizations issue policy directives, whereas others issue handbooks that combine policy, regulations, standards, and guidance.

Many organizations issue policy on key areas of computer security, such as life-cycle management, contingency planning, and network security. If the policy and associated standards and guidance are too rigid, cost-effective implementations and innovation could be negatively affected. For an example of programme-framework policy, consider a typical organization policy on contingency planning. An organization might require that all contingency plans categorize the criticality of computer programs and IT processes according to a standard scale. This will assist the organization in preparing a master plan (in case the physical plant is destroyed) by supporting prioritization across departmental boundaries. Programme-framework policies might consist of components similar to those contained in programme-level policy but could be in different formats (organizational handbooks and so forth). Examples of possible programme-framework policies include these:

- Business continuity planning (BCP) framework (see Chapter 6, "Business Continuity Planning and Disaster Recovery Planning")

- Physical security requirements framework for data centers (see Chapter 7, "Law, Investigations, and Ethics")

- Application development security framework (see Chapter 13, "Software Development Security")

Issue-Specific Policies

Issue-specific policies identify and define specific areas of concern and state an organization's position or posture on the issue. Depending on the issue and its controversy, as well as potential impact, issue-specific policy can come from the head of the organization, the top management official, the chief information officer (CIO), or the computer security programme manager (such as CISO).

Keeping Up With Ever-Changing Technology

Trying to stay on top of ever-evolving technology and the security risks posed by these technologies is one of the most challenging aspects of being an IT security professional. For example, handheld PDAs, laptop computers, tablets, and cellphones have become ubiquitous in private medical offices, clinics, hospitals, and even blood banks because of the convenience and ease of wireless local area networks (WLANs). They allow physicians and nurses to access patient records remotely, add observations and diagnoses, and check on medications, among other things. This increased access poses new and difficult security questions:

- How can office managers be sure that no unauthorized computers can eavesdrop on the wireless communications?

- How can patients be sure that the doctor's convenience is not at the price of patient record privacy?

Covered healthcare entities need to consider whether they should postpone deploying an initial WLAN until planned improvements in wireless network security standards are adopted and have been implemented in commercial products. Those who are charged with maintaining the security of healthcare information systems carry a heavy burden. As technology changes constantly, covered entity managers and their lawyers are required to regularly evaluate the impact of those changes on the security of their networks (source: www.giac.org/paper/gsec/3214/implementing-hipaa-compliant-wireless-network/105333). Issue-specific policies focus on areas of current relevance and concern to an organization. Although programme-level policy is usually broad enough that it requires little modification over time, issue-specific policies require more frequent revision because of changes in technology and related factors. As new technologies are developed, such as the advent of the cloud and the use of social media such as Facebook and Twitter, some issues diminish in importance, and new ones continually appear. For example, issuing a policy on the proper use of a cutting-edge technology (such as Wi-Fi networks) might be appropriate because the security vulnerabilities are still being addressed.

A useful structure for issue-specific policy is to break the policy into its basic components:

- An issue statement defines a security issue, along with any relevant terms, distinctions, and conditions. For example, an organization might want to develop an issue-specific policy on the use of "Internet access," which might define what Internet activities it will permit and those it won't permit. Additionally, other distinctions and conditions might need inclusion, such as

Internet access that's gained using a personal dial-up or broadband ISP connection from an employee's desktop PC that makes the internal network vulnerable to interlopers when the connection is alive.

- A statement of the organization's position clearly gives an organization's position on the issue. Continuing with the example of Internet access, the policy should state what types of sites are prohibited in all or some cases (for example, pornography sites, blog sites, or brokerage sites); whether further guidelines govern approval and use; or whether case-by-case exceptions will be granted, by whom, and on what basis.

- Applicability clearly states where, how, when, to whom, and to what a particular policy applies. For example, the hypothetical policy on Internet access might apply only to the organization's own on-site resources and employees, and not to contractor organizations with offices at other locations. Additionally, the policy's applicability to employees traveling among different sites or working at home who require Internet access from multiple sites might require further clarification.

- Roles and responsibilities assigns roles and responsibilities to the issue. Continuing with the Internet example, if the policy permits private ISP access, given the appropriate approvals, then the approving authority should be identified. The office or department(s) responsible for compliance should also be named.

- Compliance describes the infractions and states the corresponding penalties. Penalties must be consistent with organizational personnel policies and practices, and need to be coordinated with appropriate officials, offices, and perhaps employee bargaining units.

- Points of contact and supplementary information lists the names of the appropriate individuals to contact for further information and lists any applicable standards or guidelines. For some issues, the point of contact might be a line manager; for other issues, it might be a facility manager, technical support person, or system administrator. Yet for other issues, the point of contact might be a security programme representative. Using the Internet access example, we can say that employees need to know whether the point of contact for questions and procedural information is the immediate superior, a system administrator, or a computer security official. The following are examples of an issue-specific policy:

  - Email acceptable use
  - Internet acceptable use
  - Laptop security policy
  - Wireless security policy

System-Specific Policies

Programme-level policies and issue-specific policies both address policies from a broad level, usually involving the entire organization. System-specific policies, on the other hand, are much more focused because they address only one system. System-specific policy is normally issued by the manager or owner of the system (which could be a network or application) but may originate from a high-level executive or official. This is especially true if all affected departments don't agree with the policy and might be tempted to create conflicting policies addressing their own needs, to the detriment of the overall organization. System-specific policies do the following:

- State security objectives of a specific system

- Define how the system should be operated to achieve the security objectives

- Specify how the protections and features of the technology will be used to support or enforce the security objectives

Many security policy decisions apply only at the system level. Examples include these decisions:

- Who is allowed to read or modify data in the system?

- Under what conditions can data be read or modified?

- Are users allowed to connect the computer system from home or on the road?

Developing and Managing Security Policies

To develop a comprehensive set of system security policies, a management process is required that derives security rules from security goals, such as a three-level model for system security policy:

- Security objectives

- Operational security

- Policy implementation

Security Objectives

The first step is to define the security objectives. This step must extend beyond analyzing the need for confidentiality, integrity, and availability. Security objectives must be more specific and concrete. They should be clearly stated to achieve the objective. The security objectives should consist of a series of statements to describe meaningful actions about specific resources. These objectives should be based on system functionality or mission requirements, but should also state the security actions to support the requirements.

Operational Security

The next section is concerned with the operational policies that list the rules for operating a system. Using data integrity as an example, we can say that the operational policy would define authorized and unauthorized modification: who (by job category, organization placement, by name) can do what (modify, delete, or add) to which data (specific fields or records), and under what conditions (for example, peak or off-peak operational hours). Managers need to decide clearly in developing this policy because not all security objectives likely will be fully met. Cost, operational, technical, and other constraints will intervene.

Also worth consideration is the degree of formality needed in documenting the policy. Again, the more formal the documentation, the easier it will be to enforce and follow policy. Formal policy is published as a distinct policy document; less formal policy can be written in memos. Informal policy might not be written at all. As expected, unwritten policy is extremely difficult to follow or enforce. On the other hand, very granular and formal policy at the system level can also be an administrative burden. In general, good practice suggests a granular formal statement of the access privileges for a system because of its complexity and importance. Documenting access control policy makes it substantially easier to follow and to enforce.

Another area that normally requires a granular and formal statement is the assignment of security responsibilities. Some less formal policy decisions can be recorded in other types of computer security documents, such as risk analyses, accreditation statements, or procedural manuals. However, any controversial or uncommon policies might need formal policy statements. Uncommon policies include any areas in which the system policy differs from organization policy or from normal practice within the organization (either more or less stringent). Uncommon policies should also contain a statement explaining the reason for deviating from the organization's standard policy.

An example of the need for an uncommon policy or standard arises when a specialty computer system might not be able to meet the organization's overall policy on password lengths. Suppose this oddball system allows only five-character passwords using only letters of the alphabet, but the organizational policy on passwords states that passwords must be eight or more characters in length and must contain at least one number and one special character. In this case, a standard might be developed that requires additional controls over this system, to mitigate the risk of the inability to comply with the organizational policy.

Policy Implementation

Finally, the organization must determine the role technology plays in enforcing or supporting the policy. Security is normally enforced through a combination of technical and traditional management methods. This is especially true in the areas of Internet security, where security devices protect the perimeter of the company's information management systems. Although technical means are likely to include the use of access control technology, other automated means of enforcing or supporting security policy exist.

For example, technology can be used to block telephone systems users from calling certain numbers. Intrusion detection software can alert system administrators to suspicious activity or take action to stop the activity. Personal computers can be configured to prevent using a USB device. Automated security enforcement has both advantages and disadvantages. A computer system, properly designed, programmed, and installed, consistently enforces policy, although users can't be forced to follow all procedures. In addition, deviations from the policy might sometimes be necessary and appropriate. This situation occurs frequently if the security policy is too rigid.

Providing Policy Support Documents

Although policies are defined as statements of management's intent, the embodiment of policies and details on how to comply with them show up in other documents derived from policy statements. These documents provide levels of detail supporting the policy and explain the system development, management, and operational requirements. Procedures then provide a recipe for the execution of steps that are intended to comply with a policy directive. These supporting documents include the following:

- **Regulations:** Laws passed by regulators and lawmakers

- **Standards and baselines:** Topic-specific (standards) and system-specific (baselines) documents that describe overall requirements for security

- **Guidelines:** Documentation that aids in compliance with standard considerations, hints, tips, and best practices in implementation

- **Procedures:** Step-by-step instructions on how to perform a specific security activity (configure a firewall, install an operating system, and others)

Regulations

Often, the nature of an organization's business dictates the standards related to InfoSec. The Federal Trade Commission (FTC) and Department of Commerce govern U.S. retail operators, among others. Federal banking standards regulate U.S. banks (FFIEC, or the Federal Financial Institutions Examination Council), U.S. medical device manufacturers or suppliers fall under Federal Drug Administration (FDA) regulations, and so forth. By selecting the most robust or strictest sets of published standards governing a particular business, an organization is most likely to meet the requirements outlined by any applicable less stringent standards.

In 2004, the Sarbanes-Oxley Corporate Responsibility and Accountability Act—passed by the U.S. Senate in the wake of the collapse of Enron, Arthur Anderson, WorldCom, and several other large firms—gained the attention of all U.S. corporate CEOs. The act requires internal controls to foster regulator confidence in the integrity of financial statements to the Securities and Exchange Commission (SEC) and shareholders. It also requires that CEOs attest to the integrity of financial statements to the SEC.

Because of this mandate, controls related to information processing and management have been placed under a magnifying glass, underscoring the need for a comprehensive library of current operating documents.

Many of the regulations on the books are drawn from existing and evolving sources of information security industry standards and best practices. Policies and standards are always changing as best practices are learned, documented, and shared with others in the same industry.

In Practice

Understanding HIPAA Privacy

The Health Insurance Portability and Accountability Act of 1996 (HIPAA) includes a section titled "Medical Privacy Rule" that specifies new privacy protections for patients and lays out the privacy obligations for employers and healthcare providers. Because of the privacy rule, healthcare providers and health plan providers can no longer release protected health information to patients' employers unless certain conditions are met. Human resources departments in all companies that offer employee health-care coverage must now look at HIPAA as it relates to workers compensation, drug testing, physical exams, Family Medical Leave Act (FMLA), maternity leave, sick days, and healthcare plan communications.

Suddenly, developers of HR systems are no longer immune from privacy and security controls, and retrofitting existing (legacy) systems is not only costly, but also detracts from new development work and adds new risks of security controls that might not be well implemented. Demands on security specialists are increased, too, as companies are forced to bring these old systems into compliance.

IT security policies and standards have been around for many years, and many are already available as de facto (accepted practices in the industry) and de jure (official standards passed by international and industry standards committees). One such standard that is regularly used in IT security is ISO/IEC 17799, "Code of Practice for Information Security Management" (www.iso.org/iso/home/store/catalogue_ics/catalogue_detail_ics.htm?csnumber=39612). ISO/IEC 17799 is based on British Standard (BS) 7777, Part I (since revised in 2005 to ISO 27002, to align with the ISO 27000 series). It defines a series of domains or subject areas, similar to the CISSP CBK, that management is expected to address, and is more suggestive in nature (for example, management should address the area of pre-employment background checks). On the other hand, British Standard 7799, Part II is the actual standard that prescribes activities that management must address to be compliant to the standard. It refers to dictates, such as management *shall* put into place pre-employment background checks, and can be used as an assessment tool to verify compliance.

Although ISO/IEC 17799 and BS 7799 are widely used throughout the industry, other documents prepared by international and industry bodies are available for the asking. The National Institute of Standards and Technology, formerly the National Bureau of Standards, has a complete library of documents that serve as the basis for IT security within U.S. federal agencies and the Federal Information Processing Standards (FIPS).

The Control Objectives for Information and Related Technology (COBIT) is another widely accepted set of documents that is commonly found as the basis for an information security programme throughout the world. COBIT is an initiative from the Information Systems Audit and Control Association (ISACA) and is preferred among IT auditors.

The U.S. National Security Telecommunications and Information Systems Security Committee (NSTISSC) Standard 4011, otherwise known as National Training Standard for Information Systems Security Professionals, establishes the minimum training standard for the training of information systems security professionals in the disciplines of telecommunications and automated information systems security. The body of knowledge listed in the standard can be obtained from a variety of sources (including the National Cryptologic School, contractors, and adaptations of existing department/agency training programs) or a combination of experience and formal training. The instruction is applicable to all departments and agencies of the U.S. government, their employees, and contractors who are responsible for the security oversight or management of national security systems during each phase of the life cycle. For more on NSTISSC Number 4011, see https://www.cnss.gov/CNSS/openDoc.cfm?0gdXIf1iTgVIfrSAZ2epkQ==.

Standards and Baselines

The IT industry has an old saying about standards being great because you have so many to choose from. The point, you don't need to reinvent your own standards when you can simply reuse what people have found to be best practices.

FYI: Security Experts Are Never Alone

You cannot invent best practices—you simply adopt them from others and thank those who have documented them for making mistakes that you can avoid. This is a primary reason for being fully involved in the IT security industry when you're a practitioner. It's folly to operate in a corporate vacuum, especially when others who share your concerns and problems have already traversed the trails that led them to improved processes and technologies. Security is not an area in which competition is admired. Companies are better served by not competing on security when interdependence is present. For example, a bank offering better security on credit card payments is not helping the industry as a whole if it uses security as a market differentiator. If any bank suffers a breach in security, the entire banking industry is adversely affected. Below the layer of policies, you'll find a more populated layer of standards and baselines (refer to Figure 4.1). Often you'll see the terms *standards* and *baselines* interchanged. A standard refers to specific security requirements, or what a system or process needs to be considered secure. An example is a password standard that covers the requirements for password creation, distribution, use, change, and revocation in support of the policy that mandates appropriate access controls and accountability measures. A baseline is a specific set of requirements for a technology implementation, such as Windows Server 2012 security settings or Oracle DBMS protection mechanisms.

Baselines and standards are the enforceable element in the security programme. Compliance with standards and baselines is what the auditors check, and exceptions are filed against a baseline or a standard. If a standard cannot be met because of time or budget constraints to implementing a control, an exceptions or variance process is usually present to accommodate the messy reality of software development and implementation. Exceptions should be temporary and should include a plan for meeting compliance to the standard. In any event, the risks of failing to comply with a standard must be understood, and compensating controls to contain these risks should be implemented.

Guidelines

Guidelines, guidance documents, and advisories provide the people who need to implement a standard or baseline more detailed information and guidance (hints, tips, processes, advice, and so forth) to aid in compliance. These documents are optional in a library but are often helpful.

Procedures

Procedures are the detailed, step-by-step activities in implementing a process or configuring a system for compliance to a guideline. They may also be step-by-step security processes that ensure repeatability and accountability of personnel performing the procedure.

Suggested Standards Taxonomy

Standards are formal written documents that describe several security concepts that are fundamental to all successful programmes. The highest level includes the following:

- Asset and data classification

- Separation of duties

- Pre-employment hiring practices

- Risk analysis and management

- Education, awareness, and training

For a complete taxonomy of standards that would be expected in a comprehensive library, see Appendix B.

Asset and Data Classification

Businesses and agencies need asset and data classification to help determine how much security is needed for appropriate protection. A rule of thumb states that one should never spend more on security than the value of the asset being protected. Sometimes determining value is straightforward, but other times, such as when trying to place a value on a brand icon, the value is not so clear. That's where classification helps.

Some of the obvious benefits to a classification system are as follows:

- Data confidentiality, integrity, and availability are improved because appropriate controls are used throughout the enterprise.

- Protection mechanisms are maximized.

- A process exists to review the values of company business data.

- Decision quality increases because the quality of the data upon which the decision is being made has been improved.

In the military, a strict classification system exists to protect national secrets and information. Chapter 5, "Security Architecture and Design," covers this classification system in depth, but a common taxonomy for commercial businesses might provide for the following classes:

- **Public information:** Information intended for public dissemination. This might include marketing content on a website, direct mail inserts, directories of contact information, published annual reports, and so forth.

- **Business sensitive or business confidential:** Information employees and other insiders need to perform their duties. This can include company directories (address books, email addresses, and so forth), invoice information, department budget information, internal policies, and so forth.

- **Customer confidential:** Information that identifies individual customers of the business or institution and can include their purchase activity, account-specific information, credit card numbers, social security numbers (when needed), grades or course information (in the case of a university), or any other information considered personally identifiable information (PII) that dictates need-to-know or least privilege controls to ensure confidentiality and integrity.

- **Trade secret:** Information that is severely restricted and protected through more strict need-to-know controls than customer confidential information. Some examples of trade secret information include the recipe for Coca-Cola, employee disciplinary actions, prereleased financial statement information, or proprietary secrets that offer a competitive advantage to the business.

Separation of Duties

Separating duties within a business or organization helps limit an individual's ability to cause harm or perpetrate theft. For an illegal act to succeed, two or more employees would be forced to conspire. This concept is similar to accounting controls: It's imprudent, for example, for a person approving an invoice to also be responsible for preparing a vendor payment.

FYI: U.S. Regulations Covering PII

Many of the newly enacted regulations by the U.S. Congress are aimed at protecting PII. Two notable regulations are the Gramm-Leach-Bliley Act (GLBA) for banking, insurance, and finance, and the Health Insurance Portability and Accountability Act (HIPAA) for healthcare providers, pharmacies, and healthcare insurance providers. HIPAA caused a flurry of activity throughout 2002 to 2004. To comply with the act, healthcare providers required all patients to sign a release form that authorized them to share personal health-related information for purposes of treatment. You might remember signing these forms each time you used a healthcare service (dentists, doctors, pharmacy visits, and so forth).

You might also remember mass mailings by your credit card issuers of privacy statements that detailed your rights as a user of a credit product. This activity was in response to the enforcement date of GLBA, which took effect in late 2003.

No one person should be responsible for completing a task involving sensitive, valuable, or critical information from beginning to end. Likewise, a person must not be responsible for approving his or her own work. Following are some suggestions for separating critical activities:

- Separate development, testing, and production environments, and different personnel to manage and operate these environments

- Separate security management and audit mechanisms and personnel

- Separate accounts payable and accounts receivable processing and personnel

- Separate controls over encryption key generation or changing of keys (split knowledge—see Chapter 11, "Cryptography," for more details)

- Separate encryption keys into two (or more) components, each of which does not reveal the contents to the two (or more) key signing officers (dual control—see Chapter 11 for more details)

Employment Hiring Practices

Policies, standards, and procedures issued by human resources should address internal information security processes and functions. These documents should address pre-employment screening and background checks, processes for handling employee termination, creation and revocation of employee accounts, email and voice mail forwarding after departure, lock keys and safe combination changes, system password changes, and company property collections upon departure (for badges, credit cards, and so forth).

Employee Screening

Companies hiring people into areas of responsibility (especially security personnel) should have policies and practices in place to perform background checks or to get a new employee cleared by the government with security clearances when acting as a contractor for the government. Pre-employment background checks should refer to public records because they often provide critical information needed to make the best hiring decision. Conducting these and other simple checks verifies that the information provided on the application is current and true, and gives the employer an immediate measurement of an applicant's integrity.

The following are other items that can easily be checked:

- Credit report
- SSN searches
- Worker's compensation reports
- Criminal records
- Motor vehicle report
- Education verification and credential confirmation

- Reference checks

- Previous employer verification

Military Security Clearance

One of the most meticulous background checks is the U.S. Department of Defense (DOD) security clearance. The steps are contained in the 30-page Defense Industrial Personnel Security Clearance Review. A defense security clearance is generally requested only for individuals in the following categories whose employment involves access to sensitive government assets:

- Members of the military

- Civilian employees working for the Department of Defense or other government agencies

- Employees of government contractors

A DOD review, known as the Personnel Security Investigation, can take a year or longer and includes these activities:

- Search of investigative files and other records held by federal agencies, including the FBI and, if appropriate, international checks

- Financial check

- Field interviews of references (in writing, by telephone, or in person), to include coworkers, employers, personal friends, educators, neighbors, and other individuals

- A personal interview with the applicant, conducted by an investigator

Risk Analysis and Management

Security in any system should be in proportion to the risk under which it operates. The process to determine which security controls are appropriate and cost effective is often a complex and sometimes subjective matter. One of the prime functions of security risk analysis is to examine this process on a more objective basis.

Two basic types of risk analysis exist: quantitative and qualitative.

Quantitative Risk Analysis

Quantitative or quasi-subjective risk analysis attempts to establish and maintain an independent set of risk metrics and statistics. Some of the calculations used for quantitative risk analysis include these:

- **Annualized loss expectancy (ALE):** Single loss expectancy (SLE) multiplied by annualized rate of occurrence (ARO)

- **Probability:** Chance or likelihood, in a finite sample, that an event will occur or that a specific loss value might be realized if the event occurs

- **Threat:** An event whose occurrence could have an undesired impact

- **Control:** Risk-reducing measure that acts to detect, prevent, or minimize loss associated with the occurrence of a specified threat or category of threats

- **Vulnerability:** The absence or weakness of a risk-reducing safeguard

To compute risk value, multiply the probability of an event occurring by the likely loss it would incur. The result is a single value called the annual loss expectancy (ALE). Risk managers use the ALE to rank events by magnitude of risk and to make investment decisions based on this ranking. The problems with quantitative risk analysis are usually associated with the unreliability and inaccuracy of the data. Probability can rarely be precise and, in some cases, can promote complacency. In addition, controls and countermeasures often tackle a number of potential events, and the events themselves are frequently interrelated.

Qualitative Risk Analysis

Qualitative risk analysis is the most widely used approach to risk analysis. Probability data is not required, and only estimated potential loss is used. Most qualitative risk analysis methodologies make use of interrelated elements:

- Threats

- Vulnerabilities

- Controls

Threats are things that can go wrong or that can "attack" the system. Examples include fire or fraud. Threats are present for every system, no matter what you try to do to eliminate them completely.

Vulnerabilities make a system more prone to attack or make an attack more likely to have some success or impact. For example, fire vulnerability would be the presence of flammable materials (for example, paper).

Controls are the countermeasures for vulnerabilities and come in five types:

- Deterrent controls reduce the likelihood of a deliberate attack.

- Preventative controls protect vulnerabilities and either make an attack unsuccessful or reduce its impact.

- Corrective controls reduce the effect of an attack.

- Detective controls discover attacks and trigger preventative or corrective controls.

- Recovery controls restore lost computer resources or capabilities to recover from security violations.

A risk is real when there is a presence of threat (such as a willing and capable attacker), a vulnerability that the attacker can exploit, and a high likelihood that the attacker will carry out the threat.

Figure 4.2 illustrates the qualitative risk analysis process.

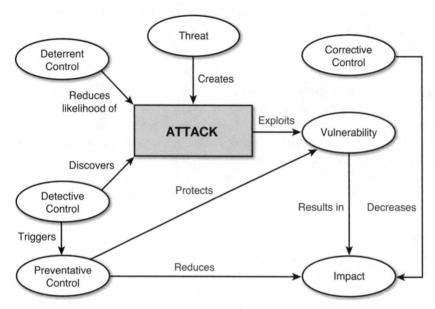

FIGURE 4.2   A model of the risk analysis process.

Risk analysis is required because it's impossible to protect assets if you do not know what you are protecting against. A risk analysis answers three fundamental questions:

- What am I trying to protect?
- What is threatening my system?
- How much time, effort, and money am I willing to spend?

After risks are classified either as metrics or relative to one another, you can develop policies and procedures needed to reduce them.

Education, Training, and Awareness

Because people are the weakest link in any security-related process, it's crucial that a security programme address user education, awareness, and training on policies and procedures that affect them. Education must be driven top down and must be comprehensive, all the way from high-end servers down to the desktop systems, mobile devices, peripherals, and hard copies of business documents.

Training can be offered in any number of forms and formats, including paper-based, intranet-based, classroom-based, and self-study methods. It should also include mechanisms to make sure that management keeps track of which employees have completed security training and which have agreed to live up to the programme expectations. Furthermore, training must be ongoing (at least annually) and should also take place whenever policies change. All employees (including contractors and third-party service providers) need to be made aware of changes.

Training materials and content vary by the roles or job duties of personnel. A computer user, for example, might need only basic security training (do not write down or share passwords, and so forth), whereas a developer would require application development security training, and IT support personnel or administrators would require more technical security training on the specific assets for which they're responsible.

Who Is Responsible for Security?

Everyone who uses information technology is responsible for maintaining the security and confidentiality of information resources and must comply with security policies and procedures. Certain individuals, however, have specific information security responsibilities that are established by the security programme:

- **Chief information security officer (CISO):** Establishes and maintains security and risk-management programmes for information resources.

- **Information resources manager:** Maintains policies and procedures that provide for security and risk management of information resources.

- **Information resources security officer:** Directs policies and procedures designed to protect information resources (identifies vulnerabilities, develops security awareness programme, and so forth).

- **Owners of information resources:** Have the responsibility of carrying out the programme that uses the resources. This does not imply personal ownership. These individuals might be regarded as programme managers or delegates for the owner.

- **Custodians of information resources:** Provide technical facilities, data processing, and other support services to owners and users of information resources.

- **Technical managers (network and system administrators):** Provide technical support for security of information resources.

- **Internal auditors:** Conduct periodic risk-based reviews of information resources security policies and procedures.

- **Users:** Have access to information resources in accordance with the owner-defined controls and access rules.

For a comprehensive example of a policy and standards library that is open to the public, visit the University of Houston Security Manual website at www.uh.edu/infotech/php/template.php?nonsvc_id=268.

Summary

The Security Management Practices domain is most concerned with the establishment and ongoing operation of the organization's security programme. This programme begins with documentation in the form of policies, standards, baselines, procedures, and guidance for compliance.

An effective security programme includes top-down sponsorship to establish and enforce these policies and standards and to develop and maintain procedures within a comprehensive library of documents that clearly spell out the responsibilities and consequence of noncompliance for all users of IT resources.

The library of documents is arranged as a hierarchy, with the highest level consisting of a few policies, followed by an increasing number of standard and baseline documents. It is further supplemented with guidance documents to aid in implementation and, finally, lots of procedure documents that explicitly describe how to implement a security control or process.

Dedicated personnel who are experts in the subject matter related to the organization's industry or mission should develop and manage the library. Because information security does not stand still for long, policies and standards libraries must be living and breathing to be effective in preventing, detecting, and responding to security risks.

Test Your Skills

MULTIPLE-CHOICE QUESTIONS

1. Which of the following choices is *not* part of a security policy?

    A. A definition of overall steps of information security and the importance of security

    B. A statement of management intent, supporting the goals and principles of information security

    C. A definition of general and specific responsibilities for information security management

    D. A description of specific technologies used in the field of information security regulations

2. Which of the following is the first step in establishing an information security programme?

    A. Adoption of a corporate information security policy statement

    B. Development and implementation of an information security standards manual

    C. Development of a security awareness training program for employees

    D. Purchase of security access control software

3. An effective information security policy should *not* have which of the following characteristics?

    A. It should include separation of duties.

    B. It should be designed with a short- to midterm focus.

    C. It should be understandable and supported by all stakeholders.

    D. It should specify areas of responsibility and authority.

4. What is the difference between advisory and regulatory security policies?

    A. There is no difference between them.

    B. Regulatory policies are high-level policy, whereas advisory policies are very detailed.

    C. Advisory policies provide recommendations.

    D. Advisory policies are mandated, whereas regulatory policies are not.

5. Which of the following terms can best be defined as high-level statements, beliefs, goals, and objectives?

    A. Standards

    B. Policies

    C. Guidelines

    D. Procedures

6. A deviation or exception from a security standard requires which of the following?

    A. Risk acceptance

    B. Risk assignment

    C. Risk reduction

    D. Risk containment

7. Why would an information security policy require that communications test equipment be controlled?

    A. The equipment is susceptible to damage.

    B. The equipment can be used to browse information passing on a network.

    C. The equipment must always be available for replacement, if necessary.

    D. The equipment can be used to reconfigure network devices.

8. Which of the following terms best describes step-by-step instructions used to satisfy control requirements?

    A. Policy

    B. Standard

    C. Guideline

    D. Procedure

9. Which of the following embodies all the detailed actions that personnel are required to follow?

    A. Standards

    B. Guidelines

    C. Procedures

    D. Baselines

10. Which of the following would be defined as an absence or weakness of a safeguard that could be exploited?

    A. A threat

    B. A vulnerability

    C. A risk

    D. An exposure

11. Within IT security, which of the following combinations best defines risk?

    A. A threat coupled with a breach

    B. A threat coupled with a vulnerability

    C. A vulnerability coupled with an attack

    D. A breach coupled with an attacker

12. Which of the following statements best describes IT security measures?

    A. IT security measures should be complex.

    B. IT security measures should be tailored to meet organizational security goals.

    C. IT security measures should make sure that every asset of the organization is well protected.

    D. IT security measures should not be developed in a layered fashion.

13. Which of the following should not be addressed by employee termination practices?

    A. Removal of the employee from active payroll files

    B. Return of access badges

    C. Employee bonding to protect against losses due to theft

    D. Deletion of assigned logon ID and passwords to prohibit system access

14. Which of the following statements best defines risk management?

    A. Risk management is the process of eliminating the risk.

    B. Risk management is the process of assessing the risks.

    C. Risk management is the process of reducing risk to an acceptable level.

    D. Risk management is the process of transferring risk.

15. Which of the following statements best describes controls?

    A. Controls eliminate risk and reduce the potential for loss.

    B. Controls mitigate risk and eliminate the potential for loss.

    C. Controls mitigate risk and reduce the potential for loss.

    D. Controls eliminate risk and eliminate the potential for loss.

16. Which of the following is an advantage of a qualitative risk analysis?

    A. A qualitative risk analysis prioritizes the risks and identifies areas for immediate improvement in addressing the vulnerabilities.

    B. A qualitative risk analysis provides specific quantifiable measurements of the magnitude of the impacts.

    C. A qualitative risk analysis makes a cost-benefit analysis of recommended controls easier.

    D. A qualitative risk analysis can easily be automated.

17. Which of the following terms best describes an event that could cause harm to the information systems?

    A. A risk

    B. A threat

    C. A vulnerability

    D. A weakness

18. One purpose of a security awareness program is to modify which of the following?

    A. Employees' attitudes and behaviors

    B. Management's approach

    C. Attitudes of employees toward sensitive data

    D. Corporate attitudes about safeguarding data

19. Which of the following should be given technical security training?

    A. Operators

    B. Security practitioners and information systems auditors

    C. IT support personnel and system administrators

    D. Senior managers, functional managers, and business unit managers

EXERCISES

EXERCISE 4.1: Analyzing Security Organizational Structures

1. Using your school or employer, document the organizational structure of the department responsible for IT security management.

2. Which security concepts (separation of duties, risk management, and so forth) do you find have influenced the current structure?

3. Which security concepts (if any) appear to be missing from the structure?

EXERCISE 4.2: Analyzing Security Policy Manuals

1. Locate the security policy manual for your organization or school.

2. How does its content compare to the content described in this chapter?

3. How does its structure compare to the structure described in this chapter?

EXERCISE 4.3: Understanding Security Awareness and Training

1. Describe the education, awareness, and training activities you have encountered as an employee or student.

2. Describe the opportunities for education and awareness that are offered to you as an employee or student.

EXERCISE 4.4: Finding Analogies to Separation of Duties

1. Explain the principle of separation of duties.

2. How does this principle compare to checks and balances found within the U.S. government?

3. How does this principle compare to checks and balances found within your state government?

EXERCISE 4.5: Applying Risk Analysis

1. Apply the information related to qualitative risk analysis to your personal or family vehicle as an asset.

2. Which risks can you determine, and how would you manage each one?

3. What might you do differently after you complete the exercise?

PROJECTS

PROJECT 4.1: Comparing Standards Libraries Across Organizations

1. Visit the University of Houston Information Security Manual website, at www.uh.edu/infotech/php/template.php?nonsvc_id=268.

2. Compare what you find there to the taxonomy of documents presented in this chapter.

3. Do you find many differences? How might you attribute differences between security manuals for corporations and those for educational organizations?

4. What are some of the similarities?

PROJECT 4.2: Understanding Best Practices Standards

1. Visit the InfoSec Reading Room at SANS.org (www.sans.org/rr).

2. Search for documented best practices in information security.

3. What types of best practices are commonly documented?

4. How could you incorporate these best practices into the development of a security manual?

5. How would you distribute these to personnel requiring the information?

PROJECT 4.3: Understanding Employee Prescreening and Termination Processes

1. Develop a list of recommended steps to include in a pre-employment hiring process.

2. Develop a list of recommended steps to include in an employee termination process.

3. Which areas within the organization need to be included?

4. Suggest some ways for the security department to communicate with these other departments, to ensure that nothing falls through the cracks.

5. How would you help ensure that outside departments follow these recommendations?

Chapter | 5

Security Architecture and Design

Chapter Objectives

After reading this chapter and completing the exercises, you will be able to do the following:

- Summarize the concept of a trusted computing base (TCB)
- Illustrate the concept of rings of trust
- Distinguish among the protection mechanisms used in a TCB
- Defend the purposes of security assurance testing
- Apply the Trusted Computer Security Evaluation Criteria (TCSEC) for software evaluations
- Apply the Trusted Network Interpretation of the TCSEC
- Categorize the role of the Federal Criteria for Information Technology Security
- Apply the Common Criteria for Information Security Evaluation
- Summarize the principles behind confidentiality and integrity models, as well as their role in security architectures

Introduction

The Security Architecture and Design domain of the Common Body of Knowledge contains the concepts, principles, structures, and standards used to design, monitor, and secure operating systems, equipment, networks, and applications. It also contains the controls used to enforce various levels of availability, integrity, and confidentiality. These ideas and controls stem from research in computer science and the development of systems requiring strict attention to computer security.

This domain introduces several new terms and concepts, including the concepts of trusted computing base (TCB), formal security evaluations and testing, and models of access control behavior.

Defining the Trusted Computing Base

Chapter 10, "Access Control Systems and Methodologies," covers the tools and methodologies used to implement access controls, but this chapter explores the principles behind these mechanisms.

The Trusted Computing Base (TCB) is the totality of protection mechanisms within a computer system, including hardware, firmware, and software. A TCB consists of one or more components that together enforce a unified security policy over a product or system. It describes the isolation of objects on which the protection is based, following the concept of the reference monitor. The reference monitor is a software model or abstract machine that mediates all access from any subject (user or other device) to any object (resource, data, and so forth); it cannot be bypassed. An abstract machine mediates accesses to objects by subjects. In principle, a reference monitor should be

- Complete, to mediate every access

- Isolated from modification by other system entities (objects and processes)

- Verifiable, doing only what it's programmed to do and not being susceptible to circumvention by malicious acts or programmer error

A security kernel is an implementation of a reference monitor for a specific hardware base, such as Sun Solaris, Red Hat Linux, or Mac OS X. The TCB, reference monitor, and security kernel are essential for military- and government-grade information technology (IT) security to prevent unauthorized access or threats to the integrity of programs, operating systems, or data.

According to the TCB, a trusted system is a system that can be expected to meet users' requirements for reliability, security, and effectiveness because it has undergone formal testing and validation. Trusted computing is an essential element for governments and agencies managing national secrets. Because no single person is responsible for data ownership when it comes to national secrets (because this is a commercial setting), the operating systems that are relied on use a concept called mandatory access control (MAC) to decide who may gain access to what. MAC requires that access control policy decisions stay beyond the control of the individual owner of an object, thus requiring the system to make the decisions. The reference monitor makes these decisions and permits or denies access based on labels and clearance levels.

An object is something within a trusted system that people want to access or use (such as a program). Objects are labeled with a sensitivity level (see Chapter 4, "Governance and Risk Management"). Subjects (people or other processes) that want to access these objects must be cleared to the same level of classification or higher. Several security models covered later in this chapter have been developed to address confidentiality and integrity.

Rings of Trust

The TCB concept is illustrated using what is called a ring of trust. Trust in a system moves from the outside to the inside in a unidirectional mode. The ring model of security (see Figure 5.1) was originally derived from the concept of execution domains developed by the Multics project.

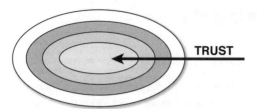

FIGURE 5.1   The unidirectional layered model of trust.

FYI: What Is Multics?

Multics (Multiplexed Information and Computing Service) was a time-sharing operating system project begun in 1965 as a joint project by MIT Project MAC, Bell Telephone Laboratories, and General Electric. Multics never enjoyed much commercial attention, but its many novel and valuable ideas had a powerful impact on the computer field. In particular, the UNIX system (produced by Bell Labs personnel who had worked on Multics), the GNU project, and, much later, the Linux kernel are partly descended from Multics.

Among its new ideas, Multics was the first operating system to provide a hierarchical file system, a feature that's now found in virtually every operating system. It had numerous features intended to result in high availability, to produce a computing utility, similar to the telephone and electricity services.

Figure 5.2 shows the rings of trust concept in the context of a single computer system. In this model, outer rings contain a lower level of security, and systems requiring higher levels of security are located inside the inner rings. Extra security mechanisms must be navigated to move from an outer ring into an inner ring. The operating system (OS) enforces how communications flow between layers using the reference monitor (within the kernel) to mediate all access and protect resources.

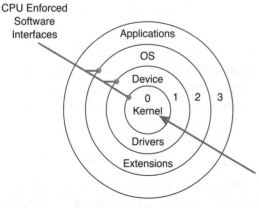

FIGURE 5.2   Rings of trust in stand-alone systems.

It's also possible to use the concepts of rings of trust to design security domains or operating environments for networks of systems. Figure 5.3 illustrates this concept.

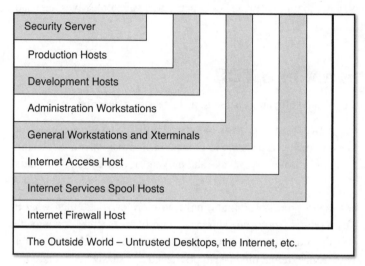

Security Server

Production Hosts

Development Hosts

Administration Workstations

General Workstations and Xterminals

Internet Access Host

Internet Services Spool Hosts

Internet Firewall Host

The Outside World – Untrusted Desktops, the Internet, etc.

FIGURE 5.3   Rings of trust in networked environments.

This model divides the hosts into rings, based on the security rating of the services they provide to the network, and then uses these rings as the basis for trust between hosts.

To help determine the hierarchy of the rings, some questions must be answered:

- Is the host in a physically secure computer room?
- Does the host have normal (as opposed to privileged) user accounts?
- Is this host at a remote site and, hence, less trustworthy than the ones in the central computer room?
- Does this host operate software that relies on data obtained from the Internet?
- Does this host provide mission-critical services? How many people in the company would be affected by downtime on this host?

The following general rules apply to constructing rings of trust in networked systems:

- Each host trusts hosts in a more inner ring than its own.
- No host trusts any host in a more outer ring than its own.
- Each host may trust hosts in the same ring as its own.
- Where a ring has been segmented into separate subnetworks, a host in one segment does not trust hosts in other segments.

As you can see, rings of trust apply equally well for stand-alone systems, small business or home networks, and large-scale corporate and government networks where security requirements are absolute.

To implement the rings of trust model, a number of software constructs and design objectives are used for security and resource protection.

Protection Mechanisms in a TCB

A TCB involves standard design concepts and software processes, as this section describes.

Process isolation is a design objective in which each process has its own distinct address space for its application code and data. Such a design makes it possible to prevent each process from accessing another process's data. This prevents data or information leakage and prevents modification of the data while in memory.

The principle of least privilege dictates that a process (program) have no more privilege than what it really needs to perform its functions. Any modules that require supervisor or root access (that is, complete system privileges) are embedded in the operating system kernel. The kernel handles all requests for system resources and mediates the access from external modules to privileged modules when required.

Hardware segmentation specifically relates to the segmentation of memory into protected segments. The kernel allocates the required amount of memory for the process to load its application code, its process data, and its application data. The system prevents user processes from accessing another process's allocated memory. It also prevents user processes from accessing system memory.

Layering is a process operation that is divided into layers by function. Each layer deals with a specific activity. The lower (outer) layers perform basic tasks, whereas the higher (inner) layers perform more complex or protected tasks.

Abstraction is a process that defines a specific set of permissible values for an object and the operations that are permissible on that object. This involves ignoring or separating implementation details to concentrate on what is important to maintain security.

Data hiding, also known as information hiding, is a mechanism used to ensure that information available at one processing level is not available in another, regardless of whether it is higher or lower. It is also a concept in the object-oriented programming (OOP) technique when information is encapsulated within an object and can be directly manipulated only by the services provided within the object.

Information storage refers to the parts of a computer system that retain a physical state (information) for some interval of time, possibly even after electrical power to the computer is removed. A number of types are used for data or information storage, including these:

- Primary storage is the computer's main memory that is directly addressable by the central processing unit (CPU). Primary storage is a volatile storage medium, meaning that the contents of the physical memory are lost when the power is removed.

- Secondary storage is a nonvolatile storage format that can store application and system code plus data when the system is not in use. Examples of secondary storage are disk drives or other persistent data storage mechanisms (including Flash [USB] drives, memory sticks, and tapes).

- Real memory refers to a definite storage location for a program in memory and direct access to a peripheral device. This is common with database management systems that control how storage is used outside the operating system's control.

- Virtual memory extends the volume of primary storage by using secondary storage to hold the memory contents. In this way, the operating system can run programs larger than the available physical memory. Virtual memory (memory contents stored on disk) is swapped in and out of primary memory when needed for processing.

- Random memory is the computer's primary working and storage area. It is addressable directly by the CPU and stores application or system code in addition to data.

- Sequential storage is computer memory that is accessed sequentially. An example of this is magnetic tape.

- Volatile memory experiences a complete loss of any stored information when the power is removed.

Closed systems are proprietary in nature. They use specific operating systems and hardware to perform the task and generally lack standard interfaces to allow connection to other systems. The user is generally limited in the applications and programming languages available.

An open system, on the other hand, is based on accepted standards and employs standard interfaces to allow connections between different systems. It promotes interoperability and gives the user full access to the total system capability.

Multitasking is a technique used by a system that is capable of running two or more tasks in a concurrent performance or interleaved execution.

A multiprogramming system permits the interleaved execution of two or more programs on a processor.

Multiprocessing provides for simultaneous execution of two or more programs by a processor (CPU). This can alternatively be done through parallel processing of a single program by two or more processors in a multiprocessor system that all have common access to main storage.

A finite-state machine is any device that stores the status or state of something at a given time that can operate based on inputs to change the stored status and/or cause an action or output to take place. The importance of finite-state machines is that the machine has distinct states that it remembers. In Multics, for example, a state was associated with each ring of trust. Each computer's data register also stores a state. The read-only memory from which a boot (computer start-up) program is loaded stores a state. In fact, the boot program is an initial state. The operating system is itself a state, and each application that it runs begins with some initial state that can change as it handles input. Thus, at any moment in time, a computer system can be seen as a complex set of states and each program in it as a state machine. In practice, however, state machines are used to develop and describe specific device or program interactions for purposes of discovery or evaluation.

System Security Assurance Concepts

When considering IT security systems (firewall software, intrusion detection devices, access control mechanisms, and so forth), the requirements or needs, decided by those who sponsor the development, appear in two forms: functional requirements and assurance requirements.

Functional requirements describe what a system should do by design. Assurance requirements describe how the functional requirements should be implemented and tested. Both sets of requirements are needed to answer the following questions:

- Does the system do the right things?
- Does the system do the right things in the right way?

These are the same questions others in noncomputer industries face with verification and validation. You need both answers to gain confidence in products before launching them into a wild, hostile environment such as the Internet or using them to protect national secrets and data (such as income tax returns). Both types of requirements must be tested (and retested) and are included in the scope of security assurance testing.

Software testing that focuses only on functionality testing for user acceptance will uncover errors (bugs) in how the software operates. If the system responds to input in the ways the users expect it to respond, it's stamped as ready to ship. If the system responds differently, the bugs are worked out in successive remediation and retesting until it behaves as desired.

Goals of Security Testing

Security testing flips this technique on its head and takes it a step further. It not only verifies that the functions designed to meet a security requirement operate as expected, but also validates that the implementation of the function is not flawed or haphazard.

This kind of security testing can be performed effectively only by experts, never by casual users or developers. Programmers can't uncover flaws in their own programs that affect security; they can only find the flaws in its operation.

Security assurance and testing is laced with odd concepts and principles that truly do fly in the face of conventional thinking and are foreign to most people involved in IT development. Gaining confidence that a system does *not* do what it's *not* supposed to do is akin to proving a negative, and almost everyone knows that you can't prove a negative! You can, however, subject a system to brutal security testing—and with each resistance to an attack, you gain additional confidence that it was developed with security in mind.

Formal Security Testing Models

Beginning with the widespread adoption of affordable computers by both the military and government bodies, the Trusted Computer System Evaluation Criteria (TCSEC) was born in the United States in the early 1980s. During the succeeding decade, other countries around the world began the work of developing their own evaluation criteria, building upon the concepts of the TCSEC but adding more flexibility to adapt to evolving computing technology.

In Europe, the European Commission published Information Technology Security Evaluation Criteria (ITSEC) version 1.2 in 1991 after joint development by France, Germany, the Netherlands, and the United Kingdom. In Canada, the Canadian Trusted Computer Product Evaluation Criteria (CTCPEC) version 3.0 was published in early 1993 as a combination of the ITSEC and TCSEC approaches.

The United States published the draft Federal Criteria for Information Technology Security (FC) version 1.0 in early 1993 as an attempt to develop criteria to replace the TCSEC and harmonize North American and European concepts for security evaluation criteria. A draft version of the Federal Criteria was released for public comment in December 1992 but was supplanted by the Common Criteria standardization efforts.

Beginning with TCSEC, the next few sections examine the evolution of security testing models that led to today's Common Criteria standard.

The Trusted Computer Security Evaluation Criteria

The U.S. Department of Defense (DOD) Trusted Computer System Evaluation Criteria (TCSEC) was a collection of criteria used to grade or rate the security claimed for a computer system product. The now-obsolete TCSEC was often called the Orange Book because of its orange cover. The last version is dated 1985 (DOD 5200.28-STD, Library No. S225,711). TCSEC is one part of a series of DOD documents called the Rainbow Series because of the multicolored covers on each document.

TCSEC is most interested in confidentiality and sets forth criteria to rate the effectiveness of trusted systems in terms of how well they can protect the secrecy of objects contained within them.

The TCB in the Orange Book is a complete description of all the protection mechanisms computer systems use. The combination of all protection mechanisms enforces security policy. The TCB consists of the hardware, software, and firmware that make up the system. Security policy is a formal description of the rules for subjects and objects that a trusted system needs to determine whether a given subject is authorized to access a specific object. Trusted systems are evaluated products (hardware, software, or combinations of the two) that are expected to meet the requirements for reliability, security, and operational effectiveness. They're both verified and validated as being implemented correctly through formal evaluation methods that use established criteria for testing.

The earlier efforts to formalize security assurance included groupings of requirements that described the desired levels of security for a product or a system. TCSEC and other assurance criteria documents outlined both security functional requirements (what functions must be present) and security assurance requirements (how thoroughly the functions should be tested) to arrive at an overall rating.

TCSEC provided classes (or divisions) of trust that are roughly equivalent to object classifications of Unclassified, Secret, Top Secret, and beyond Top Secret, using the letters D, C, B, and A, respectively.

Division D: Minimal Protection

TCSEC reserves Division D for systems that have been formally evaluated but fail to meet the requirements for a higher evaluation class. This classification is also used for unrated or untested systems. TCSEC does not contain specific requirements for Division D evaluations, but some of the TCSEC interpretation documents (including other Rainbow Series documents) do permit specifying Division D levels of evaluation.

Division C: Discretionary Protection

Classes in Division C provide for discretionary protection, based on the need-to-know or least privilege principle, and for audit control mechanisms that enforce the personal accountability of subjects for the actions they take while using the system. In the commercial world, discretionary protection shelters objects from unauthorized subjects through the assignment of privilege to the subject by the object's owner. In other words, a data owner (human being) gets to decide who is authorized to access his or her objects (data, programs, and so forth).

Class C1: Discretionary Security Protection

The TCB of a Class C1 system satisfies the discretionary access control requirements by separating users and data. It incorporates mechanisms that are capable of enforcing access limitations on an individual basis. C1 requirements are suitable for giving users the capability to protect project or private information and to keep other users from accidentally reading or destroying their data. Class C1 systems are typically used among a group of users who share the same level of clearance (such as workgroups).

Class C2: Controlled Access Protection

Systems in this class enforce a more finely grained discretionary access control than C1 systems, making users individually accountable for their actions through login procedures, auditing of security-relevant events, and resource isolation. This means that no program can gain access to the memory areas other programs use.

Security assurance divisions above Division C are usually reserved for governmental systems and are rarely found in the commercial world unless the company acts as a subcontractor to government agencies requiring such protections. Similarly, assurance levels in the Common Criteria above Evaluation Assurance Level (EAL) 4 are typically reserved for national government systems.

Division B: Mandatory Protection

A major requirement in this division is that a TCB must preserve the integrity of sensitivity labels and use them to enforce a set of mandatory access control rules. Systems in this division must carry the sensitivity labels (Secret or Top Secret, for example) with major data structures in the system. The system developer provides the security policy model on which the TCB is based and furnishes a specification of the TCB. Evidence is needed to demonstrate that the reference monitor concept has been implemented. The reference monitor refers to the concept of an abstract machine (a machine within a machine) that mediates the access of subjects to objects. The reference monitor must be protected from unauthorized changes, must always be used to mediate all access (cannot be circumvented), and must be verified as implemented correctly.

Mandatory protections are what the military is most interested in to protect national secrets. With mandatory access controls, the system or TCB decides who can access what according to the security policy implemented by the reference monitor.

Class B1: Labeled Security Protection

Class B1 systems require all the features Class C2 systems require. In addition, an informal statement of the security policy model, data labeling, and mandatory access control over named subjects and objects must be present. The system must have the capability to accurately label exported information from the system, and any flaws identified during testing must be removed.

Class B2: Structured Protection

In Class B2 systems, the TCB is based on a clearly defined and documented formal security policy model that requires extending the discretionary and mandatory access control enforcement in Class B1 systems to all subjects and objects in the system. In addition, covert channels are addressed. Covert channels are possible wherever a system has an opportunity to provide unintended communications. One example of a covert channel is a back door in a system that circumvents the security mechanisms and enables moving data from a higher classification level to an area where lower classifications of data are accessible.

The TCB must be carefully structured into protection-critical and non-protection-critical elements. The TCB interface is well defined and well understood, and the TCB design and implementation should enable the system to be subjected to more thorough testing and more complete review. During this testing and review, authentication mechanisms are strengthened, trusted facility management is offered via an interface for system administrator and operator functions, and strict configuration management controls are imposed. The system is then deemed relatively resistant to penetration.

Class B3: Security Domains

For Class B3, the TCB must satisfy the reference monitor requirements to do the following:

- Mediate all accesses of subjects to objects
- Resist tampering
- Have a small enough size that it can be subjected to analysis and tests

To this end, the TCB is structured to exclude program code that's not essential to security policy enforcement. This requires significant system engineering during TCB design and implementation, with the goal of minimizing its complexity. A security administrator role is supported, audit mechanisms are expanded to signal (trace) security-relevant events, and system recovery procedures are required. This system is deemed highly resistant to penetration.

Division A: Verified Protection

Division A is characterized by the use of formal security verification methods to ensure that the mandatory and discretionary security controls employed within the system effectively protect classified or other sensitive information that the system stores or processes. Extensive documentation is required to demonstrate that the TCB meets the security requirements in all aspects of design, development, and implementation.

Class A1: Verified Design

Systems in Class A1 are functionally equivalent to those in Class B3, with no additional architectural features or policy requirements added. The distinguishing feature of systems in this class is the analysis derived from formal design specification and verification techniques and the resulting high degree of assurance that the TCB is correctly implemented. This assurance is developmental in nature, starting with a formal model of the security policy and a formal top-level specification of the design. Class A1 systems must meet five important criteria for design verification, independent of the particular specification language or verification system used:

- A formal model of the security policy must be clearly identified and documented, including a mathematical proof that the model is consistent with its axioms and is sufficient to support the security policy.

- A formal top-level specification must be produced that includes abstract definitions of the functions the TCB performs and of the hardware and/or firmware mechanisms that support separated execution domains.

- The formal top-level specification of the TCB must be shown to be consistent with the model using formal techniques where possible (when verification tools exist) or informal ones when formal techniques are unavailable.

- The TCB implementation (in hardware, firmware, and software) must be informally shown to be consistent with the formal top-level specification. The elements of the formal top-level specification must be shown, using informal techniques, to correspond to the elements of the TCB. The formal top-level specification must express the unified protection mechanism required to satisfy the security policy. The elements of this protection mechanism are mapped to the elements of the TCB.

- Formal analysis techniques must be used to identify and analyze covert channels. Informal techniques can identify covert timing channels (unwanted communications based on temporal activities). The developer must justify any continued existence of identified covert channels in the system.

To preserve the extensive design and development analysis of the TCB required of systems in Class A1, additional stringent configuration management is required, along with procedures for securely distributing the system to sites. System security administrator functions are also required.

The Trusted Network Interpretation of the TCSEC

The Trusted Network Interpretation (TNI) of the TCSEC is also referred to as the Red Book of the Rainbow Series. The TNI restates the requirements of the TCSEC in a network context as contrasted with TCSEC on stand-alone and non-networked environments. For more information on the purpose and meaning of TNI, consult the Rainbow Books description of TNI at www.fas.org/irp/nsa/rainbow/tg005.htm.

The Information Technology Security Evaluation Criteria

The Information Technology Security Evaluation Criteria (ITSEC) is a European-developed criterion that fills a role roughly equivalent to the TCSEC for use throughout the European Community. Although the ITSEC and TCSEC have many similar requirements, they also have some important distinctions. The ITSEC places increased emphasis on integrity and availability and attempts to provide a uniform approach to the evaluation of both products and systems.

ITSEC introduces the concept of the target of evaluation (TOE), which refers to the product or system under evaluation. It adds to the TCB security-relevant functions in addition to security-enforcing functions (such as TCSEC). ITSEC provides for functionality classes, assurance classes, and profiles for systems. It also introduces the security target (ST), a written document that contains these components:

- A system security policy
- Required security-enforcing functions
- Required security mechanisms
- Claimed ratings of minimum strength
- Target evaluation levels, expressed as both functional and evaluation (F-xx and E-yy)

Comparing ITSEC to TCSEC

ITSEC functionality and assurance classes map closely to the TCSEC divisions and classes (see Table 5.1). You can use these to roughly compare implementations and testing requirements between products manufactured in the United States and ones made in Europe.

ITSEC classes are hierarchical; each class adds to the class above it and contains specific functions and mechanisms that correspond to TCSEC. ITSEC also supports other specialized classes that stand alone (nonhierarchical):

- F-IN for high-integrity

- F-AV for high-availability

- F-DI for high data integrity

- F-DC for high data confidentiality

- F-DX for networks that require high demands for confidentiality and integrity during data exchanges

These five classes describe only additional functional requirements beyond the preset requirements in Table 5.1.

ITSEC Assurance Classes

The assurance classes, listed as the second value in Table 5.1 for ITSEC, describe the testing requirements (see Table 5.2).

TABLE 5.1   TCSEC and ITSEC Classes Compared

TCSEC Classes	ITSEC Functional and Assurance Classes
C1	F-C1, E1
C2	F-C2, E2
B1	F-B1, E3
B2	F-B2, E4
B3	F-B3, E5
A1	F-B3, E6

TABLE 5.2   ITSEC Assurance Classes

C Assurance Class	Description
E0	Inadequate assurance; fails to meet E1 requirements
E1	Security target document that provides an informal description of the TOE's architectural design and functional testing that the TOE satisfies target requirements
E2	E1 requirements, plus an informal description of detailed designs, testing evidence, configuration control requirements, and approved distribution procedures
E3	E2 requirements, plus source code and drawings that are evaluated and testing evidence of security mechanisms that are evaluated

C Assurance Class	Description
E4	E3 requirements, plus a formal model of security policy, semiformal specification of security enforcing functions, architectural design documents, and detailed design documents
E5	E4 requirements, plus evidence of close correspondence between detailed design and source code (traceability of design into implementation)
E6	E5 requirements, plus a formal specification of security-enforcing functions and architectural design, along with consistency with the formal security policy model

The Canadian Trusted Computer Product Evaluation Criteria

In August 1988, the Canadian System Security Centre (CSSC) at the Communications Security Establishment of the Government of Canada was formed to develop a set of criteria and to set up a Canadian evaluation capability, among other tasks. In April 1992, a draft of version 3.0 of the Canadian Trusted Computer Product Evaluation Criteria (CTCPEC) was published.

The Canadian Trusted Computer Product Evaluation Criteria is the Canadian equivalent of the TCSEC. It is somewhat more flexible than the TCSEC (along the lines of the ITSEC), while maintaining fairly close compatibility with individual TCSEC requirements. The CTCPEC and its approach to structure security functionality separate from assurance functionality influenced international standardization through the Common Criteria. In January 1993, the final and last version (version 3) of CTCPEC was published.

The Federal Criteria for Information Technology Security

To further meet organizational needs for handling both classified and unclassified information, the Federal Criteria for Information Technology Security (Federal Criteria, or FC) was developed as a joint project by the National Institute of Standards and Technology (NIST) and the National Security Agency (NSA). The Federal Criteria was an attempt to develop a set of newer criteria to replace the aging TCSEC. It introduces the concept of a protection profile (PP) that empowers users or buyers of technology to specify their security requirements for hardware and software.

A draft version of the FC was released for public comment in December 1992. The effort was supplanted by the international Common Criteria development efforts, and the Federal Criteria never moved beyond the draft stage (although the Common Criteria retains many of its ideas). No final version of the FC was ever published.

The Common Criteria

Joint efforts among the United States (TCSEC), Canada (CTCPEC), and Europe (ITSEC) began in 1993 to harmonize security evaluation criteria to enable true comparability for the results of independent security evaluations. These joint activities were designed to align international separate criteria into a single set of IT security criteria that could be broadly used. The activity, named the Common Criteria (CC) Project, was intended to resolve the conceptual and technical differences in the various source criteria and to deliver the results to the International Organization for Standardization (ISO) as a proposed international standard under development.

> ### FYI: Formal Security Testing in the Real World
>
> These concepts and processes might seem a bit of overkill, but serious buyers of security products should never ignore assurance of commercial products. To better understand how security evaluations work in practice and what their value is to government and commercial buyers of security products, visit the Common Criteria Portal at www.commoncriteriaportal.org.

Representatives of the sponsoring organizations formed the CC Editorial Board (CCEB) to develop the CC, and the CCEB and ISO Working Group 3 (WG3) established a liaison relationship. The CCEB contributed several early versions of the CC to WG3 via the liaison. As a result of the interaction between WG3 and the CCEB, successive versions of the CC were adopted as working drafts of the various parts of the CC beginning in 1994. Work continued for the next 5 years to harmonize requirements. In June 1999, the Common Criteria for IT Security Evaluation became ISO International Standard 15408. It focuses on security objectives, the related threats (malicious or otherwise), and the functional requirements relevant to security.

The market force driving the need for harmonized criteria is best understood by an example. Imagine that a vendor of firewalls in Germany wanted to sell its ITSEC-evaluated product to an American government agency. If the U.S. agency required the product for a classified government system, the German firewall vendor would have no choice but to sponsor a separate evaluation of its product in the United States using TCSEC criteria, adding tremendous cost and time to the process of successfully selling its products beyond the German border.

The Common Criteria addresses this problem through a mutual recognition of the final certificates granted to successfully evaluated products and eliminates the need for multiple evaluations and their associated costs and time requirements.

The Common Criteria, also known as ISO 15408, combines the best features of the TCSEC with the ITSEC and the CTCPEC, and synergizes them into a single international standard.

Many countries and organizations participated in the development of the Common Criteria:

- **Canada:** Communications Security Establishment
- **France:** Service Central de la Securite des Systémes d'Information

- **Germany:** Bundesamt fur Sicherheit in der Informationstechnik

- **The Netherlands:** Netherlands National Communications Security Agency

- **United Kingdom:** Communications-Electronics Security Group

- **United States:** National Institute of Standards and Technology and the National Security Agency

The CC provides a common language and structure to express IT security requirements and enables the creation of catalogs of standards broken down into components and packages. The CC breaks apart the functional and assurance requirements into distinct elements that users can select for customized security device implementation.

Packages permit the expression of requirements that meet an identifiable subset of security objectives. Packages are reusable and can be used to construct larger packages as well. Using the CC framework, users and developers of IT security products create protection profiles (PPs) as an implementation-independent collection of objectives and requirements for any given category of products or systems that must meet similar needs (such as firewalls). Protection profiles are needed to support defining functional standards and serve as an aid in specifying needs for procurement purposes.

Whereas protection profiles work as a generic description of product and environmental requirements, targets of evaluation (TOE) are the specific products or systems that fall into an evaluation against an existing PP. The sets of evidence about a TOE and the TOE itself form the inputs to a security target (ST) that certified independent evaluators use as the basis for evaluation.

Again, two types of security requirements exist: functional and assurance. Functional requirements describe what a product needs to do, and assurance requirements describe how well it meets the functional requirements. Consumers need both pieces of data to effectively judge the merits of one product over another.

In defining security requirements for a trusted product or system, users and developers need to consider the threats to the environment. The Common Criteria provides a catalog of components (Part 2 of the CC) that developers of PPs use to form the requirements definition. Assurance requirements (defined in Part 3 of the CC) contain two classes from which evaluation assurance requirements can be selected, along with a class for assurance maintenance.

Protection Profile Organization

A protection profile is organized as follows:

- Introduction section, which provides descriptive information needed to identify, catalog, register, and cross-reference a PP. The overview provides a summary of the PP as a narrative.

- Target of evaluation (TOE) description, which describes the TOE to aid in understanding its security requirements and addresses the product type and general features of the TOE, providing a context for the evaluation.

- Security environment, which consists of three subsections:

  - Assumptions

  - Threats

  - Organizational security policies

These sections describe the security aspects of the environment in which the TOE will be used and the manner in which it will be used. Assumptions describe the security aspects of the environment in which the TOE will be used, including information about the intended usage, aspects about the intended applications, potential asset value, and possible limitations of use. The threats section covers all the threats for which specific protection within the TOE or its environment is needed. It includes only threats that are relevant to secure TOE operation. Organizational security policies identify and explain any security policies or rules that govern the TOE or its operating environment.

- Security objectives address the entire security environment aspects identified in earlier sections of the PP. These objectives define the intent of the TOE to counter identified threats and include the organizational security policies and assumptions. This section defines in detail the security requirements that by the TOE or its environment must satisfy. TOE security requirements describe the supporting evidence needed to satisfy security objectives. Functional requirements are selected from the CC functional components (Part 2).

- Assurance requirements are stated as one of the evaluation assurance levels (EALs) from the CC Part 3 assurance components.

- Rationale presents the evidence used by a PP evaluation. This evidence supports the claims that the PP is a complete and cohesive set of requirements and that a compliant TOE provides an effective set of IT security countermeasures within the security environment.

Security Functional Requirements

The following are classes of security functional requirements (component catalog):

- **Audit:** Security auditing functions involve recognizing, recording, storing, and analyzing information related to security-relevant activities. The resulting audit records can be examined to determine which security-relevant activities took place and which user is responsible for them.

- **Cryptographic support:** These functions are used when the TOE implements cryptographic functions in hardware, firmware, or software.

- **Communications:** These functional requirements are related to ensuring both the identity of a transmitted information originator and the identity of the recipient. These functions ensure that an originator cannot deny having sent the message, nor can the recipient deny having received it.

- **User data protection:** This class of functions is related to protecting user data within a TOE during import, export, and storage.

- **Identification and authentication:** These functions ensure that users are associated with the proper security attributes (including identity, groups, and roles).

- **Security management:** These functions are intended to specify the management of several aspects of the TOE security functions security attributes and security data.

- **Privacy:** These requirements protect a user against discovery and misuse of identity by other users.

- **Protection of the TOE security functions (TSF):** These requirements relate to the integrity and management of the mechanisms that provide the TSF and to the integrity of TSF data.

- **Resource utilization:** These functions support the availability of required resources such as CPU and storage capacity. Fault tolerance protects against unavailability of capabilities caused by failure of the TOE. Priority of service ensures that the resources will be allocated to the more important or time-critical tasks and cannot be monopolized by lower-priority tasks.

- **TOE access:** These requirements control the establishment of a user's session.

Evaluation assurance classes include the following:

- Configuration management helps ensure that the integrity of the TOE is preserved through required discipline and control in the processes of refinement and modification of the TOE and other related information. Configuration management prevents unauthorized modifications, additions, or deletions to the TOE and provides assurance that the TOE and documentation used for evaluation are the ones prepared for distribution.

- Delivery and operation classes define the requirements for the measures, procedures, and standards concerned with secure delivery, installation, and operational use of the TOE. This ensures that the security protection the TOE offers is not compromised during transfer, installation, startup, and operation.

- Development classes define the requirements for the stepwise (proceeding in steps) refinement of the TOE security functions (TSF) from the summary specification in the security target, down to the actual implementation. Each of the resulting TSF representations provides information to help the evaluator determine whether the functional requirements of the TOE have been met.

- Guidance documents define the requirements for coherence, coverage, and completeness of the operational documentation the developer has provided. This documentation, which provides two categories of information (for users and for administrators), is an important factor in the secure operation of the TOE.

- Lifecycle support defines the requirements for adopting a well-defined lifecycle model for all the steps of the TOE development, including flaw remediation procedures and policies, correct use of tools and techniques, and the security measures used to protect the development environment.

- Tests cover the testing requirements needed to demonstrate that the TSF satisfies the TOE security functional requirements. This class addresses coverage, depth of developer testing, and functional tests for independent lab testing.

- Vulnerability assessment defines the requirements directed at identifying exploitable vulnerabilities. Specifically, it addresses vulnerabilities introduced in the construction, operation, misuse, or incorrect configuration of the TOE.

- Protection profile evaluation demonstrates that the PP is complete, consistent, and technically sound, and that an evaluated PP is suitable as the basis for developing an ST.

- Security target evaluation demonstrates that the ST is complete, consistent, and technically sound, and is suitable as the basis for the corresponding TOE evaluation.

- Maintenance of assurance provides the requirements intended for application after a TOE has been certified against the Common Criteria. Maintenance of assurance requirements help ensure that the TOE will continue to meet its security target as changes are made to the TOE or its environment. Such changes include the discovery of new threats or vulnerabilities, changes in user requirements, and the correction of bugs found in the certified TOE.

Evaluation Assurance Levels

Assurance levels define a scale for measuring the criteria for evaluating PPs and STs. Evaluation Assurance Levels (EALs) provide an increasing scale that balances the levels of assurance claimed with the cost and feasibility of acquiring such assurance. Table 5.3 indicates the CC EAL levels, along with backward compatibility to the Orange Book and ITSEC criteria levels.

TABLE 5.3   Security Criteria Compared

Common Criteria Assurance Level	Orange Book Criteria Level	ITSEC Criteria Level
—	D: Minimal protection	E0
EAL1	—	—
EAL2	C1: Discretionary security protection	E1
EAL3	C2: Controlled access protection	E2
EAL4	B1: Labeled security protection	E3
EAL5	B2: Structured protection	E4
EAL6	B3: Security domains	E5
EAL7	A1: Verified design	E6

Evaluation Assurance Level 1

EAL1 applies when some confidence in correct operation is required, but the threats to security are not viewed as serious. It is valuable when independent assurance is required to support the contention that due care has been exercised in protecting personal or similar types of information. The intention is that an EAL1 evaluation can be successfully conducted without assistance from the developer of the TOE, at a low cost. An evaluation at this level provides evidence that the TOE functions in a manner consistent with its documentation and that it provides useful protection against identified threats. Think of EAL1 as kicking the tires on a vehicle that you're considering for purchase.

Evaluation Assurance Level 2

EAL2 requires a developer's cooperation in terms of the delivery of design information and test results, but it does not demand more effort from the developer than is consistent with good commercial practice; it also should not require a substantially increased investment of money or time. EAL2 is applicable when developers or users require a low to moderate level of independently assured security, in the absence of ready availability of the complete development record. Such a situation might arise when securing legacy systems or when access to the developer is limited.

Evaluation Assurance Level 3

EAL3 permits a conscientious developer to gain maximum assurance from positive security engineering at the design stage without substantial alteration of existing sound development practices. EAL3 applies when developers or users require a moderate level of independently assured security; it requires a thorough investigation of the TOE and its development without substantial reengineering.

Evaluation Assurance Level 4

EAL4 permits a developer to gain maximum assurance from positive security engineering based on good commercial development practices that, though rigorous, do not require substantial specialist knowledge, skills, and other resources. EAL4 is applicable when developers or users require a moderate to high level of independently assured security in conventional off-the-shelf TOEs. Additional security-specific engineering costs could be involved.

Evaluation Assurance Level 5

EAL5 permits a developer to gain maximum assurance from security engineering based on rigorous commercial development practices supported by moderate application of specialist security engineering techniques. Such a TOE likely is designed and developed with the intent of achieving EAL5 assurance. EAL5 is applicable when developers or users require a high level of independently assured security in a planned development and require a rigorous development approach without incurring unreasonable costs for special security engineering techniques.

Evaluation Assurance Level 6

EAL6 permits developers to gain high assurance from applying security engineering techniques to a rigorous development environment, to produce a premium TOE for protecting high-value assets against significant risks. EAL6 is applicable to developing security TOEs in high-risk situations, when the value of the protected assets justifies additional costs.

Evaluation Assurance Level 7

EAL7 applies to the development of security TOEs for application in extremely high-risk situations, when the value of such assets justifies the costs for higher assurance levels.

After an ST is independently evaluated and is found to meet the desired assurance level, the CC provides for a certification process that's recognized across all CC-using countries. The implication is that products developed and tested abroad can compete on equal footing with similar products developed within the United States.

The Common Evaluation Methodology

The Common Evaluation Methodology Editorial Board (CEMEB), with members from all the organizations that produced the Common Criteria for Information Technology Security Evaluation, is responsible for producing an agreed-upon methodology for conducting evaluations to apply the CC to security targets.

The Common Evaluation Methodology (CEM) is a companion document to the CC. It focuses on the actions evaluators must take to determine that CC requirements for a TOE are present. CEM is an evaluation tool to ensure consistent application of the requirements across multiple evaluations and multiple schemes. As such, it is an important component of the Mutual Recognition Arrangement (MRA) that enables any country to accept a certified evaluation from any other member country. So far, agreement has been reached for evaluation levels EAL1 to EAL4, which are deemed adequate for most commercial security products. The CCMEB is continuing the work on common evaluations for levels EAL5, EAL6, and EAL7.

The CEM contains three parts:

- **Part 1: Introduction and General Model:** This part describes agreed-upon principles of evaluation and introduces agreed-upon evaluation terminology dealing with the process of evaluation.

- **Part 2: CC Evaluation Methodology:** This part is based on CC Part 3 evaluator actions. It uses well-defined assertions to refine CC Part 3 evaluator actions and tangible evaluator activities to determine requirement compliance. In addition, it offers guidance to further clarify the intent evaluator actions. Part 2 provides for methodologies to evaluate the following:

  - PPs
  - STs
  - EAL1
  - EAL2
  - EAL3
  - EAL4
  - EAL5

- EAL6

- EAL7

- Components not included in an EAL

- **Part 3: Extensions to the Methodology:** These extensions are needed to take full advantage of the evaluation results. This part includes topics such as guidance on the composition and content of evaluation document deliverables.

The Common Criteria is currently in use worldwide and is rapidly gaining acceptance and use in common commercial off-the-shelf (COTS) systems. Several large software and hardware developers have embraced the CC, and their products (including Oracle databases, Apple Computer's MAC OS X, Windows Server 2012, and others) are poised for widespread government procurement activities.

Confidentiality and Integrity Models

Security models are mathematical representations of abstract machines that describe how a reference monitor is designed to operate and to help evaluators determine whether the implementation meets the design requirements. The following are some of the more commonly used models:

- Bell-LaPadula model

- Biba integrity model

- Clark and Wilson model

- Noninterference model

- State machine model

- Access matrix model

- Information flow model

The Bell-LaPadula model and the Biba integrity model are explained in-depth next because they were major influencing models for TCSEC and ITSEC. Other models that follow are minor improvements to Bell-LaPadula and Biba or provide more analysis tools.

Bell-LaPadula Model

Leonard J. LaPadula and David E. Bell developed this early and popular security model in the 1970s. It forms the basis of the TCSEC. This model is a formal one of security policy that describes a set of access control rules. By conforming to a set of rules, the model inductively proves that the system is secure. A subject's access (usually a user) to an object (usually a file) is allowed or disallowed by comparing the object's security classification with the subject's security clearance.

Bell-LaPadula is a confidentiality model intended to preserve the principle of least privilege. It is a formal description of allowable paths of information flow in a secure system and defines security requirements for systems handling data at different sensitivity levels. The model defines a secure state and access between subjects and objects in accordance with specific security policy.

Biba Integrity Model

The Biba model covers integrity levels, which are analogs to the sensitivity levels from the Bell-LaPadula model. Integrity levels cover inappropriate modification of data and prevent unauthorized users from making modifications to resources and data.

The Biba model uses a read-up, write-down approach. Subjects cannot read objects of lesser integrity and cannot write to objects of higher integrity. Think of CIA analysts and the information they need to perform their duties. Under the Biba model, an analyst with Top Secret clearance can see only information that's labeled as Top Secret with respect to integrity (confirmed by multiple sources, and so forth); likewise, this analyst can contribute information only at his or her clearance level. People with higher clearances are not "poisoned" with data from a lower level of integrity and cannot poison those with clearances higher than theirs.

Advanced Models

Some of the other models improve upon earlier models or provide more in-depth analysis tools.

- **Clark and Wilson model:** Proposes "well formed transactions." It requires mathematical proof that steps are performed in order exactly as they are listed, authenticates the individuals who perform the steps, and defines separation of duties.

- **Noninterference model:** Covers ways to prevent subjects operating in one domain from affecting each other in violation of security policy.

- **State machine model:** Acts as an abstract mathematical model consisting of state variables and transition functions.

- **Access matrix model:** Acts as a state machine model for a discretionary access control environment.

- **Information flow model:** Simplifies analysis of covert channels. A covert channel is a communication channel that allows two cooperating processes of different security levels (one higher than the other) to transfer information in a way that violates a system's security policy.

As you can see, security models are required to help developers and evaluators with widely accepted criteria and functions that are proven reliable and acceptable for even a nation's most closely guarded secrets.

FYI: How Does a Covert Channel Work?

Consider this example of a human covert channel: Several managers decide they don't want to waste too much time with an interview of a prospective employee and have come up with a communications protocol to let other interviewers know of their impression of the interviewee, to either continue the interview or cut it short.

The managers decide to cough if they decide to end the interview and sneeze if they are interested in pursuing the candidate. Without the candidate having any idea what they're up to, the managers can quickly agree to make the best use of their time.

Now consider an example of a computer-based covert channel: a couple of internal developers devise a scheme to alter a program specifically to violate the security policy. The scheme could work as follows: One programmer creates a program change to communicate with another program written by a different, colluding programmer to violate the system's security policy. One possible motivation for doing so is to span a "Chinese Wall" that separates a banking company from a brokerage company, for example. The companies then could share information about a high-value customer, with the intent of defrauding that person beyond the scope of the business. The programmers agree in advance on a protocol to use. Then, when the example program PostCreditToBill wants to send covert data to program SellStock, PostCreditToBill can be programmed to cause a lot of sudden CPU activity; SellStock can detect that and begin reading memory channels or communication channels to gain information about checking account data that would not appear in the brokerage system.

Summary

The Security Architecture and Models domain of the Common Body of Knowledge embodies the study of formal models for the design and evaluation of systems needed for the highest levels of information security. This includes systems that protect national secrets and other government property.

The trusted computing base, or TCB, is the portion of a computer system that contains all elements of the system responsible for supporting the security policy and ensuring the isolation of objects on which the protection is based. Included are several mechanisms, properties, and concepts that are required for a formal evaluation before they are used to protect resources and information.

Several evolving models of evaluation and assurance cover various aspects of confidentiality, integrity, and availability. TCSEC, otherwise known as the Orange Book, is primarily concerned with confidentiality and is based on the Bell-LaPadula model. ITSEC adds concerns about integrity and availability. The Canadian Criteria (CTCPEC) advances the work of TCSEC and ITSEC.

Finally, the Common Criteria harmonizes the work of the various international efforts into a unified evaluation methodology that replaces the former methods.

Test Your Skills

MULTIPLE-CHOICE QUESTIONS

1. Which of the following terms best defines the sum of protection mechanisms inside the computer, including hardware, firmware, and software?

    A. Trusted system

    B. Security kernel

    C. Trusted computing base

    D. Security perimeter

2. Which of the following statements pertaining to protection rings is false?

    A. They provide strict boundaries and definitions on what the processes that work within each ring can access.

    B. Programs operating in inner rings are usually referred to as existing in a privileged mode.

    C. They support the CIA triad requirements of multitasking operating systems.

    D. They provide users with a direct access to peripherals.

3. Which of the following places the Orange Book classifications in order from most secure to least secure?

   A. Division A, Division B, Division C, Division D

   B. Division D, Division C, Division B, Division A

   C. Division D, Division B, Division A, Division C

   D. Division C, Division D, Division B, Division A

4. The Orange Book describes four hierarchical levels to categorize security systems. Which of the following levels require mandatory protection?

   A. Divisions A and B

   B. Divisions B and C

   C. Divisions A, B, and C

   D. Divisions B and D

5. Which Orange Book rating represents the highest security level?

   A. B1

   B. B2

   C. F6

   D. C2

6. Which Orange Book security rating introduces security labels?

   A. C2

   B. B1

   C. B2

   D. B3

7. The Orange Book is founded upon which security policy model?

   A. Biba model

   B. Bell-LaPadula model

   C. Clark-Wilson model

   D. Common Criteria

8. The Information Technology Security Evaluation Criteria (ITSEC) was written to address which of the following that the Orange Book did not address?

   A. Integrity and confidentiality

   B. Confidentiality and availability

   C. Integrity and availability

   D. None of the above

9. What does CC stand for?

   A. enCrypted Communication

   B. Common Criteria for Information Security Evaluation

   C. Certificate Creation

   D. Circular Certificate rollover

10. Which of the following terms best describes a computer that uses more than one CPU in parallel to execute instructions?

    A. Multiprocessing

    B. Multitasking

    C. Multithreading

    D. Parallel running

11. Which of the following storage types is best described as a condition in which RAM and secondary storage are used together?

    A. Primary storage

    B. Secondary storage

    C. Virtual storage

    D. Real storage

12. Which of the following terms best describes the primary concern of the Biba security model?

    A. Confidentiality

    B. Reliability

    C. Availability

    D. Integrity

13. Which of the following terms is *not* a method to protect subjects, objects, and the data within the objects?

    A. Layering

    B. Data mining

    C. Abstraction

    D. Data hiding

14. Which of the following terms best describes the primary concern of the Bell-LaPadula security model?

    A. Accountability

    B. Integrity

    C. Confidentiality

    D. Availability

15. Which of the following statements best defines a covert channel?

    A. A covert channel is an undocumented back door that a programmer has left in an operating system.

    B. A covert channel is an open system port that should be closed.

    C. A covert channel is a communication channel that allows transfer of information in a manner that violates the system's security policy.

    D. A covert channel is a Trojan horse.

EXERCISES

EXERCISE 5.1: Trusted Computing Base

1. Describe the concept and main features of the trusted computing base (TCB).

2. What elements are found in the TCB?

3. What types of software should implement the concept of the TCB?

EXERCISE 5.2: Security Evaluations

1. Describe the concept of security evaluation (security assurance).

2. What are some of the general criteria used for evaluation?

EXERCISE 5.3: **TCSEC (Orange Book)**

1. Describe TCSEC in terms of its overall purposes.

2. What are the different TCSEC divisions and classes?

3. Why are different classes needed for different types of security classifications?

EXERCISE 5.4: **ITSEC**

1. Describe ITSEC in terms of purposes and differences in classes.

2. How does ITSEC differ from TCSEC?

EXERCISE 5.5: **Common Criteria (CC)**

1. Describe the Common Criteria in terms of its purpose.

2. How does the CC differ from TCSEC and ITSEC?

PROJECTS

PROJECT 5.1: **Security Testing for Obvious Vulnerabilities**

1. Research the Internet for several common software vulnerabilities (such as buffer overflow conditions, cross-site scripting, and SQL injection).

2. Describe several ways security testing can uncover the conditions.

3. Describe the limitations of security testing.

4. To what degree should testing be performed if the software is intended for commercial uses?

5. To what degree should testing be performed if the software is intended for commercial, governmental, and military uses?

PROJECT 5.2: **MS Windows and Common Criteria Testing**

1. Visit the Microsoft website, at www.microsoft.com.

2. Search for what Microsoft is doing with the Common Criteria for Windows Operating Systems.

3. How does Microsoft involvement in CC testing fit into the company's Trustworthy Computing Initiatives?

4. What advantages does a CC-certified version of Windows provide?

5. What criticisms of the CC-certified versions of Windows can you find?

PROJECT 5.3: **Trusted Computing in the Marketplace**

1. Research a few of the user authentication products in the marketplace:

   Microsoft's PhoneFactor: www.phonefactor.com

   Computer Associates eTrust: www.ca.com

   BMC Software's Control SA: www.bmc.com

2. What elements of trusted computing can you find in these products?

3. What kinds of commercial security testing have these products undergone?

4. Which product(s) are certified?

Chapter | **6**

Business Continuity Planning and Disaster Recovery Planning

Chapter Objectives

After reading this chapter and completing the exercises, you will be able to do the following:

- Distinguish between the business continuity plan (BCP) and the disaster recovery plan (DRP)
- Follow the steps in the BCP
- Explain to business executives why planning is important
- Define the scope of the business continuity plan
- Identify types of disruptive events
- Outline the contents of a business impact analysis (BIA).
- Discuss recovery strategies and the importance of crisis management
- Explain backup and recovery techniques, including agreements for shared sites and alternate sites

Introduction

When reading this chapter, you might feel like you are preparing for a project management role instead of an information security role, but you'll soon see that the interests of those who manage the business and those who safeguard it are intertwined. This chapter deals with business management concerns: how to prepare for an emergency or calamity and how to respond and continue operations under suboptimal business conditions.

In this chapter, you learn about the goals of sound business continuity planning and disaster recovery planning, see how these two types of planning differ, investigate the types of threats that could invoke emergency planning and procedures, and explore several of the more prominent techniques organizations are using to plan for and hopefully prevent a disruption in business activities.

Overview of the Business Continuity Plan and Disaster Recovery Plan

In the early 1990s, most businesses concerned about the health and safety of their organization and its continued operation focused on disaster recovery planning. This type of planning primarily included information technology (IT) systems and applications, application data, and the networks supporting the IT infrastructure. In the case of highly regulated industries such as government, healthcare, and financial services, organizations had to meet recovery-time and recovery-point objectives to minimize the loss of operations and the transaction data upon which they depend.

As the millennium change (or Y2K) approached, such organizations began to broaden their approach to disaster recovery planning, implementing more encompassing business continuity planning to address fail points not just in IT operations, but throughout the organization. Such a shift in view from a strictly IT-centric to a company-wide plan accelerated after the September 11, 2001, terrorist attack, when the loss of life dramatically emphasized the need to protect an organization's most important resource: its employees.

The business continuity plan (BCP) describes the critical processes, procedures, and personnel that must be protected in the event of an emergency. The corresponding business impact analysis (BIA) evaluates risks to the organization and prioritizes the systems in use for purposes of recovery. Mission-critical systems—systems that are essential for the ongoing operation of the business—are at the top of the list, followed by less critical systems and then "nice to have" systems that are nonessential for the business to remain in business.

The disaster recovery plan (DRP) describes the exact steps and procedures personnel in key departments, specifically the IT department, must follow to recover critical business systems in the event of a disaster that causes the loss of access to systems required for business operations. For example, one credit card company's mission-critical system is the authorization system for charge requests at the point of sale; without this capability, the company could not generate revenue and would be out of business in a matter of days or weeks.

Business continuity planning and disaster recovery planning share the common goal of keeping a business running in case of an emergency or interruptions. Both the BCP and DRP strive to prevent costly disruptions in critical business processes after disaster strikes.

Anticipating, planning for, and preventing problems is generally less costly than simply reacting to them after they occur. At a minimum, outages to IT systems can cost millions of dollars in lost revenue, lost productivity, and lost resources because of legal issues. According to the Gartner Group, "two out of every five enterprises that experience a disaster go out of business within five years." Failing to plan is indeed planning to fail when it comes to business and IT operations. At the extreme, a sustained outage can threaten the viability of an organization.

Business and security experts must take the following steps when creating a business continuity plan. They are designed to ensure continued operations and to protect people and property within the business in case of an emergency:

1. They must identify the scope and boundaries of the business continuity plan while communicating the importance of such a plan throughout the organization. What critical aspects of the business must be considered as part of the plan? This step typically involves an audit analysis of the organization's assets, including people, facilities, applications, and IT systems, along with a risk analysis that identifies the types of threats to the organization, both man-made and natural.

2. Using the results of this thorough analysis, they must create the business impact assessment (BIA). The BIA measures the operating and financial loss to the organization from a disruption to critical business functions (you get a more thorough explanation of the BIA later in this chapter).

3. When the BIA is complete, those responsible for creating the plan must sell the concept of the BCP to key senior management and obtain organizational and financial commitment. Without the support of top management, the BCP remains an abstraction—mere words on a page. The presenters must be prepared to answer questions such as whether the BCP is cost-effective and practical. If the cost of implementing the plan outweighs the benefit derived from it, the BCP must be reviewed and modified where appropriate. If the plan is too cumbersome and impractical to implement, its chances of success are slim.

4. After the BCP has gained the approval of upper management personnel who have signed off on the plan and released the necessary resources to implement it, each department needs to understand its role in the plan and support and help maintain it. This happens through a thorough examination of best practices within the organization and the tasks, processes, roles, and resources needed to meet the stated objectives of the continuity plan.

5. Finally, the BCP project team must implement the plan. This includes the necessary training, testing, and ongoing review and support of the BCP in both financial and practical terms. Business processes are rarely static, and the project team must ensure that the BCP adapts to changes within the organization.

Why the BCP Is So Important

The BCP reduces the risk to the business in case of a disruption in the continuity of business (you get more on exactly what these disruptions can be shortly). Many of the same reasons we plan for emergencies in our personal lives apply to the BCP: to save time and money, reduce stress, maintain a steady flow of income, protect lives, and minimize disruptions.

Businesses, however, have responsibilities beyond personnel and property. They are chartered with protecting shareholder investments while meeting federal and state legal requirements. They also have to worry about public image. Any significant disruption in business will quickly drive away partners, investors, and consumers. You may have heard the phrase "due diligence" in the workplace or in your coursework. Although the phrase has no precise definition, the intent is that a business will act responsibly and protect its assets according to generally accepted business practices and management. In fulfilling this responsibility, being proactive is preferable to being reactive.

According to Continuity Central (www.continuitycentral.com/feature0660.html), the international business continuity information portal, the lack of business continuity planning and disaster recovery planning results in some telling statistics:

- Eighty percent of businesses without a recovery plan either close or never reopen within 18 months.

- Seventy percent of companies go out of business after a major data loss.

- Eighty percent of companies lacking a business continuity plan fail within 2 years.

- Sixty percent of companies that lose their data shut down within 6 months of a disaster.

Types of Disruptive Events

You learn about some of the specific types of threats to a business in Chapter 8, "Physical Security Control." Part of business continuity planning involves identifying realistic threats to the business. Keep in mind that the BCP defines plans and processes to be invoked after an event occurs. Many of the preventative controls belong to the Operations Security domain, covered in Chapter 9, "Operations Security."

Natural events capable of disrupting a business include these:

- Earthquakes, fires, floods, mudslides, snow, ice, lightning, hurricanes, and tornadoes

- Explosions, chemical fires, hazardous waste spills, and smoke and water damage

- Power outages caused by utility failures, high heat and humidity, and solar flares

Examples of natural events that bring dramatic challenges to continuity planning include the 1989 San Francisco earthquake, Hurricane Hugo, the 1997 floods in the Midwestern United States, the 1998 Florida tornadoes, and Hurricane Katrina in New Orleans in 2005.

Events for which man, not nature, is directly responsible for disruptive events can include these:

- Strikes, work stoppages, and walkouts

- Sabotage, burglary, and other forms of hostile activity

- Massive failure of technology, including utility and communication failure caused by human intervention or error

Memories of the Tylenol scare in 1982; the bombings in 1992 in the London Financial District; the 1993 bombing of the World Trade Center; the Oklahoma City bombing in 1995; the Tokyo sarin gas attack in 1995; the September 11, 2001, attacks on the World Trade Center in New York and the Pentagon in Washington, D.C.; and the 2013 bombing at the Boston Marathon loom large in the minds of millions. Although these are some of the most dramatic examples of recent man-made actions resulting in significant loss of lives and money, a relatively minor event such as theft or sabotage performed by a disgruntled employee also can seriously jeopardize a business and go unnoticed for a long period of time.

Defining the Scope of the BCP

The formal implementation of the BCP requires a close examination of business practices and services that constitute the boundaries and define the scope of the plan. Obviously, for a large business or organization, this process can be time consuming and labor intensive. For that reason, one of the most overlooked but important steps is obtaining executive management buy-in and sign-off for the plan. The project team must make a business case for continuity planning, especially when the BCP is not mandatory. Team members must compare the cost of implementing the BCP with the benefits derived from meeting its objectives.

Other steps involved in defining the scope of the BCP include these:

- Identifying critical business processes and requirements for continuing to operate during an emergency.

- Assessing risks to the business if critical services are discontinued. This process is sometimes referred to as business impact analysis.

- Prioritizing those processes and assigning a value to each process. Which processes are absolutely critical and must be kept "online" without interruption? For example, keeping a continuous supply of power in a hospital emergency room is obviously more important than ensuring power in the employee cafeteria.

- Determining the cost of continuous operation and the value ascribed to each service.

- Establishing the priority of restoring critical services. Which must be restored within the hour? the day? the week? Which services cannot withstand any interruption?

- After executive management has approved the concept of the BCP and the BCP team has identified the scope and definition of the project, the team must establish the rules of engagement. This involves identifying the roles and responsibilities of the project team members and establishing the means of communication and the mechanisms for tracking progress.

Creating the Business Impact Analysis

The BIA identifies the risks that specific threats pose to the business, quantifies the risks, establishes priorities, and performs a cost/benefit analysis for countering risks. In pursuit of these goals, these are the three most important steps:

1. Prioritize the business processes, most likely at the department level, possibly using a scoring system to assign a weight or value to each process. For example, in a manufacturing environment, processes such as materials receipt, inventory, production, shipping, and accounting deserve consideration. This makes the task of prioritizing easier and hopefully less subjective, assuming that all business units accept the scoring method. This approach gives prioritization more objective scientific validity.

2. After critical processes have been identified and prioritized, determine how long each process can be down before business continuity is seriously compromised. Keep in mind that processes usually are interrelated and might need to be grouped together to assess downtime tolerance.

3. Identify the resources required to support the most critical processes. What equipment, which people, and how much money beyond normal operating costs do you need to maintain critical ("life support" in industry jargon) systems?

The committee responsible for drafting the BIA must present it to the executive team for evaluation and recommendation when it is complete. Senior management reviews the contents of the document, including the identification and prioritization of critical processes, cost/benefit analyses, and the method of supporting the plan when it has been implemented. Most important, the plan is communicated to all employees and support personnel, including outside vendors and contractors. All personnel, not just those individuals supporting the critical processes, must have a basic awareness of what the business continuity plan contains. This is one case in which on-the-job training does not work.

Disaster Recovery Planning

To keep the business running, consider the actions that must be taken until normal operations can be restored. In most organizations today, IT plays a critical role in supporting key business processes, thus the importance of the disaster recovery plan (DRP). The DRP typically involves running operations at a remote off-site location until the business deems it safe to restart at its primary location.

The goals of the DRP include these:

- Keeping the computers running. Computer services are an integral part of most businesses, especially those such as Internet service providers, where these services are the business.

- Meeting formal and informal service-level agreements (SLAs) with customers and suppliers.

- Being proactive rather than reactive. A carefully rehearsed DRP must be second nature to critical personnel. The DRP should include a comprehensive checklist of activities to perform through practice runs to make sure the people who are responsible for recovery are not caught by surprise.

Identifying Recovery Strategies

The BCP identifies the critical business processes that must be protected through the BIA documents. The function of the DRP is to identify the exact strategy for recovering those processes, specifically IT systems and services that are struck by a disaster. Because information technology is critical to almost every business these days and is the focus of this text, you need to understand several disaster recovery strategies that are available to an organization.

Understanding Shared-Site Agreements

Shared-site agreements are arrangements between companies with similar (if not identical) data processing centers. This compatibility in hardware, software, and services allows companies that enter into an agreement to back up each other when one partner has an emergency. Instead of having to build an entire infrastructure to back up its applications and data, Company A enters into an agreement with Company B to share resources in case of a disaster. Such an arrangement can save substantial time and money because the computers and software already exist and do not have to be procured. In theory, when Company A loses its data processing center resources, a figurative switch flips and it begins to run its applications on Company B's computers as if nothing had happened.

Despite the advantages of reduced costs, this scenario encounters problems. First, the data centers must be highly compatible in terms of the hardware and software they run. In fact, if Company A is not a subsidiary of Company B or they aren't regional offices of the same corporation, a shared-site agreement is difficult to implement. If the companies are not part of the same corporate charter, other difficulties arise, such as assured data security, privacy protection, and data synchronization. Shared-site agreements are feasible when companies are closely related and share common processing platforms, but the challenges are greater when this is not the case.

Using Alternate Sites

A company seeking DRP assistance can also use a third-party vendor to provide emergency backup services. Instead of entering into a reciprocal agreement with another business, the company uses the services of a vendor whose business it is to provide DRP services. You might be wondering who provides backup services for the third-party vendor. The vendor is responsible for providing backup services if the company experiences a critical failure in its systems.

These alternate-site services providers are the most commonly used form of DRP assistance and generally take one of three forms: a hot site, a warm site, or a cold site.

Hot Sites

A hot-site facility assumes the entire burden of providing backup computing services for the customer. This includes hosting the application software and data in a so-called mirror site. The vendor should be prepared to assume all responsibility for processing transactions for the customer, with little to no interruption of service. The vendor is responsible for maintaining the facility, including all environmental controls, such as heating, air conditioning, and power; hardware, including servers and printers; data backups; and all other services associated with a data processing center.

Although a hot-site facility offers several advantages, most importantly providing uninterrupted service in a relatively quick time, it can also be the most expensive solution as a DRP. In addition, the hot site poses some security risk because the data is now stored, backed up, and theoretically accessible to a third party. Still, for companies that can afford a hot-site facility, this is the most attractive solution.

Cold Sites

Unlike the hot site, the cold site provides facilities (including power, air conditioning, heat, and other environmental systems) necessary to run a data processing center without any of the computer hardware or software. The customer must deliver the hardware and software necessary to bring up the site. The cold site is a cheaper solution than a hot site, but you get what you pay for. When you consider the logistical problems of moving hardware that is highly sensitive to both temperature fluctuations and movement and then quickly installing software on it, you will appreciate the challenges that a cold-site facility poses. In the event of a true disaster, when a company cannot afford to suffer a protracted outage, the cold-site alternative, although economically feasible, might give the customer the illusion of security, even if it is not grounded in reality. Unfortunately, this lesson may be learned the hard way.

Warm Sites

As you might suspect, the warm-site facility is a compromise between the services offered by hot- and cold-site vendors. A warm-site facility provides the building and environmental services previously mentioned, with the addition of the hardware and communication links already established. However, the customer's applications are not installed, nor are workstations provided. In this case, the customer restores application software from backups using workstations it provides. Warm sites are cheaper than hot sites but require more effort. On the other hand, they are more expensive than cold-site facilities but are less labor intensive and more likely to be effective in a disaster.

An important part of the BCP is determining the constraints, both financial and operational, under which the company is working and choosing the most realistic solution that meets the minimal needs of the BCP.

Making Additional Arrangements

Several other arrangements can afford a company more options with business continuity planning:

- **Multiple centers:** Processing is distributed across multiple sites that are in-house or part of a shared-site agreement. As with distributed networks, a multiple center arrangement spreads the processing across sites and offers redundancy in processing as an added safeguard. Although less costly than a hot site, administering multiple centers could be a burdensome chore and cost-prohibitive.

- **Service bureaus:** Known for their quick response but high cost, service bureaus provide backup processing services at a remote location. Service bureaus also perform primary application processing such as payroll systems and have extra capacity available for DRP services.

- **Mobile units:** In this scenario, a third-party vendor provides a data processing center on wheels, complete with air conditioning and power systems.

- **The cloud:** Using the cloud for virtualized storage of applications and their data, the customer (especially medium-size organizations that can't afford an expensive DRP) finds its data backed up and available for immediate recovery. (Source: www.twinstrata.com/)

Testing the DRP

Testing the DRP thoroughly is an absolutely necessary and non-negotiable step in planning for a disaster. A plan might look great on paper, but until it is tested in a situation that resembles a true disaster, its value cannot be determined. Testing the plan not only shows that the plan is viable, but also prepares personnel for a disaster by teaching them their responsibilities, removing all uncertainty, and thus mitigating risk.

The Certified Information Systems Security Professional (CISSP) recognizes five methods of testing the DRP:

- **Walk-throughs:** Members of the key business units meet to trace their steps through the plan, looking for omissions and inaccuracies.

- **Simulations:** During a practice session, critical personnel meet to perform a dry run of the emergency, mimicking the response to a true emergency as closely as possible.

- **Checklists:** In a more passive type of testing, members of the key departments check off the tasks for which they are responsible and report on the accuracy of the checklist. This is typically a first step toward a more comprehensive test.

- **Parallel testing:** The backup processing occurs in parallel with production services that never stop. This is a familiar process for those who have installed complex computer systems that run in parallel with the existing production system until the new system proves to be stable. An example of this is when a company installs a new payroll system: Until the new system is deemed ready for full cut-over, the two systems operate in parallel.

- **Full interruption:** Also known as the true/false test, production systems are stopped as if a disaster occurred to see how the backup services perform. They either work (true) or fail (false), in which case the lesson learned can be as painful as a true disaster.

A Word About Testing DRPs

A well-tested DRP should anticipate the unanticipated. It should predict how employees will behave in the event of an emergency within its walls and consider how they will interact with external agents such as firemen, ambulance drivers, and policemen. The goal of the DRP is to reassure, not alarm, personnel about the outcome of a disaster and to remind them, above all, that the company will make every effort to protect them. The company must also protect its image to outsiders by proving that the DRP procedures are well thought out and tested. If the company survives a disaster in spite of its DRP rather than because of it, the message sent to customers, suppliers, and investors is not a comforting one.

Summary

Business continuity planning (BCP) and disaster recovery planning (DRP) are formal processes in any business that is concerned about maintaining its operation in the face of a disaster or interruption that prevents people from gaining access to their place of employment.

The DRP has its roots in the early 1990s, when securing IT operations was the focus of most organizations. This concern spread to other areas of the organization, with dramatic punctuation after the September 11, 2001, attack.

To implement its DRP, a company typically uses outside services such as a shared-site arrangement or a third-party vendor to replicate critical data processing services. Several of the alternatives are hot-site, cold-site, and warm-site arrangements.

Regardless of which arrangement a company chooses, the plan must be thoroughly tested using one or more of the five testing techniques, such as simulation or parallel testing. Although a true disaster cannot absolutely be re-created, a close approximation should reassure employees that their safety is the company's highest priority and also clarify their responsibilities in the event of a true disaster.

Test Your Skills

MULTIPLE-CHOICE QUESTIONS

1. Which of the following statements is *not* true about the BCP and DRP?

    A. Both plans deal with security infractions after they occur.

    B. Both plans describe preventative, not reactive, security procedures.

    C. The BCP and DRP share the goal of maintaining "business as usual" activities.

    D. They belong to the same domain of the Common Body of Knowledge.

2. According to the Gartner Group, which of the following statements is true?

    A. Organizations with sound business continuity plans will never experience an interruption of business.

    B. Approximately 40 percent of businesses experiencing a disaster of some sort go out of business.

    C. The BCP and DRP are interchangeable in most organizations.

    D. Organizations with fewer than 100 employees generally do not need a DRP.

3. Place the following steps of the BCP in the correct sequence: (a) create the BIA; (b) obtain signoff of the tested BCP; (c) identify the scope of the BCP; (d) write the BCP:

    A. a, c, d, b

    B. c, b, a, d

C. c, a, d, b

D. d, b, c, a

4. Which of the following statements best explains why the BCP is important?

A. The BCP is important because it minimizes disruption in business continuity.

B. The BCP is important because it eliminates risk in an organization.

C. The BCP is important because it has spawned a new cottage industry for business planning experts.

D. The BCP is important because the public will be unaware of problems within the organization.

5. Which of the following statements best describes the purpose of the BIA?

A. The purpose of the BIA is to create a document that helps management understand the impact a disruptive event would have on the business.

B. The purpose of the BIA is to define a strategy that minimizes the effect of disturbances and to allow for the resumption of business processes.

C. The purpose of the BIA is to emphasize the organization's commitment to employees and vendors.

D. The purpose of the BIA is to work with executive management to develop a DRP.

6. The scope definition of the BCP should include all of the following *except*:

A. Prioritizing critical business processes

B. Calculating the value and cost of continuing important business processes

C. Performing a dry run of emergency fire and medical evacuation procedures

D. Assessing the cost to the business if critical services were disrupted

7. Which of the following events is considered a man-made disaster?

A. Earthquake

B. Tornado

C. Flooding caused by a broken water main

D. Labor walkout

8. Which of the following is the number one priority of disaster response?

A. Hardware protection

B. Software protection

C. Transaction processing

D. Personnel safety

9. Which of the following is *not* a benefit of cold sites?

   A. No resource contention with other organizations

   B. Quick recovery

   C. Geographical location that is not affected by the same disaster

   D. Low cost

10. Which of the following computer recovery sites is only partially equipped?

    A. Nonmobile hot site

    B. Mobile hot site

    C. Warm site

    D. Cold site

11. An organization short on funding but long on its ability to assume risk would most likely use which of the following recovery sites?

    A. Alternate site

    B. Cold site

    C. Global site

    D. Tepid site

12. Which of the following is an advantage of using hot sites as a backup alternative?

    A. The costs associated with hot sites are low.

    B. Hot sites can be made ready for operation within a short period of time.

    C. Hot sites can be used for an extended amount of time.

    D. Hot sites do not require that equipment and systems software be compatible with the primary installation being backed up.

13. Which of the following is considered the main disadvantage of using multiple centers as a recovery site?

    A. Multiple centers are more difficult to administer than other types of recovery sites.

    B. Multiple sites share processing.

    C. Multiple centers offer redundant processing.

    D. Services can be shared between in-house and outside services.

14. Which of the following statements best describes a mobile unit site?

    A. A mobile unit site is a convenient means for employees to give blood.

    B. A mobile unit site is a fully equipped recovery site on wheels.

    C. A mobile unit site is a SWAT team that provides first-response services.

    D. A mobile unit site is a backup power supply, typically a diesel or gasoline generator.

15. Which of the following statements best describes the primary goal of the DRP?

    A. The primary goal of the DRP is to alarm employees as a call to arms.

    B. The primary goal of the DRP is to protect the image of the organization.

    C. The primary goal of the DRP is to educate employees about emergency evacuation procedures.

    D. The primary goal of the DRP is to reassure employees that the organization puts their safety above all else.

16. Which of the following is considered the most extensive type of disaster recovery testing?

    A. Checklists

    B. Full interruption

    C. Simulation

    D. Parallel testing

EXERCISES

EXERCISE 6.1: Defining the Attributes of an Effective DRP

1. Develop a DRP for an elementary school to respond to the building catching fire. Remember that the DRP must address the following concerns:

   ■ It's practical. Include useful information. Leave out unnecessary information.

   ■ It's understandable. Test instructions before implementing them.

   ■ It's accessible. Give copies to all concerned individuals, offices, and service points.

   ■ It's kept current. Revise pages as needed.

2. Share your DRP with other students in the class. What are the similarities? What are the differences?

EXERCISE 6.2: Investigating 9/11 Emergency Procedures

1. Investigate BCP/DRP disaster recovery stories from the September 11, 2001, catastrophe in New York and Washington, D.C. (for example, visit the website www.history.com/topics/9-11-attacks).

2. What did the companies that successfully recovered do right?

3. What did the companies that failed do wrong?

4. What lessons have we learned from such a calamity?

EXERCISE 6.3: Determining Local DRP Considerations

1. Identify the types of natural disasters prevalent in the area where you live.

2. Research the types of disaster recovery services ready to respond to such disasters (you might research your local government website devoted to emergency management and homeland security).

3. Do you feel that your community is prepared for such events?

EXERCISE 6.4: Revisiting a Family Emergency

Think about a particular time in your own life (for example, during a family emergency) when you feel you were not adequately prepared to respond to the event. For example, imagine that you went on an overnight backpacking trip with a small child and didn't take adequate supplies to get you through the hike.

1. What could you have done beforehand to avert some of the consequences of a lack of preparedness?

2. What could you have done to foresee events requiring contingency responses?

PROJECTS

PROJECT 6.1: Defending Your Company from Disaster

1. Create a fictitious company or organization. Describe the nature of its business, its location, the number of employees, and so forth.

2. Identify the challenges you would face in keeping your company running in the event of a disaster or interruption.

3. Prioritize the assets. Determine what mission-critical functions and systems would need to be recovered first, second, and so forth.

4. Describe some strategies for recovering these systems and processes.

PROJECT 6.2: **Developing a BCP or DRP**

1. Search the Internet to locate a business continuity plan or disaster recovery plan checklist for a small business. You might want to visit these sites:

   ■ The Business Continuity Planning & Disaster Recovery Planning Directory: www.disasterrecoveryworld.com/

   ■ Disaster Recovery Made Easy: www.disaster-recovery-plan.com/

   ■ Disaster Recovery Journal: www.drj.com

2. Draft your own business continuity plan or disaster recovery plan, including a checklist of critical recovery tasks.

3. Share your plans with your classmates.

4. What are the similarities between the plans? What are the differences?

5. How would you revise your plan(s) now that you've seen some others?

PROJECT 6.3: **Comparing Off-Site Services**

1. Using the Internet, identify two or more off-site companies that provide third-party backup services, and compare their services and costs.

2. What kind of common services do they offer?

3. Compare the costs of each third-party backup service, and describe your findings.

4. Does one company offer services that another doesn't? How do you account for this difference?

PROJECT 6.4: **Assessing New Technology for an Old Problem**

1. Research the latest trends in technology, such as cloud and mobile computing, and describe how recent advances have changed the face of disaster recovery. For example, visit the IBM site www-935.ibm.com/services/us/en/it-services/business-continuity-and-resiliency-services.html?lnk=mhse to learn what one vendor is doing to help with DRP planning.

2. Describe other technology changes that have occurred since the September 11, 2001, tragedy that have affected DRP planning.

Chapter | **7**

Law, Investigations, and Ethics

Chapter Objectives

After reading this chapter and completing the exercises, you will be able to do the following:

- Identify the types and targets of computer crime
- Summarize the major types of attacks performed by cybercriminals
- Understand the context of the computer in the legal system
- Appreciate the complexities of intellectual property law
- Discuss the issues surrounding computer security and privacy rights
- Articulate the challenges of computer forensics
- Recognize ethical issues related to information security

Introduction

This chapter focuses on the obligations and responsibilities of the information security (IS) specialist. It covers appropriate ethical behavior for working with sensitive data and systems, and it examines the laws governing the profession. IS specialists are constantly challenged to keep up with the latest laws, codes of ethics, and other rules governing the use of information technology. They rely on legal experts from both the private and public sectors that scramble to understand and respond to issues created by emerging technologies—issues that might have never existed. In most cases, the speed of technological change simply outstrips the speed at which our governing bodies can create applicable laws.

This gap between technology and the laws governing its use makes the IS specialist's role even more critical. IS specialists are duty-bound to their employers, the public, and governing bodies such as the Information Systems Security Certification Consortium (ISC)² to uphold the law and act ethically in all cases. This chapter exposes you to some of the legal and ethical implications of being an IS specialist by looking at the nature and types of computer crime, the laws created to deal with it, and the IS specialist code of ethics that governs professional behavior.

Types of Computer Crime

The pervasiveness of sensitive customer, government, and corporate information on the web has created a million-dollar cottage industry of computer crime. The losses are difficult to gauge accurately, partly because many businesses and individuals are reluctant to advertise vulnerabilities. After all, letting the world know that the company site has been hacked simply is not good advertising. Corporations shun bad news such as this because it undermines public confidence, rattles stockholders, and can result in a sell-off on Wall Street.

Still, the 2013 Verizon Data Breach Investigations Report (www.verizonenterprise.com/DBIR/2013/) represents the largest number of breaches spanning a single year: more than 47,000 reported security incidents, 621 confirmed data disclosures, and at least 44 million compromised records. Over the entire 9-year range of Verizon studies, that tally now exceeds 2,500 data disclosures and 1.1 billion compromised records.

The Verizon Data Breach report also revealed these statistics:

- Seventy-five percent of attacks were driven by financial motives.

- Seventy-one percent targeted user devices.

- Fifty-four percent compromised servers.

- Seventy-five percent were considered opportunistic attacks.

- Seventy-eight percent of intrusions were considered low difficulty.

- Sixty-nine percent were discovered by external parties.

- Sixty-six percent took months or longer to discover.

The last point is telling. Attacks have become harder to discover, and monitoring and tracking mechanisms are lacking.

Who are the victims of these acts? Practically everyone, as it turns out. According to the Certified Information Systems Security Professional (CISSP) Common Body of Knowledge, computer crimes are so widespread that identifying specific targets is too cumbersome. Instead, the CISSP has identified these major categories of computer crimes:

- **Military and intelligence attacks:** Criminals and intelligence agents illegally obtain classified and sensitive military information and police files.

- **Business attacks:** Increasing competition between companies frequently leads to illegal access of proprietary information.

- **Financial attacks:** Banks and other financial institutions provide attractive targets for computer criminals, for obvious reasons.

- **Terrorist attacks:** The U.S. Department of Homeland Security monitors the level of "chatter" on the Internet, looking for evidence of planned terrorist attacks against computer systems and geographic locations.

- **Grudge attacks:** Companies are increasingly wary of disgruntled employees who feel mistreated and exact their revenge using computer systems.

- **Thrill attacks:** Unlike grudge attackers who want some kind of revenge, thrill attackers hack computer systems for the fun of it, for bragging rights, or simply for a challenge.

Now that we've categorized the types of crimes that take place, we can take a look at how these crimes are pulled off and what the consequences might be.

How Cybercriminals Commit Crimes

Computer criminals use methods that are extensive and too numerous for complete treatment in this text, but the following are several of the most prevalent types of computer crimes:

- **Denial of service (DoS) attacks:** This tactic overloads a computer's resources (particularly the temporary storage area in computers, called the buffers) from any number of sources (referred to as a distributed denial of service, or DDoS, attack) until the system is so bogged down that it cannot honor requests. The DDoS attack in February 2000 on Yahoo! took the site down for 3 hours. A day later, eBay, Amazon.com, Buy.com, and CNN.com were hit with the same type of attack. The following day, E*TRADE and ZDNet were struck.

- **Rogue code:** The user inadvertently launches software that can log a user's keystrokes and either send them to a remote server or perform other undesirable activities, such as deleting files or destroying the operating system, rendering the computer useless.

- **Software piracy:** The attacker copies or downloads software and uses it without permission.

- **Social engineering:** Using deception, the attacker solicits information such as passwords or personal identification numbers (PINs) from unwitting victims. For example, a thief might call a help desk pretending to be a user whose password needs resetting.

- **Dumpster diving:** This no-tech criminal technique is the primary cause of ID theft. A criminal simply digs through trash and recycling bins looking for receipts, checks, and other personal and sensitive information. (If you don't shred all your receipts or lock up your recycling bin where you dispose of protected information, someone might be rummaging through your personal or proprietary information at this very moment.)

- **Spoofing of Internet Protocol (IP) addresses:** The attacker sends a message with a false originating IP address to convince the recipient that the sender is someone else. Every computer on the Internet is assigned a unique IP address. In this case, the attacker masquerades as a legitimate Internet site by using that site's IP address.

■ **Emanation eavesdropping:** The attacker intercepts radio frequency (RF) signals emanated by wireless computers to extract sensitive or classified information. This U.S. government's TEMPEST program addresses this problem by requiring shields on computers transmitting such data. Operated by the U.S. Department of Defense (DOD), the TEMPEST program has created a cottage industry of companies that create protective equipment to prevent foreign spies from collecting stray computer signals issued from DOD labs or U.S. embassies.

■ **Embezzlement:** In the movie *Office Space*, three disgruntled employees modify computer software to collect round-off amounts (fractions of a penny) from a company's accounting program. This is an old crime in new garb. Now criminals steal money by manipulating software or databases.

■ **Information warfare:** A concern of the U.S. Department of Homeland Security, information warfare includes attacks upon a country's computer network to gain economic or military advantage. You can learn more about information warfare at the Institute for the Advanced Study of Information Warfare (www.psycom.net/iwar.1.html).

The more highly publicized instances of these attacks are generally dramatic because they are so far reaching. Some familiar examples are the DoS attack against 3Com Corp and Nike.com in 2000, Kevin Mitnick's well-documented hacker exploits against phone companies, the Nigerian email fraud, the Melissa Microsoft Word virus, the Bubbleboy worm, the theft of 300,000 credit card numbers by Russian hacker Maxus in 1999, the Heartland Payment Processor breach in 2009, and the Target credit and debit card breach at the end of 2013.

More pedestrian methods also crop up: chain letters, pyramid schemes, outright fraud, cyberstalking, and phishing, in which a scammer poses as a legitimate enterprise or organization to extract personally identifying information from a naïve or gullible user.

A common theme among most of these methods is the presence of vulnerabilities because of flaws in popular computer operating systems and application software or flaws in system implementation (such as failing to activate security controls or not configuring a system properly). The Software Development Domain (see Chapter 13, "Software Development Security") covers specific vulnerabilities, but it is important to recognize now that most computer crime is preventable with sufficient, competent attention to security detail when deploying software.

The Computer and the Law

Many laws address computer crime. Legal issues have become more complex in the past decade, with attacks originating across international borders and the proliferation of companies with international or offshore sites. Computer crime issues were once strictly a matter of national law, but the movement of data across time zones and international boundaries has complicated the issue of legal jurisdiction.

As a consequence, an entirely new set of international computer security and privacy laws has been forged, yet these laws often have conflicting goals. When the European Union passed the 1998 EU Data Protection Directive, it caused a great deal of controversy in the United States. This directive contains protections and safeguards of individual privacy that are generally much stricter than they are in the United States. Instead of examining the conflicts between countries over competing computer security regulations, this text focuses primarily on the legal system within the United States; we discuss international law only in the context of how it differs from U.S. laws.

Legislative Branch of the Legal System

As you are undoubtedly aware, the three branches of government that create and administer the laws defining the legal system in the United States are the legislative, executive, and judicial branches. The legislative branches (Congress and Senate) are responsible for passing statutory laws. A statutory law is a law written through the act of a legislature declaring, commanding, or prohibiting something. Statutory laws are arranged by subject matter in the order in which they are enacted, thus they are referred to as session laws. Federal and state law codes incorporate statutes into the body of laws, and the judiciary system interprets and enforces them. State statutes govern matters such as wills, probate administration, and corporate law; federal statutes cover matters such as patent, copyright, and trademark laws.

Later in this chapter, you look at copyright law and see how a basic understanding of statutory law is important to the information security specialist.

Administrative Branch of the Legal System

Administrative law is also referred to as natural justice. We owe this legal concept to the Romans, who believed certain legal principles were "natural" or self-evident and did not need to be codified by statute. In this case, disputes are resolved before an administrative tribunal, not in a court. For example, the Workmen's Compensation Board reviews and resolves disputes between employee and employer, aiming to give workers and their dependents financial relief in the case of injuries from job-related accidents without requiring a formal court proceeding. Administrative law is expanding rapidly because it normally offers a more expeditious and inexpensive resolution to disputes.

Judicial Branch of the Legal System

Common law arose from unwritten law that developed from judicial cases based on precedent and custom. The United States inherited the common law system from England as the basis for most of its legal systems. Common law is either unwritten or written as statutes or codes. The following are three primary categories of laws within the common law system:

■ **Civil law:** Civil laws are written to compensate individuals who were harmed through wrongful acts known as torts. A tort can be either intentional or unintentional (as in the case of negligence). Common law is generally associated with civil disputes in which compensation is financial but does not involve imprisonment.

- **Criminal law:** Criminal law punishes those who violate government laws and harm an individual or group. Unlike civil law, criminal law includes imprisonment in addition to financial penalties.

- **Regulatory law:** Regulatory law is administrative laws that regulate the behavior of administrative agencies of government. Considered part of public law, regulatory law addresses issues that arise between the individual and a public entity. Regulatory laws can also exact financial penalties and imprisonment.

The common laws governing matters of information systems include laws regulating intellectual property and privacy; these are discussed next in this chapter.

Intellectual Property Law

If you have ever downloaded music from a website without paying for it, you have likely broken one of the laws protecting intellectual property—that is, you have committed copyright infringement. Such an act might seem innocuous at first. But multiply this event by millions of users and the cost of the CDs they would have purchased, and the sum of the lost revenue is staggering. The magnitude of the problem is immense, and it costs the recording industry millions of dollars in revenue yearly. According to the Irish Recorded Music Association, a nonprofit organization facilitating discussion between the Irish recording industry and the government, annual losses from downloaded music exceed €3.8 million (at the current exchange rate, about US$5 million) within the European Union. The association estimates the worldwide music piracy problem to be $5 billion annually (see www.irma.ie/piracy.htm). This is why the artists and their recording labels go to court.

It is also why you need to know something about the legal framework protecting intellectual property. The computer and its Internet connection make the theft of music, video, and software files possible. The Internet also makes plagiarism a breeze. With the sheer volume of content on the Internet, determining what is covered by copyright and what is not can be difficult at times, but more than one term paper is certain to have violated someone's copyrights.

Besides copyright protection to safeguard the distribution and reproduction rights of the owner, intellectual property law includes patent law, trademarks, and trade secrets. The following sections discuss these in detail.

Patent Law

Inventors rush to patent their ideas to prevent others from using them. Patents "grant an inventor the right to exclude others from producing or using the inventor's discovery or invention for a limited period of time" (www.uspto.gov). In the United States, a patent is good for 17 years. The Patent and Trademark Office (PTO) oversees patent law for the federal government. However, the PTO has historically resisted patenting software. In the 1970s, the PTO did not grant a patent if the invention required a computer to perform a computation. The PTO was geared to the world of processes, manufactured articles, and machinery, and it did not recognize original claims to scientific truth or mathematical expressions. (Mathematical formulas and algorithms still cannot be patented.) This reluctance did not prevent a number of companies from filing patent applications for software, however. In 1963, for example, Bell Telephone Laboratories filed an application on behalf of its employees entitled "Conversion of Numerical Information" for its method of processing data, specifically the programmatic conversion of numeric data to other data types. The patent examiner from the PTO rejected the claim because of a "lack of novelty or non-obviousness." He felt that "mental processes" and "mathematical steps" were not the stuff of statutory law (source: http://digital-law-online.info/lpdi1.0/treatise61.html).

With the rapid advance of computer technology and its rapid spread from government offices to business and public use, the PTO had to devise new guidelines to address the issue of software patents. After numerous U.S. Supreme Court challenges in the early 1980s, the PTO had, by the mid-1990s, developed new guidelines to determine when a software invention was protected by patent law. For example, the PTO now grants patents for software such as instructions on a disk that guide machines or computers.

More famously, Amazon.com won an injunction against Barnes & Noble, which used the "one click" software similar to the software Amazon.com introduced for storing buyer preferences and other identifying information. The courts overturned the injunction in 2001, but Amazon still holds six patents related to ordering books (source: www4.ncsu.edu/~baumerdl/Burgunder.04/Ch.%205.ppt#11).

Trademarks

The Trademark Act defines a trademark as "any word, name, symbol, or device, or any combination thereof" that the individual intends to use commercially and wants to distinguish as coming from a unique source. Again, the PTO was originally reluctant to sail the uncharted waters of granting trademarks to intellectual property such as software, but over time, it has done so. Software giant Microsoft currently holds more than 200 trademarks, from *Actimates* to *Zoo Tycoon*.

Trade Secrets

If you just gulped down your favorite sports drink, answered a telemarketing survey, or performed a routine task on your computer that used an obscure algorithm, chances are, you have unwittingly taken advantage of a company trade secret. Unlike trademarks or patents, trade secrets do not benefit from legal protection. As long as no one but you knows about your idea, it belongs to you. Usually, a trade secret is a patent in process, an embryonic but unofficial and legally unprotected idea.

The story of the protection of software as intellectual property is a book unto itself. Enter the keyword search "software intellectual property" on Amazon.com, and you should get almost 2,000 hits, beginning with the contentious issue of open sourcing. The courts are still debating the question of when an idea manifested as software moves from protection under intellectual property law to the public domain.

Privacy and the Law

Perhaps you have received privacy statements from your bank or other financial lenders explaining exactly what they plan to do with your personally identifying information (such as a PIN). Maybe you have signed a statement at your doctor's office agreeing that you have read and fully comprehend the fine print contained in the Health Insurance Portability and Accountability Act (HIPAA) of 1996. These privacy documents often give rise to confusion. Do you opt in or opt out when being asked to share personally identifying information? What about privacy issues you might not be aware of, such as cookies (text files that remember information about you) stored on your hard drive without your knowledge? Many privacy issues confront companies that keep personal information about customers and employees.

The Federal Trade Commission's May 2000 report "Fair Information Practices in the Electronic Marketplace" (www.ftc.gov/reports/privacy2000/privacy2000.pdf) is pertinent to this discussion. Although the FTC does not mandate privacy practices, the report lists four privacy practices that all companies engaged in electronic commerce should observe:

- **Notice/awareness:** In general, websites should tell the user how they collect and handle user information. The notice should be conspicuous, and the privacy policy should clearly state how the site collects and uses information.

- **Choice/consent:** Websites must give consumers control over how their personally identifying information is used. Abuse of this practice is gathering information for a stated purpose but using it in another way, one to which the consumer might object.

- **Access/participation:** Perhaps the most controversial of the fair practices, users would be able to review, correct, and, in some cases, delete personally identifying information on a particular website. Most companies that currently collect personal information have no means of allowing people to review what the company collected, nor do they provide any way for a person to correct incorrect information. Implementing this control would be a burden to companies to retrofit onto an existing system. As you have likely seen with commercial credit reports, inaccurate information or information used out of context can make people's lives problematic.

- **Security/integrity:** Websites must do more than reassure users that their information is secure with a "feel-good" policy statement. The site must implement policies, procedures, and tools that will prevent unauthorized access and hostile attacks against the site.

International Privacy Issues

The issue of protecting privacy in the United States has grown more complicated with the expansion of e-commerce across international borders and into the domain of different and sometimes much more rigorous and exacting privacy protection laws. The European Union's Data Protection Directive of 1998 was the result of several years of tough negotiation among E.U. members. The directive addressed the disparity between European privacy protection laws and what the E.U. viewed as the more porous and inconsistent state and federal privacy laws in the United States.

The U.S. Department of Commerce, wishing to head off a privacy law impasse with the European Union, negotiated the Safe Harbor Privacy Principles, a framework that allowed U.S. entities wanting to do business in the European Union to meet the minimum privacy controls of the E.U. directive. The International Safe Harbor Principles include the following privacy guidelines:

- **Notice:** Companies must notify individuals about what personally identifying information they are collecting, why they are collecting it, and how to contact the collectors.

- **Choice:** Individuals must be able to choose whether and how their personal information is used by, or disclosed to, third parties.

- **Onward transfer:** Third parties receiving personal information must provide the same level of privacy protection as the company from which the information is obtained.

- **Security:** Companies housing personal information and sensitive data must secure the data and prevent its loss, misuse, disclosure, alteration, and unauthorized access.

- **Data integrity:** Companies must be able to reassure individuals that their data is complete, accurate, current, and used for the stated purposes only.

- **Access:** Individuals must have the right and ability to access their information and correct, modify, or delete any portion of it.

- **Enforcement:** Each company must adopt policies and practices that enforce the aforementioned privacy principles.

Privacy Laws in the United States

Unless you are an employee of a U.S. corporation working in the European Union, you are probably more aware of privacy matters in your day-to-day life. For example, the Kennedy-Kassenbaum Health Insurance Portability and Accountability Act (HIPAA), passed in August 1996, codifies the right of individuals to control and protect their own health information. Although the European continent has adopted a more comprehensive and consistent set of privacy principles, the United States has been more willing to allow different industries, such as banking, healthcare, and different levels of government, to draft their own privacy guidelines. The effect has been a more piecemeal and disjointed approach to privacy protection. The following partial list of computer security and privacy laws shows a less than holistic approach to privacy protection in the United States:

- **1970 U.S. Fair Credit Reporting Act:** Regulates the activities of credit bureaus.

- **1986 U.S. Electronic Communications Act:** Protects the confidentiality of private message systems through unauthorized eavesdropping.

- **1987 U.S. Computer Security Act:** Congressional declaration to improve the security and privacy of sensitive information in federal computer systems and establish minimum acceptable security practices for such systems.

- **1996 U.S. Kennedy-Kassenbaum Health Insurance and Portability Accountability Act (HIPAA):** Protects the confidentiality and portability of personal health care information.

- **2000 National Security Directive 42 (NSD-42):** Established the Committee on National Security Systems (CNSS), which provides guidance on the security of national defense systems, among other roles.

- **2001 U.S. Patriot Act HR 3162:** Also known as "Uniting and Strengthening America by Providing Appropriate Tools Required to Intercept and Obstruct Terrorism (USA PATRIOT ACT) Act of 2001." The Act was passed by Congress and the Senate to deter and punish terrorist acts in the United States and around the world, to enhance law enforcement investigatory tools, and for other purposes related to international terrorism.

- **2002 Federal Information Security Management Act:** Defines the basic statutory requirements for protecting federal computer systems.

- **2010 Fair Debt Collection Practices Act:** Addresses unfair or unconscionable means to collect or attempt to collect any debt.

The sheer number of laws related to computers has made it difficult for owners, operators, legislators, and law enforcement to stay on top of all regulations because of these factors:

- Enactment of new laws in a rapidly changing technology environment sometimes causes more problems than are solved.

- Globalization of the economy results in unclear international legal boundaries and jurisdiction questions.

- Not all countries adopt standards, and conflicting security standards and practices result in varying levels of compliance and enforcement.

Without a more comprehensive and consolidated approach to privacy law, legislation in the United States most likely will continue to be a series of industry-specific rules and regulations.

Computer Forensics

Investigating crimes committed with computers is known as computer forensics. The National Data Conversion Institute specializes in facilitating the conversion and exchange of data between disparate computer systems and providing litigation data management services to law firms, corporations, and governments. This organization states that an increasing number of civil and criminal lawsuits involve computerized data stored on some form of computer medium. Sherlock Holmes never could have envisioned that the physical evidence he once detected, such as a lock of hair, a smudge on a topcoat, or mud caked on boots, would evolve into the nearly invisible world of computer evidence.

The intangibility of computer evidence makes the job of prosecuting cybercrime more difficult than with traditional crime. Specialized expert knowledge is usually required, and jurisdictions become murky because of the difficulty of determining the locus of the crime. Furthermore, gathering evidence is complicated by the high-tech sleight-of-hand computer criminals have mastered. Many know how to cover their tracks and distract investigators from their true locations.

The National Data Conversion Institute (NDCI) makes a case for using expert investigative services to solve computer crimes. The following are among the many arguments for such services:

- Successful litigation frequently depends on obtaining irrefutable computer evidence. Without solid computer evidence, you might not have a case.

- Your evidence might not be as good as the opposition's if you are using less sophisticated data detection techniques.

- Your adversaries do not want you to obtain the data you need.

- The technology used to create the data you need might have already disappeared. Time is of the essence.

Additionally, all the other requirements of successful litigation are still in play: the admissibility of evidence, the types of legal evidence, and the legal search and seizure of evidence. Those prosecuting a crime must still play by the rules when conducting an investigation. But instead of looking for a smoking gun, they may be trying to restore a hard drive that was "permanently" erased.

The Information Security Professional's Code of Ethics

Security specialists are held to a high standard because they have access to a vast amount of information that, if used improperly, could ruin lives and even nations. Ethical behavior is easier to define than display. Although most people intuitively know what proper conduct is, people also have a hard time admitting that they have done something wrong. It is tempting to find ways to reinterpret behavior when caught committing a crime. For example, is an IT security specialist with access to sensitive payroll information acting unethically when confirming that a coworker is making substantially less money than another employee with the same job grade and performance rating?

In an effort to make the ethical behavior of information security specialists more explicit, the International Information Systems Security Certification Consortium (ISC)² developed the code of conduct for Certified Information Systems Security Professionals (CISSPs).

According to the (ISC)² website, "All information systems security professionals who are certified by (ISC)² recognize that such certification is a privilege that must be both earned and maintained. In support of this principle, all Certified Information Systems Security Professionals (CISSPs) commit to fully support this Code of Ethics. CISSPs who intentionally or knowingly violate any provision of the Code will be subject to action by a peer review panel, which may result in the revocation of certification" (www.isc2.org). The (ISC)² Code of Ethics is mandatory for certified professionals. The code has four mandatory canons. General guidance is not intended to substitute for the sound ethical judgment of the professional.

- Protect society, the commonwealth, and the infrastructure.

- Act honorably, honestly, justly, responsibly, and legally.

- Provide diligent and competent service to principals.

- Advance and protect the profession.

FYI: A Security Professional's Ethical Dilemma

Suppose you're an IT employee at a pharmaceutical manufacturer, and a high-level manager's PC has been hit hard with a virus attack that requires a desk-side visit to determine the prognosis. You find that the system will no longer boot up, but with your hard-drive recovery and antivirus tools, you're able to recover her files. In the process, you discover an internal memo that the company is trying to suppress from the FDA that discusses the surprising number of deaths during the field trials of a new anticancer drug.

What should you do? Should you ignore what you've found? Should you notify someone? Should you blow the whistle through the media? How can you apply the Code of Ethics to this dilemma? Which canon(s) apply?

This type of dilemma is one you might face as an IT security professional at some point in your career. Your decision at that point will be easier if this is a scenario that you have already thought about.

Although the tools used to commit crimes may change over the years with the advances in technology, the principles of investigation and prosecution, as well as the standards of ethical behavior, remain the same.

Other Ethics Standards

The (ISC)² Code of Ethics is one of the more prominent attempts at specifying ethical conduct for computer specialists. The following are other codes:

- Computer Ethics Institute's Ten Commandments of Computer Ethics

- Internet Activities Board's Ethics and the Internet

- U.S. Department of Health, Education, and Welfare Code of Fair Information Practices

These efforts to codify ethical behavior share a common goal: to establish a code of conduct for anyone using computer resources. We cover each one in more detail next.

Computer Ethics Institute

Dr. Ramon C. Barquin originally presented the Ten Commandments of Computer Ethics in a paper titled "In Pursuit of a 'Ten Commandments' for Computer Ethics" (Computer Ethics Institute; http:// computerethicsinstitute.org/publications/tencommandments.html).

1. Thou Shalt Not Use a Computer to Harm Other People.

2. Thou Shalt Not Interfere with Other People's Computer Work.

3. Thou Shalt Not Snoop Around in Other People's Computer Files.

4. Thou Shalt Not Use a Computer to Steal.

5. Thou Shalt Not Use a Computer to Bear False Witness.

6. Thou Shalt Not Copy or Use Proprietary Software for Which You Have Not Paid.

7. Thou Shalt Not Use Other People's Computer Resources Without Authorization or Proper Compensation.

8. Thou Shalt Not Appropriate Other People's Intellectual Output.

9. Thou Shalt Think About the Social Consequences of the Program You Are Writing or the System You Are Designing.

10. Thou Shalt Always Use a Computer in Ways That Ensure Consideration and Respect for Your Fellow Humans.

Although many of these commandments are just good common sense, reminding people that unacceptable behavior has consequences is a useful practice. You might consider including these Ten Commandments in a security training and awareness program (see Chapter 4).

Internet Activities Board: Ethics and the Internet

Computer uses are pervasive; no industry or profession can survive without the aid of computer technology. Because of the potential for abuse of information or damage to resources from malicious use of computer technology, the Internet Activities Board published a standard called "Ethics and the Internet," intended for wide distribution and acceptance from the Internet-using communities. The introduction to RFC 1087, "Ethics and the Internet," reads:

> At great human and economic cost, resources drawn from the U.S. Government, industry and the academic community have been assembled into a collection of interconnected networks called the Internet…

> …As is true of other common infrastructures (e.g., roads, water reservoirs and delivery systems, and the power generation and distribution network), there is widespread dependence on the Internet by its users for the support of day-to-day research activities.

The reliable operation of the Internet and the responsible use of its resources are of common interest and concern for its users, operators and sponsors....

...Many of the Internet resources are provided by the U.S. Government. Abuse of the system thus becomes a Federal matter above and beyond simple professional ethics.

The complete RFC 1087 is available at www.faqs.org/rfcs/rfc1087.html. It outlines a statement of policy and lists unacceptable behaviors that would violate ethical behavior.

Code of Fair Information Practices

The U.S. Department of Health, Education and Welfare (now called the U.S. Department of Health and Human Services) adopted the Code of Fair Information Practices in 1973 (source: www.epic.org/privacy/consumer/code_fair_info.html). It states:

1. There must be no personal data record-keeping systems whose very existence is secret.

2. There must be a way for an individual to find out what information is in his or her file and how the information is being used.

3. There must be a way for an individual to correct information in his or her records.

4. Any organization creating, maintaining, using, or disseminating records of personally identifiable information must assure the reliability of the data for its intended use and must take precautions to prevent misuse.

5. There must be a way for an individual to prevent personal information obtained for one purpose from being used for another purpose without his or her consent.

The Code of Fair Information Practices, related more to the privacy of individuals on computerized record-keeping systems, complements the ethics standards for people to consider when using information systems. Because no one stands alone when connected to public networks, it's vital to lay the ground rules for what's acceptable and what's not (source: U.S. Department of Health, Education, and Welfare, 1973).

Summary

Laws, investigative principles, and professional ethics, often thought of as abstract topics, are as important to information security professionals as knowing how to design firewall architecture. Understanding how different laws affect security practices across the globe gives the practitioner the correct perspective to operate internationally with the same confidence as working close to home. Understanding the relationships of computer crime investigations and the laws that govern property is critical to becoming a productive member of a team that can effectively protect, detect, and respond to security incidents.

Ethics are the ties that bind one's behavior to the world of computer security, balancing the authority one is given while working in the field with the checks and balances that prevent the abuse of power.

Test Your Skills

MULTIPLE-CHOICE QUESTIONS

1. Business losses that result from computer crime are difficult to estimate for which of the following reasons?

    A. Companies are not always aware that their computer systems have been compromised.

    B. Companies are sometimes reluctant to report computer crime because it is bad advertising.

    C. Losses are often difficult to quantify.

    D. All of the above.

2. According to a 2013 Verizon Breach Investigations Report, what percentage of breaches were driven by financial motives?

    A. 75 percent

    B. 30 percent

    C. 10 percent

    D. 90 percent

3. The CISSP categorizes computer attacks by type. Which of the following is *not* one of the categories identified by the CISSP?

    A. Terrorist attack

    B. Thrill attack

    C. Subterfuge attack

    D. Business attack

4. Which type of individual is most likely to perform a grudge attack?

   A. An employee who feels that his employer has mistreated him

   B. A political exile

   C. A member of Anonymous

   D. All of the above

5. Computer crime is generally made possible by which of the following?

   A. The perpetrator's obtaining advanced training and special knowledge

   B. The victim's carelessness

   C. Collusion with others in information processing

   D. System design flaws

6. The computer criminal who calls a help desk trying to obtain another user's password is most likely a _____.

   A. Dumpster diver

   B. Black-hat hacker

   C. Social engineer

   D. Spammer

7. Which of the following computer crimes involves overtaxing a computer's resources until it is no longer functional?

   A. IP addresses spoofing

   B. Denial of service (DoS)

   C. Rogue code

   D. Information warfare

8. We inherited which of our legal systems from England?

   A. Administrative law

   B. Patent law

   C. Common law

   D. Byways

9. Computer laws have become increasingly difficult to enforce for which of the following reasons?

    A. The inability of legislation in the United States to keep pace with technological advances

    B. The globalization of the economy, resulting in unclear international legal boundaries

    C. Conflicting security standards within the United States and between the United States and other nations

    D. All of the above

10. Which of the following statements best describes natural justice?

    A. Natural justice is primitive and, thus, "natural."

    B. Natural justice is enforced by judge and jury.

    C. Natural justice is considered self-evident and thus requires no statutes.

    D. Natural justice is unsuited for arbitration.

11. The Patent and Trademark Office (PTO) resisted patenting software for years for what primary reason?

    A. Software was too intangible.

    B. Software was the product of scientific truth or mathematical expressions.

    C. The average shelf life of software was estimated to be less than the lifespan of a patent (17 years).

    D. It was too interconnected with the computer's operating system.

12. Which of the following statements is true about a trade secret?

    A. It offers legal protection just as a trademark does.

    B. It is a patent in the works.

    C. It is widely known but rarely discussed.

    D. All of the above.

13. Which of the following is *not* one of the FTC's four Fair Information Practices?

    A. Individuals should be given the choice of opting out when sharing personal information.

    B. Personal information should be accurate and stored securely.

    C. Websites must have 100 percent availability, in case users want to change their personal information.

    D. Websites must tell users how their personal information will be used and notify them of any changes to that policy.

14. Which of the following statements best reflects the European Union Data Protection Directive of 1998?

   A. The United States was exempted from privacy standards in the E.U.

   B. The directive's goal was to standardize privacy protection among the E.U. members.

   C. It resulted in the Safe Harbor Privacy Principles that allowed the United States to meet minimum privacy controls in the European Union.

   D. Both B and C are correct.

15. Which of the following definitions best describes computer forensics?

   A. Using computers to investigate crime

   B. Investigating crimes committed using computers

   C. Probing the operating system for signs of malfeasance

   D. Predicting behaviors of cybercriminals

16. Which of the following statements best describes the intentions of the $(ISC)^2$ Code of Ethics?

   A. The $(ISC)^2$ Code of Ethics helps certificate holders resolve dilemmas related to their practice.

   B. The $(ISC)^2$ Code of Ethics provides guidance on encouraging good behavior.

   C. The $(ISC)^2$ Code of Ethics provides guidance on discouraging poor behavior.

   D. All of the above.

17. Which of the following statements is true of ethical conduct?

   A. Ethical conduct is expected of all IS specialists.

   B. Ethical conduct helps define a high moral code of professional behavior.

   C. Ethical conduct speaks to the credibility of the individual.

   D. All of the above.

18. Which of the following is *not* one of the provisions of the $(ISC)^2$ Code of Ethics?

   A. Act honorably, responsibly, and legally.

   B. Provide thorough and competent service to your customers and peers.

   C. Judge not, lest you be judged.

   D. Strive to protect society and its components.

EXERCISES

EXERCISE 7.1: Researching Current Computer Crimes

1. Perform a Google search on computer crime and compile a list of recent attacks and data compromises.

2. Where possible, identify the nature and source of the attacks.

EXERCISE 7.2: Researching the Details of a Computer Crime

1. Select one type of computer attack (such as DoS) and research the details of the attack.

2. Describe what the industry has done in response to these attacks.

3. Describe what happened to the perpetrators of the crime(s).

EXERCISE 7.3: Investigating the Current State of the EU Directive

1. Investigate further the current status of the European Union's Data Protection Directive on information privacy.

2. How many countries currently belong to the Safe Harbor group?

3. In your opinion, how well is Safe Harbor working for information providers based in the United States?

EXERCISE 7.4: Investigating the Different Types of Computer-Based Legal Evidence

1. Research the different kinds of legal evidence used in computer crime investigations.

2. Describe the differences between admissible and inadmissible evidence.

3. Who should be responsible for maintaining the chain-of-custody for computer crimes evidence?

EXERCISE 7.5: Brainstorming Unethical Uses of the Computer

1. Think of ten examples of what you consider to be unethical uses of the computer.

2. How might you mitigate these threats?

3. How would a set of codified ethics that users of the computer must subscribe to before using the system help in mitigating these threats?

PROJECTS

PROJECT 7.1: **Interviewing an IS Specialist**

1. Identify and interview an IS specialist whose job it is to gather evidence for computer crimes.

2. Ask that specialist to discuss as fully as possible the nature of the crimes. (Investigators love talking about their jobs!)

3. What tools and techniques did this person use to determine the culprit(s)?

4. How successful were any prosecutions of lawsuits brought against the perpetrators?

PROJECT 7.2: **Investigating the Complexities of Intellectual Property Law**

1. Research the topic of intellectual property as related to copyright law.

2. What are some of the difficulties in proving a copyright infringement case, such as that brought by the RIAA against users who download free MP3 files?

3. What are some of the other recent and famous cases related to copyright, trademark, or trade secret infringements?

4. Who should govern the Internet to prevent intellectual property law infringements?

5. Can any person or country govern how the Internet is used (and abused)? Why or why not?

PROJECT 7.3: **Examining a Recent Governmental Privacy Act**

1. Select a government regulation such as HIPAA or the Gramm-Leach-Bliley Act (GLBA) to research the privacy aspects of the act.

2. What are some conflicting interests to businesses and the individuals related to privacy matters?

3. What privacy concerns do you have as an Internet user and shopper?

4. How will your behavior change as a result of reading this chapter?

Chapter | **8**

Physical Security Control

Chapter Objectives

After reading this chapter and completing the exercises, you will be able to do the following:

- Distinguish between logical and physical security, and explain the reasons for placing equal emphasis on both
- Recognize the importance of the Physical Security domain
- Outline the major categories of physical security threats
- Classify the techniques to mitigate risks to an organization's physical security
- Classify the five main categories of physical security controls, including their strengths and limitations
- Identify how to use smart cards for physical access control
- Categorize the different types of biometric access controls and determine their respective strengths and weaknesses

Introduction

An often-overlooked connection between physical systems (computer hardware) and logical systems (the software that runs on it) is that, to protect logical systems, the hardware running them must be physically secure. If you can't physically protect your hardware, you can't protect the programs and data running on your hardware.

Physical security deals with who has access to buildings, computer rooms, and the devices within them. Controlling physical security involves protecting sites from natural and man-made physical threats through proper location and by developing and implementing plans that secure devices from unauthorized physical contact.

Information security experts, however, usually focus more on the problems related to logical security because of the greater likelihood that remotely located computer hackers will analyze, dissect, or break into computer networks. A hacker's physical proximity to a network has less to do with its vulnerability than porous interfaces or operating systems with more holes in them than Swiss cheese.

The idea of physical security might seem almost arcane and anachronistic in an age of remote high-tech stealth and subterfuge, but no aspect of computer security can be taken for granted. We are reminded by surveys, including the National Retail Security Survey (NRSS), that employee (insider) theft is on the rise and shows no sign of abating in light of downsizing, rightsizing, and layoffs. According to the 2012 NRSS (www.nrf.com/modules.php?name=News&op=viewlive&sp_id=1389), retailers attributed more than 43.9 percent of their company's losses to employee theft, including the trafficking of proprietary information. As you shall see, physical security applies not only to external attacks, but also to inside jobs perpetrated by disgruntled employees who frequently feel that the company owes them something or by employees who are simply thieves.

The NRSS describes the more traditional view of loss of tangible goods (such as clothing, DVDs, and manufacturing parts) through theft; however, loss of intellectual property and company information complicates the more traditional definition of property and has forced organizations to take internal theft as seriously as external theft.

Some of the information in this chapter might seem intuitive or obvious. Unfortunately, too many organizations, big and small, neglect some of the most basic aspects of physical security. That is why physical security is one of the ten domains of the Certified Information Systems Security Professional (CISSP) Common Body of Knowledge (CBK).

Understanding the Physical Security Domain

The Physical Security domain includes the more traditional safeguards against threats, both intentional and unintentional, to the physical environment and the surrounding infrastructure. If you have ever worked for a large company or entered a municipal building, you most likely have experienced some of these security checks firsthand: badge readers, television monitors, bag and "airport" X-ray devices, and the ever-present armed security guards. The level of physical security is typically proportional to the value of the property being protected. Organizations such as the government and corporations conducting high-level research generally use more sophisticated physical security checks, including biometrics (explained later), because the property inside might be highly classified. Organizations that keep less sensitive information, however, still must worry about compromising customer and employee information, which could result in damaging or fatal lawsuits. Regardless of the size or the nature of the organization, the goal of the Physical Security domain is to put safeguards in place to protect an organization's assets and ensure the continuity of business in the event of man-made or natural disasters.

Challenges related to physical security center on the need to make it simple for people who belong in a building to get in and get around, but make it difficult for those who do not belong to enter and navigate. Thus, physical security, like many other areas of security, is a careful balancing act that requires trusted people, effective processes that reduce the likelihood of harm from inadvertent and deliberate acts, and appropriate technology to maintain vigilance.

If you have an interest in the security field, you must understand the following areas of physical security:

- How to choose a secure site (location) and guarantee the correct design

- How to secure a site against unauthorized access

- How to protect equipment, such as personal computers and the information contained on them, against theft

- How to protect the people and property within an installation

These four areas of physical security are the focus of this chapter.

Physical Security Threats

You need to understand the threats that physical security control systems address before you learn about design and implementation. As you learn later in this chapter, site selection depends heavily upon a list of potential physical security threats for a given location. The goal of identifying these threats beforehand is to help ensure uninterrupted business and computer services, lessen the risk of physical damage to a site from natural or man-made causes, and reduce the risk of internal and external theft. Most important, the safety of personnel takes precedence over the safety of structures, computers, data, and other systems.

The CBK defines these major categories of physical security threats:

- **Weather:** Tornadoes, hurricanes, floods, fire, snow, ice, heat, cold, humidity, and so forth

- **Fire/chemical:** Explosions, toxic waste/gases, smoke, and fire

- **Earth movement:** Earthquakes and mudslides

- **Structural failure:** Building collapse because of snow/ice or moving objects (cars, trucks, airplanes, and so forth)

- **Energy:** Loss of power, radiation, magnetic wave interference, and so forth

- **Biological:** Virus, bacteria, and infestations of animals or insects

- **Human:** Strikes, sabotage, terrorism, and war

Factors such as geographic locale determine the likelihood of specific physical security threats. A data center located in the San Francisco Bay area should be more concerned about earthquakes than a comparable data center in Kansas. And because tornados are more prevalent in Kansas than on the West Coast, data centers in the Great Plains should be more concerned about wind shears and snow and ice storms.

Providing Physical Security

The rest of this chapter discusses in some detail the five areas of physical security that address the aforementioned types of physical security threats:

- Education for personnel

- Administrative access controls, such as work area restrictions, visitor control, and site selection

- Physical security controls, such as perimeter security controls, badging, keys and combination locks, security dogs, lighting, fencing, and guards

- Technical controls, such as smart cards, audit trails, intrusion detection systems, and biometrics

- Environmental/life safety controls

Education for Personnel

An educated staff that knows about the potential for theft and misuse of facilities and equipment is the best weapon a company can have against illegitimate and accidental acts by others. Just as the staff should be prepared for the potential of unforeseen acts of nature, employees should be reminded periodically of the importance of helping to secure their surroundings:

- Being mindful of physical and environmental considerations required to protect the computer systems

- Adhering to emergency and disaster plans

- Monitoring the unauthorized use of equipment and services, and reporting suspicious or unusual activity to security personnel

- Recognizing the security objectives of the organization

- Accepting individual responsibilities associated with their own security and that of their co-workers, as well as the equipment they use and how they use it

An organization can educate its staff on the importance of their physical security through self-paced or formal instruction, security education bulletins, posters, training films and tapes, or awareness days that drive home the importance of constant vigilance.

Administrative Access Controls

The second category of physical access controls, administrative access controls, addresses the procedural and codified application of physical controls. For example, you will learn about several different physical control devices that make a site more secure. One of the administrative access controls in this section, site selection, involves planning for and designing the site before it is constructed.

Restricting Work Areas

A physical security plan, developed by executive management, department managers, and physical security site personnel as one of the many policy and standards documents that all effective security programmes require (see Chapter 4, "Governance and Risk Management"), should first identify the access rights to the site (campus) in general and then identify the various access rights each location (building) within the site requires. Within a manufacturing plant, individuals might need different access privileges, based on the department or area they are attempting to enter, even though they have gained general admittance to the plant. A single mechanism can control various levels of security access. This can be a badge reader encoded to allow the individual into specific areas of the facility based on function or business need. The important point to remember is that, just as security experts assign data to specific security classes, varying degrees of physical access can be based on security requirements within the facility.

Visitor Control

Controlling visitor access to a building is not a new concern. Most companies have long had some kind of procedure for requiring visitors to sign in and specify a purpose for their visit, and then wait for an escort who authorizes their presence before granting access to the visitor. However, with heightened post-September 11, 2001, security and the formation of the U.S. Department of Homeland Security, visitor control has taken on increased importance because of concern over foreign nationals in the workplace. The U.S. Department of Commerce (DOC) defines a foreign national as "a person who was born outside the jurisdiction of the United States, who is subject to some foreign government, and who has not been naturalized under U.S. law." In many government facilities or facilities with strong government ties, foreign nationals are not allowed unescorted access to any site within the facility. To gain access to any DOC site, for example, a foreign national must provide more than 17 identifying pieces of information, including passport number, country of issuance, and sponsor information.

For less secure and nongovernment sites, visitors typically must have a clear purpose for their visit and a confirmed contact within the site, such as an employee or another individual with the appropriate clearance. Visitors are usually required to sign in at the security desk and are given a temporary badge or other identifying moniker that clearly defines them as a visitor.

In addition, visitors might be required to pass through a metal detector and should be prepared to have handbags, satchels, and laptop briefcases checked. They also should be ready to surrender, at least temporarily, recording devices such as cameras, tape recorders, and other questionable items (for example, pocketknives).

Site Selection

Site designers and planners must make at least the following considerations when deciding on the location for a facility. This example considers the location of a data operations center for a major corporation.

- **Visibility:** How conspicuous will the facility be at a particular site? Most data centers look non-descript for a reason: They don't want to advertise what they are and attract undue attention. You will never find signs along the highway stating, "Highly Secure but Anonymous-Looking Data Operations Facility, Exit Here!" *Low-key* is the byword.

■ **Locale considerations:** A wise prospective homeowner should always inspect the neighborhood before purchasing a new house. The same rule applies to site-selection committees. What are the local ordinances and variances? What is the crime rate of the surrounding neighborhood? Are potentially hazardous sites nearby, such as landfills, hazardous waste dumps, or nuclear reactors?

■ **Natural disasters:** Several major corporations (including Charles Schwab) have moved their computer operations centers from the West Coast, particularly the San Francisco Bay area, to more geologically stable locations because of the risk of earthquakes. Other obvious natural threats to consider are tornadoes, hurricanes, floods, wildfires, chemical fires, vermin, pest damage, and snow and ice. Mother Nature's hand is far reaching, but site planners can minimize risk by examining local weather patterns, checking the history of weather-related disasters, and determining their risk tolerance.

■ **Transportation:** Are transportation routes such as airports, highways, and railroads nearby? If so, are they navigable? A good transportation system is important not only for the delivery of goods and services, but also for emergency evacuation procedures as part of a disaster recovery plan (DRP).

Physical Security Controls

Spectrums of physical controls are needed to support the principle of defense in depth. These include controls for the perimeter of the data center, employee and visitor badging, guard dogs when deemed appropriate, and building lighting.

Perimeter Security Controls

Controls on the perimeter of the data center are designed to prevent unauthorized access to the facility. These types of controls might have different "states" or behaviors based on the time of day or the day of the month. For example, a gate might allow controlled access during the day but be locked or closed at night.

In some respects, fences model the various levels of security in the virtual world. A fence 3 to 4 feet high will discourage the casual passerby. A fence 6 to 7 feet high will deter general intruders. A fence 8 feet high topped with concertina wire signals an even greater need to keep intruders out (and sometimes, unfortunately, to keep people in). A perimeter intrusion and detection assessment system (PIDAS) is fencing that uses passive vibration sensors to detect intruders or any attempts to compromise the system.

Turnstiles are less effective than either gates or fences. They dissuade rather than prevent intruders from entering a site without authorization. Anyone who has ever taken the New York City subway system undoubtedly has witnessed individuals leaping over the turnstile without depositing a token or, in today's age, swiping a Metro card. Turnstiles usually do not authenticate a user; they simply control access based on the use of a token.

Mantraps, as the name implies, are enclosed areas with a secure door on either end that literally "trap" an individual between doors. They address the problem of "piggybacking," in which an individual without proper authorization enters a secure area behind an authorized person. To pass through the second door of the mantrap, the individual must pass a second level of validation—perhaps the authorization of a security guard, the entering of a password, or some other mechanism (see Figure 8.1 for an example of a mantrap).

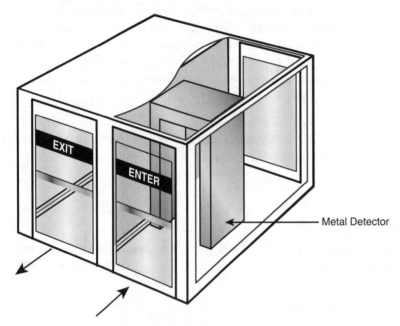

FIGURE 8.1   Example of a mantrap.

Badging

Issued by a site security office, the photo identification badge is a perimeter security control mechanism that not only authenticates an individual, but also continues to identify the individual while inside the facility. Most sites issuing photo identification require that the individual display the badge where it is most visible, usually on the upper torso. The badge alone is no guarantee that unauthorized individuals are denied access—badges can be stolen and photos replaced—but combined with other perimeter controls, the badge offers a familiar and comfortable sense of security in most organizations.

Keys and Combination Locks

Keys and combination locks are how most people know physical security, mainly because they are the least complicated and expensive devices. Beyond the mechanical door lock opened with a key, locks can be programmed and opened with a combination of keys (such as the five-key pushbutton lock once popular in IT operations), a security badge with a magnetic strip, or some other mechanism. Locks are typically unguarded and are meant to delay intruders, not to deny them access. For that reason, you rarely find these devices in areas that require a high level of access authorization.

Security Dogs

Dogs are not just man's best friend—they also make great security guards. Dogs can be unflinchingly loyal and rely on all their senses to detect intruders. They can also be trained to perform specialized services, such as sniffing out drugs or explosives at airports or alerting the blind to fire. The picture of the German Shepherd tethered to a door behind an auto junkyard might be the first image that comes to mind when thinking about security dogs, but dogs are a highly effective form of perimeter security control when handled properly and humanely.

Lighting

Lighting is another form of perimeter protection that discourages intruders or other unauthorized individuals from entering restricted areas. You are likely familiar with how shopping malls use streetlights to discourage parking lot break-ins, and many homeowners have motion-detector lights installed on garages and back porches. Critical buildings and installations should use some form of lighting as a deterrent, whether floodlights, streetlights, or searchlights. According to the National Institute of Standards and Technology, critical areas (fire escapes, emergency exits, and so forth) require safety lighting to be mounted 8 feet high and burn with a candlepower of 2 candelas (the equivalent of a strong spotlight).

Technical Controls

The next group of physical security controls involves using computer hardware and software to protect facilities. The following are prominent technical controls:

- Smart/dumb cards
- Audit trails/access logs
- Intrusion detection
- Biometric access controls

Smart Cards

A smart card resembles a regular payment (credit) card, but it carries a semiconductor chip with logic and nonvolatile memory (see Figure 8.2). Unlike a security access card (badge with magnetic strip), the smart card has many purposes, including value for consumer purchases, medical identification, travel ticketing and identification, and building access control. The card can also store software that detects unauthorized tampering and intrusions to the chip itself and, if detected, can lock or destroy the contents of the chip to prevent disclosure or unauthorized uses.

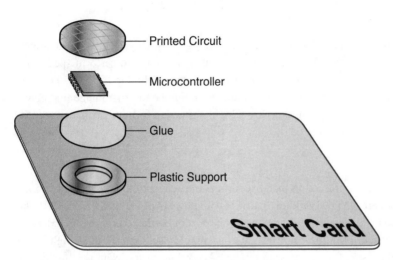

- Printed Circuit
- Microcontroller
- Glue
- Plastic Support

Smart Card

FIGURE 8.2   A smart card.

FYI: A Taxonomy of Smart Cards

Smart cards are essentially working computers with an infinite possibility of uses. On the physical level, smart cards are classified as contact, contactless, or combinations of the two. Contact smart cards require a reader (and/or writer) in which the card is inserted when it's needed. Contactless cards contain an antenna read by remote receivers. Combination cards can be used both ways, depending on the applications intended. Logically, you'll find smart cards classified three different ways. Memory cards (the simplest form) are used to store values for future uses.

The most common example of a memory card is a prepaid phone card redeemable through the bright-yellow reader slot found on modern pay phones. Protected memory cards require entry of a secret code or PIN before a stream of data can be sent to or received from the chip. Microprocessor cards contain a semiconductor chip to hold microcode that defines command structures, data file structures, and security structures. They are present when more intelligence or information storage is needed, and they often show up in multiapplication products and services, such as combined access and stored-value cards.

Smart cards, used much more extensively in Asia and Europe than in the United States, can also store banks of passwords. For example, users can store network, application, and Internet URLs and login passwords on a smart card. When smart cards are integrated with a biometrics login (such as a fingerprint, as discussed in more detail later in this chapter), security is further enhanced (see Chapter 5, "Security Architecture and Design").

Smart cards can also facilitate file encryption by storing the user's private key for use with a public key infrastructure (or PKI, a mechanism allowing the use of one private key and one public key to lock and unlock files—see Chapter 11, "Cryptography"). They work well for mobile users because such users are inclined to carry their smart card with them as they would one of their credit cards. This means that the user's encryption keys are not stored on a workstation, so the environment is more secure than when the cryptographic functions are performed on the workstation itself. Workstations are subject to Trojan horse attacks, in which a seemingly innocuous object contains something harmful to the interests of the recipient.

Still, smart cards alone are not completely secure. If an attacker steals a user's PIN or password along with the card, he or she gains complete access to the network. However, using a fingerprint along with the card to authenticate the user greatly reduces the chance for intrusion.

The use of smart cards in conjunction with biometrics authentication, such as fingerprint readers or retinal scan techniques, can be extremely effective, especially when controlling physical access is of the utmost importance. This kind of layered security goes beyond the use of passwords or passwords and smart cards alone. A company that has already committed to using smart cards for many of its applications could benefit from adding a level of security using a biometrics logon.

So why aren't these techniques more widely used? Factors such as cost, reliability, and practicality have hampered the deployment of smart cards and biometrics. However, as more companies build smart card readers into their workstations, and as the use of biometrics increases in manageability and flexibility and decreases in price, their use will become increasingly important and prevalent.

Audit Trails and Access Logs

In financial settings such as banks, audit trails enable examiners to trace or follow the history of a transaction through the institution. For example, bank auditors or examiners can determine when information was added, changed, or deleted within a system, to understand how an irregularity occurred and hopefully correct it. The immediate goal is to detect the problem in order to prevent similar problems in the future. The audit trail should contain the following information:

- The user ID or name of the individual who performed the transaction
- Where the transaction was performed (hopefully using a fixed terminal ID)
- The time and date of the transaction
- A description of the transaction—that is, what function the user performed and on what device

Creating an audit log is not enough to protect a site, however. The retention period of the audit logs, recovery time (how long it takes to recall an archived log file), and, perhaps most important, the integrity of the data must also be considered, and the logging system must be designed appropriately.

Intrusion Detection

Intrusion detection is another type of technical control. In this case, intrusion detectors and alarms alert security personnel when an unauthorized person attempts to access a system or building. Unlike the security guards, guard dogs, and security fencing discussed in the section on facility access control, this type of physical security control distinguishes itself by using technology. The burglar alarm is the most commonly known intrusion detection device, but as you can imagine, the technology has become much more sophisticated since the first devices were used. Consider the two categories of devices:

- **Perimeter intrusion detectors:** These devices are based on dry contact switches or photoelectric sensors. The former consists of metallic foil tape placed on windows or doorframes using contact switches. Disturbing the switches sets off an alarm. Dry contact switches are used in residential homes and shop fronts, where cost is important. Photoelectric sensors receive light beams, typically infrared, from a light-emitting device. When an intruder breaks the beams of light, he or she trips an alarm. This type of intrusion detection device is more expensive and usually found in larger facilities.

- **Motion detectors:** These devices detect unusual movements within a well-defined interior space. Included in this category of intrusion detection devices are wave pattern detectors that detect changes to light-wave patterns and audio detectors that passively receive unusual sound waves and set off an alarm.

Alarm Systems

The implementation of a series of the aforementioned intrusion detectors is referred to as an alarm system. A local alarm system sets off an alarm on the premises, alerting guards. Private security firms manage central-station systems, such as home alarms from ADT and other well-known home security companies. They monitor a system 24 hours a day and respond to alerts from a central location.

Company-established, -owned, and -operated alarm systems (also called dedicated alarm systems) resemble a commercial central station system; they serve many customers, but the focus is on the company exclusively. Dedicated systems might be more sophisticated than a local alarm system and share many of the same features as the centralized version. Additional alarms can be triggered at police or fire stations, with the permission and knowledge of the company being protected.

Biometrics

The use of biometrics (the Greek word for "life measurements") in conjunction with more standard forms of authentication such as fixed passwords and PINs is beginning to attract attention as the cost of the technology decreases and its sophistication increases. In fact, the traditional scheme of password-based computer security could lose stature as the use of smart card–based cryptographic credentials and biometrics authentication becomes commercially viable. Companies such as the American Biometrics Corporation claim that using an individual's unique physical characteristics along with other identification and authentication (I&A) techniques can almost unequivocally authenticate a user. Biometrics authentication uses characteristics of the human face, eyes, voice, fingerprints, hands, signature, and even body temperature; naturally, each technique has its strengths and weaknesses.

Once the domain of TV spy shows and science fiction stories, the use of human characteristics to allow access to secure systems has become a reality. (If you have ever seen Tom Cruise in any of his *Mission Impossible* movies, you will recognize many of these devices; science fiction often is several decades ahead of reality.)

Any security system, especially biometrics systems, must balance convenience with security. A system that is too intrusive or cumbersome will discourage or prevent an authorized user from accessing a system. A security system should also be scalable. In other words, not all systems and users need the same level of security, and security procedures and techniques should be flexible enough to reflect this. Still, any computer system requires a minimal level of security, and that is where authenticating the user at system logon becomes an issue.

A user's first access to a PC is during system logon, thus much attention focuses on the use of passwords, PINs, and, more recently, biometrics. Older versions of PC desktop operating systems, such as Windows 98 and Windows Me, did not require system logon, so whoever had physical access had complete control over the operating system and all the programs and data on the PC. Windows NT was one of the first popular PC operating systems to require a network-level logon, which can be secured by authenticating a user's credentials on an authentication server before that user can access the operating system and its file system.

How Best Can Authentication Be Achieved?

Today, the use of fingerprints appears to be the cheapest and most reliable form of biometrics authentication, although techniques such as retina scanning and thermal patterns are currently being developed. Apple's latest iPhone 5s has the capability to register the user's fingerprint with the device to unlock its functionality instead of using a PIN. The tip of the finger has characteristics called friction ridges, enclosures, and bifurcation points that uniquely differentiate one print from the print of any other individual. Because the fingerprint can vary in appearance throughout the day due to changes in temperature, skin moisture, dryness, oiliness, or cuts and abrasions, a direct comparison of digital images of the fingerprint cannot guarantee true authentication. Doing so would also require storing a complete image of the fingerprint in a database, which would attract the attention of civil liberties groups and government agencies.

Instead, fingerprints are compared based on their previously described characteristics and are thus characterized. How does this process work? The following steps generally describe the use of authenticating an individual using a fingerprint:

1. Multiple images of the individual's fingerprint are taken, using the center of the image as the reference point for the orientation and placement of other features.

2. The minutia features (ridges and other points) of importance surrounding the center of the image are computed as coordinate (XY) points and are catalogued in a database.

3. Each sample is scored based on the number and quality of coordinate values. The image with the highest (best sample) score becomes the "template" for the individual. This template is stored on a database and becomes the user's baseline or foundational template. Because it contains only a subset of the fingerprint detail, the template cannot be used to reconstruct the fingerprint or impersonate a sample fingerprint.

4. When a user wants to authenticate, an algorithm is used to process the template stored in the database against the minutiae of the sample fingerprint. The level of security required determines the number of coordinate values that must match.

Environmental/Life Safety Controls

Think of the infrastructure required to maintain the optimal operating environment for man and machine, and you have environmental and life safety controls. The three most critical areas follow:

■ Power (electrical, diesel)

■ Fire detection and suppression

■ Heating, ventilation, and air conditioning (HVAC)

Each of these areas is discussed briefly next. For a more complete discussion, see the CISSP Common Body of Knowledge description (www.isc2.org/).

Power

Whereas human beings can light candles when the power goes out, computers depend on an uninterrupted and regulated supply of power for constant voltage and current—computer equipment is highly sensitive to fluctuations in either voltage or current. We hardly need to mention the importance of electricity in our working and private lives, but whereas the consumer patiently waits for the lights to come back on, businesses count the minutes in terms of lost revenue and productivity. As part of their DRP (see Chapter 6, "Business Continuity Planning and Disaster Recovery Planning"), most sites have backup power sources such as diesel generators, a kind of private energy source that kicks in when the primary power source is interrupted or inadequate. Threats to power systems include noise (more specifically electrical radiation in the system), brownouts when a prolonged drop in voltage occurs, and humidity. When the humidity is too high (normally, above 60 percent), condensation on computer parts can occur, resulting in lost efficiency.

Fire Detection and Suppression

It is outside the scope of this book to discuss at length the details surrounding this extremely important technical control. If you plan to study more about physical security, you will need to understand these particulars. We briefly touch on the main areas of this control here, but you should consult one of the websites or CISSP exam prep books recommended throughout this text for further information.

■ **Fire types:** Fires are classified according to the type of combustibles and recommended methods of suppression. The four types of fires include common combustibles (wood, paper, and so forth), liquids (petroleum products, coolants, and so forth), electrical, and combustible metal (such as magnesium).

- **Fire detectors:** Fire detectors can be one of several types. Heat-sensing systems respond to either a predetermined threshold or a rapid rise in temperature. Flame detectors sense infrared energy or the pulsation of the flame. Smoke detectors use photoelectric sensors to respond to variations in the light hitting the photoelectric cells.

- **Fire-extinguishing systems:** When a fire occurs, the heating, ventilation, and air conditioning system (HVAC) must be stopped immediately to prevent the flow of oxygen. To extinguish the fire, either a water-sprinkler system or a gas-discharge system is used.

Water-sprinkler systems have four classifications: wet pipe, dry pipe, deluge, and preaction. Wet pipe systems hold water in the pipes that is released when heat opens a valve. Dry pipe systems do not have standing water in the pipes, so they eliminate the potential damage of a flood from a burst pipe in a wet pipe system. When water is needed, a central valve outside the data center is opened (automatically when a fire is sensed), and water flows into the plumbing only when it's required to extinguish a fire. The deluge system is a dry pipe system with a substantially higher volume of water. The preaction system combines elements of both wet and dry pipe systems and is the recommended fire-extinguishing system for computer rooms.

Heating, Ventilation, and Air Conditioning (HVAC)

The classifieds always seem to have ads for HVAC repairmen. That's because reliable and uninterrupted heating, ventilation, and air conditioning systems are critical environmental controls. Computers are particularly sensitive to the smallest fluctuations in temperature and humidity. We frequently take HVAC environmental controls for granted, but the IT manager or the person(s) responsible for these systems should know exactly what to do and whom to contact in the event of failure. Routine maintenance of critical infrastructure systems should prevent any significant failure of HVAC systems.

Summary

Security experts often underemphasize physical security when discussing strategies for protecting critical resources such as computers and the data stored on them. The ability of intruders and unauthorized personnel to access computer systems remotely does not take anything away from the need to secure physical sites. The Physical Security domain includes traditional safeguards against intentional and unintentional threats. Physical security threats can be man-made (such as labor strikes) or natural (such as earthquakes). Educating personnel about the importance of emergency response and accepting responsibility for their actions is critical. One type of physical security control is administrative access controls that use procedural and codified applications of physical security controls.

Another type of physical security control involves mechanisms such as fences and gates to control access to a facility. Yet another type of physical security control, technical controls, uses computer hardware and software such as smart cards to protect facilities. One rapidly growing area of technical security controls is biometrics, the use of human traits such as fingerprints to identify and authenticate an individual.

Test Your Skills

MULTIPLE-CHOICE QUESTIONS

1. Physical security pertains to which of the following?

    A. Guaranteeing the safety of equipment before people

    B. Mandating annual health checkups for all employees

    C. Protecting an organization's assets and ensuring the continuity of business in case of a disaster

    D. Installing smoke alarms in every doorway of every building

2. Which of the following statements is true of level of physical security?

    A. Physical security has no limits.

    B. Physical security is proportional to the value of the property being protected.

    C. Physical security depends on management involvement.

    D. Physical security is indexed to employee insecurities.

3. Which of the following does *not* pertain to physical security?

    A. Site selection

    B. Securing a site against unauthorized access

    C. Protecting people and property

    D. Installing firewalls on all computers

4. Which of the following events are considered natural disasters?

    A. Earthquakes

    B. Chemical fires

    C. Rat infestations

    D. All of the above

5. Why is it important to educate personnel on the physical security of their facility?

    A. Doing so makes them more employable if they seek a career in facility management.

    B. They are protecting shareholder investments.

    C. They become more aware of the safety of coworkers and equipment.

    D. None of the above.

6. Which of the following is *not* a major concern when reviewing site selection?

    A. Local crime rate

    B. Proximity of restaurants, banks, and other conveniences for employees

    C. Transportation systems

    D. Weather

7. Why might San Francisco not be an optimal site for a data center?

    A. The cost of doing business is often higher in San Francisco than in other parts of the country.

    B. San Francisco is near a major earthquake fault zone.

    C. Employees are easily distracted by local attractions.

    D. A and B.

8. Which of the following is not considered a physical security protection device?

    A. Mantrap

    B. Concertina wire

    C. German Shepherd

    D. Police helicopter

9. Which of the following statements is true of security dogs?

    A. Security dogs are always German Shepherds.

    B. When trained, security dogs provide effective perimeter control.

    C. Security dogs are best utilized as a form of an environmental/life safety control.

    D. None of the above.

10. Which of the following statements are true of smart cards?

    A. Smart cards are used more extensively in Europe and Asia than in the United States.

    B. Smart cards can store passwords such as personal identification numbers (PINs).

    C. Although they promise great strides in authenticating users, smart cards are not infallible.

    D. All of the above.

11. Which of the following statements best describes an audit trail?

    A. An audit trail is a fitness path for quality inspectors.

    B. An audit trail is a sound recording of conversations taped through perimeter devices.

    C. An audit trail is a history of transactions indicating data that has been changed or modified.

    D. All of the above.

12. Which of the following is *not* true about the use of fingerprints for identification and authentication (I&A)?

    A. Fingerprints are an infallible physical security control.

    B. Fingerprints contain friction ridges and minutia points.

    C. Fingerprints change based on fluctuations in temperature, skin moisture, and dryness.

    D. The practice has alarmed civil libertarians.

13. Environmental controls include which of the following elements?

    A. Heating and air conditioning

    B. Barometers

    C. Diesel backup generators

    D. Both A and C

14. Which of the following statements is true of power supplies?

    A. Power supplies need to be clean and uninterrupted.

    B. Power supplies come in unlimited quantities.

    C. Power supplies are not a major physical security concern because municipalities are responsible for supplying power.

    D. Power supplies are becoming increasingly inexpensive.

15. Which of the following statements best describes HVAC?

   A. HVAC is a backup computer power supply system.

   B. HVAC is an acronym used to describe a medical response team.

   C. HVAC is a type of environmental control system.

   D. None of the above.

EXERCISES

EXERCISE 8.1: Examining Your Personal Security Systems

1. Develop a checklist for your home or place of employment to help you decide whether the level of physical security is adequate to protect your personal assets or your business's assets and data.

2. Complete the checklist by taking a walk around your site.

3. Recommend what you think needs to be done to improve the physical site's security.

EXERCISE 8.2: Explaining the Codependency of Physical and Logical Security Controls

1. Describe how physical security controls are needed to augment logical security controls in a typical data center.

2. What physical security controls would you recommend for server rooms or network switching equipment closets if a full-blown data center is not practical?

EXERCISE 8.3: Observing the Security Controls Around You

1. Pick a typical day, and from dawn to dusk, make note of the ways in which you interact with security controls (for example, you used a badge reader to enter an office building). Remember that security controls include the unseen as well as the visible.

2. After you complete your list of security controls, describe how you feel about your observations.

3. Do you feel like your personal privacy is being invaded, or are the security controls necessary in the highly technological age in which we live?

EXERCISE 8.4: Evaluating a Locale for a Data Center Operation

1. Select a specific geographic location (perhaps your hometown or the place where a friend or relative lives), and describe the suitability of the location for a major data center operation.

2. What criteria does the location meet for a viable operations center?

3. What are the drawbacks/limitations?

4. How do you go about weighing the advantages against the disadvantages?

EXERCISE 8.5: Evaluating the Practicality of Biometrics

1. Research an aspect of biometrics (such as palm print recognition) and discuss the practicality of the security control.

2. Are specific biometric devices more realistic than others?

3. If so, what factors determine the reliability of a biometric control?

PROJECTS

PROJECT 8.1: Touring Your School's Enrollment Systems

1. Arrange for a tour of your local school's information-keeping systems for student and faculty records.

2. Determine whether their systems of controls seem appropriate for the nature and sensitivity of their record keeping.

3. Write down your impressions of their physical security controls to share with the class.

4. How do your findings differ from the findings of other students in the class?

PROJECT 8.2: **Comparing Built-in Physical Security to Add-on Physical Security**

Tiger Industrial (www.brb.tigerindustrialrentals.com/?gclid=CP_e3q78yrcCFRHhQgodEHUAXA) is just one example of a company specializing in the design and implementation of blast-resistant building materials for government buildings (the U.S. embassy in Moscow is the company's signature project).

1. Describe how a company such as Tiger Industrial builds in physical security.

2. How does the company's approach differ from add-on physical security devices and protections?

3. For what types of installations is this approach required?

4. Who is the company's largest customer?

PROJECT 8.3: **Researching the Effectiveness of Home Alarm Systems**

1. Americans spend millions of dollars each year on antitheft systems for their homes and offices from companies such as ADT (www.adt.com). In your opinion, how effective are these systems? (For example, consider whether you believe home alarm systems are worth their cost or whether you believe money is simply wasted on these systems.) Explain your reasoning.

3. What impacts do home alarm systems have on homeowner insurance premiums?

4. How much security is enough security? How can you determine how much of a system you should buy?

Chapter | 9

Operations Security

Chapter Objectives

After reading this chapter and completing the exercises, you will be able to do the following:

- Outline the types of controls needed for secure operations of a data center
- Explain the principle of least privilege.
- Differentiate between the principle of least privilege and the principle of separation of duties
- Define the control mechanisms commonly found in data center operations
- Create a model of controls that incorporates people-, process-, and technology-based control mechanisms

Introduction

Operations security is used to identify the controls over software, hardware, media, and the operators and administrators who possess elevated access privileges to any of these resources. Operations security is primarily concerned with data center operations processes, personnel, and technology, and is needed to protect assets from threats during normal use. Audits and monitoring are the mechanisms that permit the identification of security events, define the key elements of these events, and serve as the source of pertinent event information given to the appropriate individual, group, or process.

Specific types of controls are needed to implement the security necessary to protect assets. This chapter covers the following controls:

- Preventative controls reduce the frequency and impact of errors and prevent unauthorized intruders.
- Detective controls discover errors after they've occurred.

- Corrective or recovery controls help mitigate the impact of a loss.

- Deterrent controls encourage compliance with external controls.

- Application-level controls minimize and detect software operational irregularities.

- Transaction-level controls provide control over various stages of a transaction.

Operations Security Principles

The principle of least privilege, or need to know, defines a minimum set of access rights or privileges needed to perform a specific job description. For example, a system administrator should have the necessary privileges to install server operating systems and software but should not have the role to add new users to the server. Separation of duties is a type of control that shows up in most security processes to make certain that no single person has excessive privileges that could be used to conduct hard-to-detect business fraud or steal secrets from a government system. The idea is to force collusion among two or more insiders in order for them to perpetrate fraud or theft.

Separation of duties is one of the six key elements of a strong system of security controls. It is similar in scope and practice to the financial systems for internal controls (for example, accounting departments). These six elements are listed here:

- Employing competent, trustworthy people with clear lines of authority and responsibility

- Having adequate separation of job and process duties

- Having proper procedures for authorizing transactions or changes to information

- Maintaining adequate documents and records

- Maintaining appropriate physical controls over assets and records

- Executing independent checks on performance

A primary benefit of separation of duties is that it enables one person's work to serve as a complementary check on another person's work. This implies that no single person has complete control over any transaction or process from beginning to end.

Separation of duties is important within all security-related processes for two fundamental reasons. First, people are an integral part of every operations process. They authorize, generate, and approve all work that is needed. Having different people engaged in critical positions within the process is a common, sensible practice that ensures consistent and successful execution of the process. Second, people have shortcomings. When individuals perform complementary checks on each other, an enhanced opportunity arises for someone to catch an error before a process is fully executed and before a decision is made based on potentially erroneous data or activity. In spite of these checks and balances, some people might still be inclined to engage in fraud, theft, or malicious activities. They usually do so because they possess the following:

- **Motivation:** Usually caused by some financial crisis that results from health problems, drugs, overspending, gambling, extortion, or relationship problems, for example.

- **Justification:** A sense that they have not been treated fairly, the employer owes them, or any other explanation that they use to give good reason for their actions

- **Opportunity:** Knowledge or belief that a fraud can be committed and remain undetected ("I'll never get caught") either because internal controls are not in place or are inadequate, or because they believe no one is minding the store.

FYI: Separation of Duties

Separation of duties is essential to maintain the integrity of production operations. A typical computer operation in most companies divides separation of duties into various environments: one environment for the software developers, another for quality assurance testing, and a third for production, or the environment that end users access, to perform their duties. As software is deemed ready, it's promoted from environment to environment by systems and security administration personnel, not the programmer. This separation of duties prevents a programmer from launching into production software that can perpetrate fraud or cause damage to production data or resources.

Operations Security Process Controls

Process controls are necessary for secure data center operations. They help ensure that the principles outlined previously are implemented in human-based process activities and software-based utilities and other data center management systems (such as backup libraries and program directories).

Trusted recovery controls ensure that security is not breached when a computer system crashes. Fail-secure system controls preserve the state of the system before the crash and prevent further damage or unauthorized access to the system. One example of this is a bank vault located in a high-security room. The trusted recovery control is the room itself, which can detect any attempt at an unauthorized entry and lock the perpetrator in an area where he cannot escape (see the discussion on mantraps in Chapter 8, "Physical Security Control").

Configuration and change management controls are used for tracking and approving changes to a system. This process identifies, controls, and audits any changes by administrative personnel to reduce the threats or negative impacts of security violations. One threat to configuration and change management is called a block upgrade. In this situation, a requestor asks for a large number of simultaneous changes during an upgrade, but because change management is impossible, it is bypassed. To prevent the threats from a block upgrade, changes should be packaged so they are readily managed and easily understood to preserve system security and integrity. You can read more on configuration and change management in the "Operations Security Controls in Action" section later in this chapter.

Personnel security involves pre-employment screening and mandatory vacation time. This prevents people from hiding illegal activities while performing their duties. (For instance, when other people take over the work while the person is on vacation, they might detect hidden activity.) Other personnel security measures include job rotation and a series of escalating warnings that lead up to termination of employment or prosecution in the criminal justice system in cases of unauthorized or illegal activity.

Record retention processes refers to how long transactions and other types of computerized or process records should be retained. These controls deal with computer files, directories, and libraries of software and utilities.

Resource protection is needed to protect company resources and assets. Some resources that require protection are modem pools, network routers, storage media, and documentation.

Privileged entity controls are given to operators and system administrators as special access to computing resources. Included are controls to ensure individual accountability for all actions taken while logged in as administrator.

In Practice

Controlling Privileged User IDs

To best control administrative rights and access to a system, it is essential to issue individual accounts (IDs) and passwords that can be tied to a single person. Those accounts can then be granted account privileges of an administrator. Instead of sharing the password associated with a default account ID administrator or root (UNIX-based systems), a better practice is to tag the default account so that it cannot be used (or delete it entirely, if possible) and make sure that each administrator has a unique and personally identifiable account to perform his or her duties.

Media viability controls are needed for properly marking and handling assets. These include clearly marking media with contents, dates, classification (if needed), and other information to help operators locate and use the correct media more often.

Operations process controls are a necessary element in the overall security of a computer installation. Because operators tend to possess privilege beyond other users, it's vital to impose controls to limit the damage they can cause and protect them from themselves.

FYI: Sarbanes-Oxley and Data Center Security

The Sarbanes-Oxley (SOX) Act of 2002, passed by the U.S. Congress after the accounting scandals at firms such as Enron and WorldCom, captured the attention of internal auditors and CEOs nationwide. SOX requires executives to review and modernize companies' financial reporting systems to comply with its regulations. One specific section of SOX (Section 404) calls for company executives and third-party auditors to certify the effectiveness of technologies and processes (internal controls) that are put in place to ensure the integrity of financial reports.

Complying with Section 404 means looking into situations in which sensitive corporate data might be accessible, processed, or stored. Statement on Standards for Attestation Engagements (SSAE) No. 16, Reporting on Controls at a Service Organization, was finalized by the Auditing Standards Board of the American Institute of Certified Public Accountants (AICPA) in January 2010. SSAE 16 effectively replaces SAS 70 as the authoritative guidance for reporting on service organizations. SSAE 16 was formally issued in April 2010 and became effective on June 15, 2011. SSAE 16 was drafted with the purpose of updating the U.S. service organization reporting standard so that it mirrors and complies with the new international service organization reporting standard, ISAE 3402. SSAE 16 also establishes an Attestation Standard, called AT 801, which contains guidance for performing the service auditor's examination. Many service organizations that previously had an SAS 70 service auditor's examination (SAS 70 audit) performed converted to the new standard in 2011 and now have an SSAE 16 report instead; this is also referred to as a Service Organization Controls (SOC) 1 report (source: http://ssae16.com/SSAE16_overview.html).

Operations Security Controls in Action

The Achilles' heel of many organizations is failure to pay close and ongoing attention to operations security. The following section provides more details on specific areas of operations used as protection against this vulnerability. It emphasizes the principles needed for secure operations of data center assets. Without a robust set of controls, it is easy to undermine expensive security measures. This could be because of poor documentation, old user accounts, conflicting software versions or products, or poor control over the maintenance of default accounts that come preloaded on new computer systems.

To ensure operations security, the individuals in charge of information security must keep these considerations in mind at all times:

- Software support
- Configuration and change management
- Backups
- Media controls
- Documentation
- Maintenance
- Interdependencies

The following sections discuss each of these in depth.

Software Support

Software is the heart of an organization's computer operations, regardless of the size and complexity of the system. As such, it is essential that software functions correctly and is protected from corruption. Several elements of control are needed for software support.

One type of control within this category is to limit what software is used on a given system. If users or systems personnel can load and execute any software on any system, these systems become more vulnerable to viruses, worms, malware, unexpected software interactions, or software that can subvert or bypass security controls.

A second method of controlling software is to inspect or test software before it is loaded (for example, to determine compatibility with custom applications or identify other unforeseen interactions). This applies to new software packages, upgrades, off-the-shelf products, and custom software. In addition to controlling the loading and execution of new software, organizations should be cautious with off-the-shelf or downloaded system utilities. Some of the system utilities are designed to compromise the integrity of operating systems or breach logical access controls.

Many organizations also include on their agendas a program to help ensure that software is properly licensed. For example, an organization might audit systems for illegal copies of copyrighted software. This problem is primarily associated with PCs and local area networks (LANs), but it can apply to any type of system.

Another element of software support involves ensuring that software is not modified without proper authorization. This involves protecting all software and backup copies. This step is often accomplished using a combination of logical and physical access controls (see Chapter 8).

Configuration and Change Management

Configuration and change management, which is closely related to software support, tracks and, if needed, approves changes to the system. It normally addresses hardware, software, networking, documentation, and other changes, and the process can be formal or informal. The primary security goal of configuration management is ensuring that users don't cause unintentional changes to the system that could diminish security. Some of the methods discussed under software support can be useful in reaching this goal (for example, inspecting and testing software changes, and periodically reviewing software security controls and parameter settings in the software).

For networked systems, configuration management should include a consideration of external connections. Is the computer system connected to a network? What other systems are involved? To what systems are these other systems and organizations connected? Note that the security goal is to know what changes occur—you cannot manage what you do not know about.

A second security goal of configuration and change management is to ensure that changes to the system are reflected in up-to-date documentation, such as the contingency or continuity plan, as discussed in Chapter 6, "Business Continuity Planning and Disaster Recovery Planning." If the change is major, it might be necessary to reanalyze some or all of the system's security.

Backups

Support and operations personnel (and sometimes users) back up software and data. This function is critical to contingency planning. The frequency of backups depends on how often data changes and the importance of those changes. Also, as a safety measure, it is useful to test the backup copies to ensure that they are actually usable. Finally, backups should be stored securely and off site.

Users of smaller systems are often responsible for their own backups. However, they do not always perform backups regularly or thoroughly. In some organizations, support personnel are charged with making backups periodically for smaller systems, either automatically (through server software) or manually (by visiting each machine).

Media Controls

Media controls include a variety of measures to provide physical and environmental protection and accountability for tapes, optical media, USB (Flash) drives, printouts, and other media. From a security perspective, media controls should be designed to prevent the loss of confidentiality, integrity, or availability of information, including data or software, when stored outside the system. This can include storage of information before it is input into the system and after it is output.

The extent of media control depends on many factors, including the type of data, the quantity of media, and the nature of the user environment. Physical and environmental protection prevents unauthorized individuals from accessing media and also protects against such factors as heat, cold, or harmful magnetic fields. When necessary, logging the use of individual media (such as CDs and DVDs) provides detailed accountability, to hold authorized people responsible for their actions. The next sections describe some of the common media controls.

Marking

Controlling media might require some form of marking or physical labeling. The labels can be identify media with special handling instructions, locate needed information, or log media (for example, with serial/control numbers or bar codes) to support accountability. Colored labels often identify media, and banner pages are used on printouts.

If labeling is used for special handling instructions, it is critical that people dealing with the labeled material are appropriately trained. The marking of PC input and output is generally the responsibility of the user, not the system support staff; marking backup media can help prevent them from being accidentally overwritten.

Logging

Logging media supports accountability. Logs can include control numbers (or other tracking data), the times and dates of transfers, names and signatures of individuals involved, and other relevant information. Periodic spot checks or audits can be conducted to determine that no controlled items have been lost and ensure that all are in the custody of individuals named in control logs. Automated media tracking systems are helpful in maintaining inventories of media libraries.

Integrity Verification

When electronically stored information is read into a computer system, you might need to determine whether it has been read correctly or subjected to any modification. You can verify the integrity of electronic information using error detection and correction or, if intentional modifications are a threat, cryptographic-based technologies. In addition, the integrity of backup media should be tested periodically so that no surprises arise when it's time to rely on them to restore normal operations.

Physical Access Protection

Media can be stolen, destroyed, replaced with a look-alike copy, or lost. Physical access controls that limit these problems include locked doors, desks, file cabinets, and safes. If the media requires protection at all times, it may be necessary to actually output data to the media in a secure location (for example, printing to a printer in a locked room instead of to a general-purpose printer in a common area).

Physical protection of media should extend to backup copies stored offsite. These offsite backup copies should generally be accorded an equivalent level of protection as media containing the same information stored onsite. Equivalent protection does not mean that the security measures need to be exactly the same: The controls at the off-site location are quite likely to be different from the controls at the regular site, but adequate controls must be present to preserve the integrity of media or systems used at off-site facilities.

Environmental Protection

Magnetic media, such as CDs, DVDs, and other optical media, require environmental protection because they are sensitive to temperature, liquids, magnetism, smoke, and dust. Other media, such as paper and other storage, have different sensitivities to environmental factors.

Transmittal

Media control can be transferred both within the organization and to outside elements. Possibilities for securing such transmittal include sealed and marked envelopes, authorized messenger or courier, or U.S. certified or registered mail.

Disposition

When media is disposed of, it might be important to ensure that information is not improperly disclosed. This applies both to media that is external to a computer system (such as USB Flash drives and optical media) and to media inside a computer system, such as a hard disk. People often throw away old media, believing that erasing the files has made the data irretrievable. In reality, however, erasing a file simply removes the pointer to that file. The pointer tells the computer where the file is physically stored. Without this pointer, the files will not appear on a directory listing—but this does not mean that the file was removed. Commonly available utility programs can easily retrieve information that is presumed deleted.

To prevent the threats from recovering information from disposed media, we turn to the technique of permanently removing information from media, called sanitization. Three techniques are commonly used for media sanitization:

- Overwriting
- Degaussing
- Destruction

Overwriting is an effective method for clearing data from magnetic media. As the name implies, overwriting uses a program to write data (1s, 0s, or a combination) onto the media. Common practice is to overwrite the media three times. Overwriting should not be confused with merely deleting the pointer to a file, which typically happens when a delete command is used (as already mentioned).

Degaussing involves magnetically erasing data from magnetic media. Two types of degaussers exist: strong permanent magnets and electric degaussers.

The final method, and the only sure method of sanitization, is destruction of the media by shredding or burning.

Documentation

Although it's the bane of most developers and IT professionals due to extra work involved, documentation of all aspects of computer support and operations is important to ensure continuity and consistency. Formalizing operational practices and procedures with sufficient detail helps to eliminate security lapses and oversights. It also gives new personnel sufficiently detailed instructions and provides a quality assurance function to help ensure that operations will be performed correctly and efficiently.

The security of a system also needs to be documented. This includes many types of documentation, such as security plans, contingency plans, risk analyses, and security policies and procedures. Much of this information, particularly risk and threat analyses, must be protected against unauthorized disclosure. Security documentation also needs to be both current and accessible. Accessibility should take special factors into account (such as the need to find the contingency plan during a disaster).

Security documentation should be designed to fulfill the needs of the different types of people who use it. For this reason, many organizations separate documentation into policy and procedures. A security procedures manual should be written to inform various system users how to do their jobs securely. A security procedures manual for systems operations and support staff can address a wide variety of technical and operational concerns in considerable detail.

Maintenance

System maintenance requires either physical or logical access to the system. Support and operations staff, hardware or software vendors, or third-party service providers can maintain a system. Maintenance can be performed onsite, or you might have to move equipment to a repair site. Maintenance can also be performed remotely via communications connections. If someone who does not normally have access to the system performs maintenance, security vulnerability is introduced.

In some circumstances, additional precautions, such as conducting background investigations of service personnel, might be necessary. Supervision of maintenance personnel might prevent some problems, such as snooping around the physical area. However, if someone gains access to the system, the potential damage done through the maintenance process is very difficult to prevent.

Many computer systems and network devices provide default maintenance accounts. These special log-in accounts are normally preconfigured at the factory with preset, widely known passwords. One of the most common methods hackers use to break into systems is to go through maintenance accounts that still have factory-set or easily guessed passwords. Changing these passwords or otherwise disabling the accounts until they are needed is critical. Procedures should be developed to ensure that only authorized maintenance personnel can use these accounts. If the account is to be used remotely, authentication of the maintenance provider can be performed using features present in most remote access that requires strong user authentication. This helps ensure that remote diagnostic activities actually originate from an established telephone number at the vendor's site.

Other techniques, including encryption and decryption of diagnostic communications, as well as strong identification and authentication techniques (such as tokens; see Chapter 10), also can help. Larger systems might have diagnostic ports. In addition, manufacturers of larger systems and third-party providers might offer more diagnostic and support services. These ports must be used only by authorized personnel and must not be accessible by hackers.

Interdependencies

Support and operations components coexist in most computer security controls:

- **Personnel:** Most support and operations staff have special access to the system. Some organizations conduct background checks on individuals who fill these positions, to screen out possibly untrustworthy individuals (see Chapter 4, "Governance and Risk Management").

- **Incident handling:** Support and operations can include an organization's incident-handling staff. Even if they are separate organizations, they need to work together to recognize and respond to incidents (see Chapter 6).

- **Contingency planning:** Support and operations normally provide technical input to contingency planning and carry out the activities of making backups, updating documentation, and practicing responses to contingencies (see Chapter 6).

- **Security awareness, training, and education:** Support and operations staff should be trained in security procedures and be aware of the importance of security. In addition, they provide technical expertise needed to teach users how to secure their systems (see Chapter 4).

- **Physical and environmental:** Support and operations staff often control the immediate physical area around the computer system (see Chapter 8).

- **Technical controls:** Support and operations staff installs, maintains, and uses the technical controls. They create the user accounts, add users to access control lists, review audit logs for unusual activity, control bulk encryption over telecommunications links, and perform the countless operational tasks needed to use technical controls effectively. In addition, support and operations staff provide needed input to the selection of controls, based on their knowledge of system capabilities and operational constraints.

- **Assurance:** Support and operations staff ensures that changes to a system do not introduce security vulnerabilities by using assurance methods to evaluate or test the changes and their effect on the system. Support and operations staff normally performs operational assurance (see Chapter 5, "Security Architecture and Design").

Paying close attention to these operations controls helps in ensuring overall secure operations and keeping auditors at bay as they review the data center's operation—which they often do in large organizations.

Summary

Operations security clarifies the controls needed to ensure secure data center operations. It covers processes concerning hardware, media, software, and the operations staff who typically possess elevated privileges to maintain data center and computer program operations. The principle of least privilege, which limits operators' access rights or privileges, is essential to prevent abuses. A clear separation of duties is necessary to prevent abuses at a transaction or business process level. Even if process and human controls in data center operations are firmly in place and operating as intended, controls ensuring the maintenance of the operation must also be present and operating successfully.

Test Your Skills

MULTIPLE-CHOICE QUESTIONS

1. Operations security seeks to primarily protect against which of the following?

   A. Object reuse

   B. Facility disaster

   C. Compromising emanations

   D. Asset threats

2. Which operations security control prevents unauthorized intruders from internally or externally accessing the system and lowers the amount and impact of unintentional errors that are entering the system?

   A. Detective controls

   B. Preventative controls

   C. Corrective controls

   D. Directive controls

3. What is the main objective of separation of duties?

   A. To prevent employees from disclosing sensitive information

   B. To ensure that access controls are in place

   C. To ensure that no single individual can compromise a system

   D. To ensure that audit trails are not tampered with

4. A violation of the "separation of duties" principle arises when the security systems software is accessed by which of the following individuals?

   A. Security administrator

   B. Security analyst

    C. Systems auditor

    D. Systems programmer

5. Which security procedure forces collusion between two operators of different categories to have access to unauthorized data?

    A. Enforcing regular password changes

    B. Management monitoring of audit logs

    C. Limiting the specific accesses of operations personnel

    D. Job rotation of people through different assignments

6. Intrusion response is a _____.

    A. Preventive control

    B. Detective control

    C. Monitoring control

    D. Reactive control

7. Which of the following are functions that are compatible in a properly separated environment?

    A. Security administration and software security testing activity

    B. Security administration and external customer service

    C. Security administration and application programming

    D. Application programming and test data creation

8. If a programmer is restricted from updating and modifying production software, what is this an example of?

    A. Rotation of duties

    B. Least privilege

    C. Separation of duties

    D. Personnel security

9. What is the most effective means of determining how controls are functioning within an operating system?

    A. Interview with a computer operator

    B. Review of software control features and/or parameters

    C. Review of operating system manual

    D. Interview with product vendor

10. Which of the following is not concerned with configuration management?

    A. Hardware

    B. Software

    C. Documentation

    D. They all are concerned with configuration management.

11. When backing up an application system's data, which of the following is a key question to be answered first?

    A. When to make backups

    B. Where to keep backups

    C. What records to backup

    D. How to store backups

12. Operations security requires the implementation of physical security to control which of the following?

    A. Unauthorized personnel access

    B. Incoming hardware

    C. Contingency conditions

    D. Evacuation procedures

13. Which of the following is the best way to handle obsolete magnetic tapes before disposing of them?

    A. Overwriting the tapes

    B. Initializing the tape labels

    C. Erasing the tapes

    D. Degaussing the tapes

14. Which of the following is *not* a media viability control used to protect the feasibility of data storage media?

    A. Clearing

    B. Marking

    C. Handling

    D. Storage

15. Which of the following is the most secure way to dispose of information stored on optical media?

    A. Sanitizing

    B. Physical damage

    C. Degaussing

    D. Physical destruction

EXERCISES

EXERCISE 9.1: Examining Separation of Duties

1. Construct a list of benefits for proper separation of duties in data center operations.

2. What threats are eliminated with a proper separation of duties?

3. What does separating duties force people who want to abuse their privilege to do?

EXERCISE 9.2: Touring a Data Center

1. Arrange for a tour of your school's or employer's data center.

2. What controls over data center personnel can you identify?

3. Are there controls you would expect to be there but are not? Describe them.

EXERCISE 9.3: Understanding the Need for Current Backups

1. Why are current backups important?

2. Outline a recommendation for work-at-home users with respect to their backup habits and practices. Consider how cloud-based solutions (such as DropBox) can affect the ability to recover from backups.

EXERCISE 9.4: Understanding Configuration and Change Control

1. Why is configuration and change management important?

2. What threats are mitigated through effective change management?

3. What are some of the activities you would expect to see in the process?

PROJECTS

PROJECT 9.1: Designing Data Center Personnel Controls

1. Create a fictitious company or organization that requires a robust data center and operations.

2. Describe the data center and its operations schedule and personnel.

3. What roles are present?

4. What operations controls would you ensure are operating correctly?

PROJECT 9.2: Sanitizing Media

Suggest some ways to erase the contents of the following types of media so that no data can be recovered. You might find the article "Guide to Understanding Data in Automated Information Systems (http://cerberussystems.com/INFOSEC/stds/ncsctg25.htm) useful.

1. Optical media (CDs, DVDs, and so on)

2. Paper-based data

3. Flash (USB) or thumb drives

4. Magnetic tape cartridges

5. PC hard drives

PROJECT 9.3: Researching Controls

1. List some preventative controls that you might expect to see in a data center.

2. List some detective controls that you might expect to see in a data center.

3. List some corrective or recovery controls that you might expect to see in a data center.

4. List some deterrent controls that you might expect to see in a data center.

5. List some application-level controls that you might expect to see in a data center.

6. List some transaction-level controls that you might expect to see in a data center.

Chapter 10

Access Control Systems and Methodology

Chapter Objectives

After reading this chapter and completing the exercises, you will be able to do the following:

- Apply access control techniques to meet confidentiality and integrity goals
- Understand and implement the major terms and concepts related to access control and tie them to system security
- Apply discretionary access controls (DAC) and mandatory access controls (MAC) techniques, as appropriate
- Choose effective passwords and avoid password limitations
- Implement password alternatives, including smart cards, password tokens, and other multifactor techniques
- Apply the goals of single sign-on concepts to business and common users
- Use the techniques described to control remote user access

Introduction

Access controls are a collection of mechanisms that work together to create a security architecture that protects the assets of an information system. One of the goals of access control is personal accountability, which is the mechanism that proves someone performed a computer activity at a specific point in time.

This chapter covers terminology and principles of authentication used in the Access Control domain, along with some of the more popular techniques and protocols used in commercial software to control access.

This chapter also covers single sign-on techniques and the methods commonly used to permit remote access to corporate and back-office systems (office networks and servers that front-office personnel access to do their jobs).

Terms and Concepts

Access control is the heart of an information technology (IT) security system and is needed to meet the major objectives of InfoSec: confidentiality and integrity.

You must be familiar with certain concepts and terms to gain an appreciation for access control needs and the techniques involved in meeting these needs. The following sections discuss these terms.

Identification

Identification credentials uniquely identify the users of an information system. Typically, identification equates to a user's offline identity through his or her name, initials, or email address, or a meaningless string of characters. Think of identification credentials in terms of how you identify yourself in the offline world: name, social security number, student ID number, and so on.

Authentication

Authentication credentials permit the system to verify someone's identification credential. Authenticating yourself to a system involves giving it the information you have established to prove that you are who you say you are. Most often this is a simple password that you set up when you receive the privilege to access a system. You might initially receive an assigned password, with the requirement that you reset it to something more personal that only you can remember. Offline, your picture on your credential (license, credit card, and so forth) allows the world to check the legitimacy of your identification claim. Your photo authenticates your identity. Another common authentication of your identity is your signature. If your signature matches the signature on your credential, the recipient can be reasonably assured that you are who your ID claims you are.

Least Privilege (Need to Know)

The principle of least privilege is the predominant strategy to ensure confidentiality. The objective is to give people the least amount of access to a system that they need to perform the job they're doing. The "need to know" concept governs the privilege (authority) to perform a transaction or access a resource (system, data, and so forth). The military has a strict methodology for implementing this concept, using sensitivity labels (see Chapter 5, "Security Architecture and Design") to stored information and clearance levels to personnel; access is granted only when the subject also has the need to know. Thus, not all users (subjects) with Top Secret clearances can gain access to all Top Secret information.

Information Owner

An information owner is one who maintains overall responsibility for the information within an information system. In the corporate world, it might be a department head or a division executive. In the academic world, it might be a dean of records or a university president. Information owners can delegate the day-to-day work to a subordinate or to an information technology department, but they cannot delegate the overall responsibility for the information and the system that maintains it. The information owner must be the one to make the decisions about who uses the system and how to recover the system in case a disaster (see Chapter 6, "Business Continuity Planning and Disaster Recovery Planning").

Discretionary Access Control

The principle of discretionary access control (DAC) dictates that the information owner is the one who decides who gets to access the system(s). This is how most corporate systems operate. DAC authority can be delegated to others who then are responsible for user setup, revocation, and changes (department moves, promotions, and so forth). Most of the common operating systems on the market today (Windows, Mac OS X, UNIX, Novell's NetWare, and so forth) rely on DAC principles for access and operation.

Access Control Lists

An access control list (ACL) is simply a list or a file of users who are given the privilege of access to a system or a resource (such as a database). Within the file is a user ID and an associated privilege or set of privileges for that user and that resource. The privileges are typically Read, Write, Update, Execute, Delete, and Rename. A system using ACLs to protect data files might encode the permissions as in Table 10.1.

TABLE 10.1   Example Users and Permissions

Filename	User ID	Permissions
ABC.dat	User01	RW
ABC.dat	User02	R
ABC.dat	Admin1	RWD

User Provisioning

The activity of bringing new employees into an organization includes granting them access to the systems that they need to perform their duties. User provisioning activities include checking management approvals for granting access. Identity management seeks to reduce the number of different IDs a person requires for accessing various systems, including email IDs, mainframe access IDs (if present), application IDs, and network IDs. User provisioning tools help managers determine what rights their employees possess and to recertify their need for ongoing access periodically (such as semiannually or annually.)

Mandatory Access Control

In a system that uses mandatory access control (MAC; also called nondiscretionary access control), the system decides who gains access to information based on the concepts of subjects, objects, and labels, as defined here. MAC is most often used in military and governmental systems and is rarely seen in the commercial world. In a MAC environment, objects (including data) are labeled with a classification (Secret, Top Secret, and so forth), and subjects, or users, are cleared to that class of access.

- **Subjects:** The people or other systems that are granted a clearance to access an object within the information system.

- **Objects:** The elements within the information system that are being protected from use or access.

- **Labels:** The mechanism that binds objects to subjects. A subject's clearance permits access to an object based on the labeled security protection assigned to that object. For example, only subjects who are cleared to access Secret objects may access objects labeled Secret or less than Secret, provided that they also possess the need to know. Subjects who are cleared for Top Secret access may access objects labeled Top Secret and objects with a lower classification label.

Role-Based Access Control

Role-based access control (RBAC) groups users with a common access need. You can assign a role for a group of users who perform the same job functions and require similar access to resources. Role-based controls simplify the job of granting and revoking access by simply assigning users to a group and then assigning rights to the group for access control purposes. This is especially helpful in companies that experience a high rate of employee turnover or frequent changes in employee roles.

The business benefits of RBAC are potentially tremendous. The most obvious is the significant time savings when combined with automated user provisioning. System and application accounts for new hires are created immediately with the correct set of access privileges needed for their job, based on predefined roles for the user's title or responsibilities. Furthermore, compliance and security controls are significantly enhanced by using role-based access control. The roles themselves are already predefined. When managers and business owners perform periodic certifications of access rights, they simply need to review a handful of roles to ensure that the user is in the correct role, instead of reviewing tens or hundreds of individual access rights. Moreover, automated tools can easily detect user privileges (excessive permissions) that are beyond the approved role and provide a mechanism for handling exceptions (see www.securitycompliancecorp.com/RBAC-SCC-InsecureMag.pdf).

Classification and Clearances in Military Security

A security clearance investigation is an inquiry into an individual's loyalty, character, trustworthiness, and reliability to ensure eligibility for access to national security secrets. All investigations consist of a national records and credit check; some investigations also include interviews with the candidate and individuals who know him or her.

In a military security model, information is ranked in a hierarchy: Unclassified, Confidential, Secret, and Top Secret. The principle of least privilege also applies; a subject has access to the fewest objects needed to successfully perform job duties. The government compartmentalizes information to enforce the need-to-know principle and might spread it over several compartments. An indication of a certain level of trust is established by a security clearance classification. A subject can access an object only if he or she holds a clearance level that is at least as high as that of the information.

Following is a definition of the U.S. government classification labels (for more, see www.dm.usda.gov/ocpm/Security%20Guide/S1class/Classif.htm):

- **Confidential:** Unauthorized disclosure of information may damage national security.
- **Secret:** Unauthorized disclosure of information may seriously damage national security.
- **Top Secret:** Unauthorized disclosure of information may cause exceptionally grave damage to national security.

Some classified information is so sensitive that even the extra protection measures applied to Top Secret information are not sufficient. This information is known as sensitive compartmented information (SCI) or special access programs (SAP). You need special SCI access or SAP approval to gain access to this information.

"For Official Use Only" is not a security classification. It is used to protect information covered under the Privacy Act and other sensitive data.

Principles of Authentication

The idea of authentication is that only the legitimate user possesses the secret information needed to prove to a system that he or she has the right to use a specific user ID. These secrets are commonly passwords, but history shows that passwords are problematic.

The Problems with Passwords

Sometimes passwords cause more problems than they solve. It is often said in the security field that people are the weakest link in the security chain. Because people are responsible for managing their passwords, problems are inherent.

- **Passwords can be insecure.** Given the choice, people will choose easily remembered and easily guessed passwords, such as names of relatives, pets, phone numbers, birthdays, hobbies, and other similar items.

- **Passwords are easily broken.** Common words in an ordinary dictionary make for poor choices of passwords. Free and widely available programs are available on the Internet to crack passwords through a dictionary attack. A dictionary attack involves rapidly cycling through words, phrases, and common permutations of words and phrases to match a password and record it for someone to exploit at some future point.

In Practice

Password Cracking

Password cracking is typically a process of recovering passwords from stored data in a computer device. The purpose of password cracking is to recover the forgotten passwords, but it also is used maliciously to gain unauthorized access to a computer system. Password cracking involves two distinct phases. In the first phase, the attacker's intention is to dump the hashes of the passwords. In the second phase, the attacker tries to crack those acquired hashes. Besides this method, attackers can use other ways to crack passwords, such as by guessing the password, using malicious tools such as keyloggers, launching phishing attacks, making use of social engineering, going dumpster diving, and staging shoulder surfing attacks, among others.

Over the last several years, attackers have used password-cracking tools such as Cain and Abel and John the Ripper to crack the password hashes. These kinds of tools use CPU core power to crack the hashes into a readable form (see http://resources.infosecinstitute.com/password-cracking-evolution/).

- **Passwords are inconvenient.** In an attempt to improve security, organizations often issue users computer-generated passwords that are difficult, if not impossible, to remember. Instead of trying to remember them, users often write them down and put them where they can see them, such as on a sticky note attached to a monitor or an index card taped to the bottom of a keyboard. Clearly, this compromises the security of the system.

- **Passwords are repudiable.** Unlike a written signature, when a transaction involves only a password, no real proof can confirm the identity of the individual who made the transaction. Repudiation is the act of denying participation in a transaction or system access. There's no way to prove whether the user shared his or her ID and password with someone else, or whether someone other than the user stumbled upon or cracked the user's password and logged on pretending to be the authorized user. Later in the chapter, you'll see a few alternatives to passwords alone that help information owners gain confidence that users are legitimate.

FYI: Creating Better Passwords

Good passwords are easy to remember and hard to crack using computerized password-cracking tools. The best way to create passwords that fulfill both criteria is to use two or more small and unrelated words or phonemes, ideally with a special character or number. Good examples include `pa55w0rd` and `!10g*me*1n`.

Don't use these elements as passwords:

- Common names, date of birth, spouse's name, phone number, pet name, and so forth
- Words found in dictionaries
- `Password` as a password
- System default passwords (`administrator`, `field-support`, and so forth).

Passwords are an example of single-factor authentication, which is simply something someone knows that is used to gain access to a system with no further requirements for proving identity.

Multifactor Authentication

It's possible to add more sophistication to authenticating users than using passwords alone. With two or three factors (multifactor authentication) to authenticate, an information owner can gain confidence that users who access their systems are indeed authorized to access those systems. This is accomplished by adding more controls or devices to the password authentication process.

Two-Factor Authentication

With a two-factor authentication system, a user has a physical device (a card, token, smart card, USB flash drive, and so forth) that contains his or her credentials, protected by a personal identification number (PIN) or a password that the user keeps secret. This condition is described as something you have plus something you know (SYH/SYK). An example is your debit card and PIN used to access an automated teller machine (ATM) at your bank. The card identifies you as the account holder, and the PIN authenticates you to the device. Because these PINs are usually only four characters long and usually consist of only numbers, the number of possibilities (entropy) of the system is 10,000 (0000 to 9999). Because a brute-force attack will eventually hit the right PIN, the ATM permits only three tries before it retains the card and notes the attempted breach of your account, forcing the user to contact the bank to restore the ATM privilege.

> ## FYI: What's a Password Token?
>
> An example of two-factor authentication is a password token, a mechanism that generates changing passwords every minute or so. These devices are protected by a password so that when they're in use, a user is challenged to provide the one-time-password (OTP) displayed on the device at that moment in time as the "dynamic" password plus the password only the user knows (a static password to prove that the device holder is the authorized user of the device). The mechanism behind these devices employs secret key cryptography (discussed in Chapter 11, "Cryptography") that encrypts and decrypts a unique time stamp each time the device is used. You learn more about these devices in the section "Remote User Access and Authentication."

Three-Factor Authentication

In a three-factor system, unique information related to the user is added to the two-factor authentication process. This unique information might be a biometric (fingerprint, retinal scan, and so forth) needed for authentication. These systems are common for physical access to secured areas and can be replicated for computer or logical access. The three-factor mechanism is described as something you have plus something you know plus something you are (SYH/SYK/SYA). For example, a person trying to access a data center door might be required to swipe a card (a badge), enter a PIN on a keypad to prove that she's the owner of the badge, and offer a fingerprint or iris or retinal scan to prove that she is the person assigned the badge and PIN.

Biometrics

Biometric methods of identification work by measuring unique human characteristics as a way to confirm identity. The following are common biometric techniques in use today:

- Fingerprint recognition
- Signature dynamics
- Iris scanning
- Retina scanning
- Voice prints
- Face recognition

The most common biometric in use is fingerprint recognition. Consider some advantages of fingerprints:

- Fingerprints can't be lent out like a physical key or token and can't be forgotten like a password.
- Fingerprints are a good compromise in ease of use, cost, and accuracy.

■ Fingerprints contain enough inherent variability to enable unique identification even in very large databases (think millions of records).

■ Fingerprints last virtually forever—or at least until some extraordinary circumstance prevents their use (amputation, dismemberment, and so forth).

■ Fingerprints make network login and authentication effortless.

The following are practical applications for biometric identification/authentication:

■ Handling network access control

■ Tracking staff time and attendance

■ Authorizing financial transactions

■ Distributing government benefits (Social Security, public assistance, and so forth)

■ Verifying identities at point of sale

■ Working in conjunction with ATM cards, credit cards, or smart cards

■ Controlling physical access to office buildings or homes

■ Protecting personal property

■ Preventing kidnapping in schools, play areas, and other locations

■ Protecting children from fatal gun accidents

■ Controlling voting, passports, visas, and immigration

Single Sign-On

All the methods to authenticate described in this chapter assume that every system a user needs access to requires a unique ID and password, thus requiring the user to maintain a number of ID/password pairs. Internet sites exacerbate this problem by requiring users to register and create a user ID and password. A single sign-on (SSO) system can simplify this. In an SSO system, users have one password for all corporate and back-office systems and applications that they need to perform their jobs. That way, they can remember and use one consistent password, thus increasing the security of the overall system of access controls. Although this goal sounds reasonable, it's actually quite difficult to implement.

One common approach to managing IDs and passwords is to create a password or PIN vault. These programs use secure methods to locally store IDs and passwords that are protected by a master password that unlocks the vault when it's needed. A free, open-source version of this concept, developed by Bruce Schneier, a well-known industry expert on cryptography, is available from Sourceforge.com. You can download a copy of it, called Password Safe, from http://sourceforge.net/projects/passwordsafe/.

Some mechanisms used to implement single sign-on include Kerberos (developed at MIT and described next), proprietary mechanisms that mimic Kerberos, and custom-developed solutions that actually maintain the discrete IDs and passwords. These types of programs make it transparent to users that different IDs and passwords are being used for access to different systems.

Kerberos

Kerberos is a network authentication protocol named for the three-headed dog that guarded the entrance to Hades in Greek mythology.

Kerberos is designed to provide authentication for client/server applications by using symmetric key cryptography (described in Chapter 11). A free implementation of Kerberos is available from the Massachusetts Institute of Technology (MIT). Kerberos is available in many commercial products as well. The Kerberos protocol uses robust cryptography so that a client can prove his or her identity to a server (and vice versa) across an insecure network connection, such as the Internet. After a client and server have used Kerberos to prove their identities, they can also encrypt all their communications to ensure privacy and data integrity as they go about their business. Kerberos works by assigning a unique key, called a ticket, to each user who logs on to the network. The ticket is then embedded in messages that permit the receiver of the message (programs or other users) to positively identify the sender of the message.

When using Kerberos, users need to log in only once, and each resource they want to access checks their tickets for currency and validity when a request for access is made.

For a view of the Kerberos Ticket Exchange Process, see Figure 10.1.

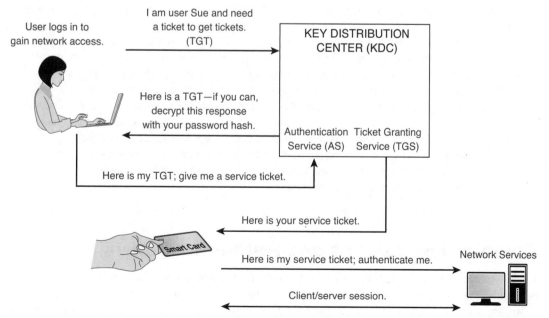

FIGURE 10.1   The Kerberos ticket exchange process.

Federated Identities

So far, you have learned about mechanisms to implement single sign-on to manage the multiple corporate IDs and passwords needed to perform a job. But what about users who require multiple identities and passwords to access e-commerce and websites for conducting personal business?

Today's common Internet user likely maintains a slew of IDs and passwords to access travel sites, online banking sites, credit card management sites, online brokerage sites, and so forth. All too often, users tire of trying to remember all these IDs and passwords and use the same IDs and passwords on each site, increasing their risk if a theft or compromise of their credentials occurs. With modern problems such as identity theft, e-scams, phishing, and offline social engineering attacks on consumers, users need to take extra precautions with their credentials to limit their risks. Some examples of federated identity include Facebook, where sites that have an arrangement with Facebook can log in users to their site without requiring them to create a unique ID and password. Other examples of federated identity providers include Google and LinkedIn.

FYI: What Is Phishing?

Internet scammers casting about for people's financial information have a way to lure unsuspecting victims: They go phishing.

Phishing is a high-tech scam that uses spam or pop-up messages to deceive you into disclosing your credit card numbers, bank account information, debit card PINs, social security number, passwords, or other sensitive information.

According to the Federal Trade Commission (FTC), phishers send an email or pop-up message that claims to be from a business or organization that you deal with—for example, your Internet service provider (ISP), your bank, an online payment service, or even a government agency. The message usually says that you need to "update" or "validate" your account information. It might threaten some dire consequence if you don't respond. The message directs you to a website that looks just like a legitimate organization's site, but it isn't. The purpose of the bogus site is to trick you into divulging your personal information so the operators can steal your identity and run up bills or commit crimes in your name. A newer class of crimes, called spear phishing, entails building a profile of the intended target to customize a message increases the likelihood that the user will open and act upon it. This insidious effort to subvert human trust has caused a number of costly security incidents and breaches, including a large-scale breach of RSA Security in 2011 (see https://blogs.rsa.com/anatomy-of-an-attack/).

Remote User Access and Authentication

When working at remote locations or telecommuting from home, additional security problems arise because of the use of insecure networks (such as the Internet) to create a connection to the corporate local area network (LAN). Addressing these problems requires additional access control mechanisms to protect both the LAN and the users.

Remote Access Dial-In User Service

Remote Access Dial-In User Service (RADIUS) is a client/server protocol and software that enables remote access users to communicate with a central server to authenticate dial-in users and authorize their access to the requested system or service. For example, you might need to dial up an external network to gain access so that you can perform work, deposit a file, or pick up a file. The earliest versions of America Online (AOL) used RADIUS, or RADIUS-like technology, to authenticate legitimate AOL users. RADIUS allows a company to maintain user profiles in a central database that all remote servers can share. RADIUS allows a company to set up a policy that can be applied at a single administered network point. Having a central service also means it's easier to track usage for billing and network statistics. RADIUS is the de facto industry standard for many network product companies and is in wide use throughout corporate networks primarily for system and network administrators to log in and manage remote devices (routers, servers, and so on).

Authenticating to a RADIUS server might require using an ID/password combination or, more often, a token or smart card for multifactor authentication.

Virtual Private Networks

A virtual private network (VPN) is the more common means for remote users to access corporate networks. With a VPN, a user connects to the Internet via his or her ISP and initiates a connection to the protected network, creating a private tunnel between the endpoints that prevents eavesdropping or data modification. VPNs often use strong cryptography to both authenticate senders and receivers of messages and to encrypt traffic so that it's invulnerable to a man-in-the-middle (MitM) attack.

You'll find more details about VPNs in Chapter 12.

Summary

Access control is a central theme of information security. It is needed to meet the goals of confidentiality, integrity, and user accountability, all essential for trust in an information system.

Access controls differentiate between identifying users of a system and authenticating them. This is done using discretionary means: An information owner decides who obtains access rights to the assets they control. Mandatory access control means the computer system itself decides access rights based on classifications and clearance. Role-based means that groups of people with a similar need for access are placed in a group, and the group itself is provided the access rights. If a person is in the group, they are given access to the resource or asset.

Passwords are the most common method people use to authenticate their identities, but problems with passwords have led to the development of alternatives, such as tokens that use one-time passwords and smart cards that use cryptography to prove a person's identity. Identification and authentication techniques sometimes use biometric information to add further confidence that users are legitimate when attempting physical or logical access to system resources.

Single sign-on and associated technologies and protocols aim to reduce the proliferation of IDs and passwords, to better control the security of access control mechanisms both within and outside the organization.

Finally, remote access control technology, such as RADIUS and virtual private networks, permits travelers and work-at-home employees to access corporate networks without the need for expensive dial-up connections or additional hardware.

Test Your Skills

MULTIPLE-CHOICE QUESTIONS

1. Which of the following terms best describes the verification that the user's claimed identity is valid?

    A. Authentication

    B. Identification

    C. Integrity

    D. Confidentiality

2. Which access model is most appropriate for companies with high employee turnover?

    A. Role-based access control

    B. Mandatory access control

    C. Lattice-based access control

    D. Discretionary access control

3. Which of the following statements is true?

   A. Identification establishes user accountability for the actions on the system.

   B. Identification establishes top management accountability for the actions on the system.

   C. Identification establishes IT department accountability for the actions of users on the system.

   D. Identification establishes authentication for actions on the system.

4. Which of the following statements is true?

   A. Controlling access to information systems and associated networks is necessary for the preservation of their authenticity, confidentiality, and availability.

   B. Controlling access to information systems and associated networks is necessary for the preservation of their confidentiality, integrity, and accountability.

   C. Controlling access to information systems and associated networks is necessary for the preservation of their integrity and availability.

   D. Controlling access to information systems and associated networks is necessary for the preservation of their authenticity, confidentiality, integrity, and availability.

5. Which access control model is also called nondiscretionary access control?

   A. Rule-based access control

   B. Mandatory access control

   C. Role-based access control

   D. Label-based access control

6. An access control policy for a bank teller is an example of the implementation of which of the following?

   A. Rule-based policy

   B. Identity-based policy

   C. User-based policy

   D. Role-based policy

7. Which of the following security models is dependent on security labels?

   A. Discretionary access control

   B. Label-based access control

   C. Mandatory access control

   D. Role-based access control

8. What can be defined as a table of subjects and objects indicating what actions individual subjects can take upon individual objects?

    A. A capacity table

    B. An access control list

    C. An access control matrix

    D. A capability table

9. Which of the following is the weakest authentication mechanism?

    A. Passphrases

    B. Passwords

    C. One-time passwords

    D. Token devices

10. Which type of password provides maximum security because a new password is required for each new logon?

    A. One-time or dynamic password

    B. Cognitive password

    C. Static password

    D. Passphrase

11. Which of the following passwords is considered the strongest?

    A. golf001

    B. Elizabeth

    C. t1me4g0lf

    D. password

12. Tokens, smart cards, and biometric devices used for identification and authentication provide robust authentication of the individual by practicing which of the following principles?

    A. Multiparty authentication

    B. Multifactor authentication

    C. Mandatory authentication

    D. Discretionary authentication

13. Access control is the collection of mechanisms that permits managers of a system to exercise a directing or restraining influence over the behavior, use, and content of a system. It does not permit management to do which of the following?

    A. Specify what users can do

    B. Specify which resources users can access

C. Specify how to restrain hackers

D. Specify what operations users can perform on a system

14. Which of the following statements is true?

  A. The three classic ways of authenticating yourself to the computer security software use something you know, something you have, and something you need.

  B. The three classic ways of authenticating yourself to the computer security software use something you know, something you have, and something you read.

  C. The three classic ways of authenticating yourself to the computer security software use something you know, something you have, and something you are.

  D. The three classic ways of authenticating yourself to the computer security software use something you know, something you have, and something you do.

15. Which of the following terms best describes the use of technologies such as fingerprint, retina, and iris scans to authenticate the individuals requesting access to resources?

  A. Micrometrics

  B. Macrometrics

  C. Biometrics

  D. Microbiometrics

16. Which of the following addresses cumbersome situations in which users need to log on multiple times to access different resources?

  A. Single sign-on (SSO) systems

  B. Dual sign-on (DSO) systems

  C. Double sign-on (DSO) systems

  D. Triple sign-on (TSO) systems

EXERCISES

EXERCISE 10.1: Understanding Access Controls and Confidentiality

1. How are access controls used to implement the security objective of confidentiality?

2. What features should a good access control system include?

3. Determine the access control model in Microsoft's Active Directory (see technet.microsoft.com/en-us/library/bb742424.aspx).

EXERCISE 10.2: Analyzing Attacks on Passwords

1. Visit the Symantec website to read the article "Password Crackers—Ensuring the Security of Your Password," at www.securityfocus.com/infocus/1192.

2. Will reading this article change the way you establish and maintain passwords? Why or why not? What might you do differently?

EXERCISE 10.3: Researching Biometrics and Privacy

People tend to resist biometrics as a method of identification because of their concerns that their privacy will be invaded or belief that the technology is too intrusive in their personal lives.

1. Research the Internet to determine some privacy problems related to biometrics.

2. Consider some mechanisms that could mitigate these problems and concerns.

3. Which method(s) of biometrics that would not meet with undue resistance from potential users would you recommend to a manager to replace password-based access controls?

EXERCISE 10.4: Evaluating Single Sign-On Technologies in the Market

1. Visit one or more of the following single-sign-on product web pages:

   Gemalto Protiva (www.gemalto.com/identity/index.html#entrance2)

   Remedy Identity Management (www.bmc.com/products/product-listing/BMC-Identity-Management-Platform.html)

   Computer Associates SiteMinder (www.ca.com/us/secure-sso.aspx)

2. Compare and contrast these single sign-on mechanisms. Which characteristics are similar among each mechanism? Which characteristics are different?

3. Which product is most appealing to manage internal users throughout an enterprise? Why? Which product would be most beneficial for Internet users? Why?

EXERCISE 10.5: Understanding Phishing

1. Search the Internet for recent reported incidents on phishing and spear phishing.

2. Which industry has companies that are the most frequent targets of phishers?

3. What measures can you find that these companies are taking to protect their customers from phishing attacks?

PROJECTS

PROJECT 10.1: **Using Password Safe**

1. On your home PC, download and install a copy of Password Safe from http://sourceforge.net/projects/passwordsafe/.

2. Input your personal information for one or two of the sites you regularly visit while surfing the Internet.

3. Visit those sites and use Password Safe to supply your credentials to log in and fill out some of the information on forms.

4. What do you think of the experience using this software? Is it easy to install and use? Is it easy to configure with your own IDs and passwords? Why or why not?

5. Would you consider using Password Safe for all your personal information management and security? Why or why not?

PROJECT 10.2: **Evaluating Kantara**

1. Visit the Kantara Initiative site, at http://kantarainitiative.org/.

2. Describe the pillars of identity relationship management.

3. List some disadvantages of trust frameworks.

4. Locate some sites that have signed on to use Identity Assurance Services for access control by their customers or users.

PROJECT 10.3: **Assessing Smart Card Access Controls**

1. Research the Internet for information about using smart cards for access controls and the Common Access Card (CAC) that the U.S. Department of Defense uses.

2. Where are they being used most frequently?

3. What are some complications in implementing smart cards for network access?

4. Which access control model seems most appropriate for smart cards?

5. What changes to infrastructure would be necessary for an enterprise-wide implementation of smart cards for PCs, mobile devices, and tablet computer access controls?

Chapter 11

Cryptography

Chapter Objectives

After reading this chapter and completing the exercises, you will be able to do the following:

- Explain common terms used in the field of cryptography
- Outline what mechanisms constitute a strong cryptosystem
- Demonstrate how to encrypt and decrypt messages using the transposition method
- Demonstrate how to encrypt messages using the substitution method
- Support the role of cryptography in e-commerce systems
- Explain the differences between symmetric and asymmetric cryptography
- Outline the mechanisms used for digital signatures
- Explain the purpose and uses of digital certificates
- Evaluate commercial implementations of public key infrastructure (PKI) products

Introduction

In the offline world, it's easy to ask someone for an ID to prove that people are who they claim to be. As a society, we've generally grown to trust photo IDs and written signatures as a way of verifying the legitimacy of certain rights, such as the right to use a credit card or drive a car.

In the online world, checking the same claims to access rights can be performed only through technology, primarily cryptography. Generally, this is accomplished by binding a person to a pair of cryptographic keys using tightly controlled and secure conditions. When the trusted key issuance process is complete, these keys are used to keep messages private, authenticate the sender, and test the integrity of messages. This achieves two objectives of security: confidentiality and integrity. Because most computer application-level security relies on cryptography, having a strong foundational understanding of this topic is essential.

Applying Cryptography to Information Systems

Applied cryptography, the science of secret writing, enables the storage and transfer of information in forms that reveal it only to those permitted to see it, while hiding that information from everyone else.

In the 20th century, international governments began to adopt the use of cryptography to protect their private and sensitive information and for communication purposes. Until the past 25 years or so, governments and military organizations were the exclusive users of cryptography: They secured their own private data and tried to crack everyone else's. The United States National Security Agency (NSA) is a large government agency devoted to developing and protecting robust cryptography to protect secrets. The NSA also uses its specialized skills in breaking cryptosystems to eavesdrop on encrypted foreign communications. Today, certain elements of cryptography are treated as munitions, so various government agencies (including the NSA) tightly control cryptography's uses and export. U.S. encryption export policy rests on three principles: review of encryption products before sale, streamlined post-export reporting, and license review of certain exports and re-exports of strong encryption to foreign governments. As of December 2004, some controls were relaxed and others were clarified in a "Commercial Encryption Export Controls" fact sheet available at www.steptoe.com/assets/attachments/1333.pdf.

Since the 1970s, academic interest in cryptography has grown at a tremendous rate. With this proliferation of research, private citizens have gained access to various cryptography techniques to protect personal information and conduct secure electronic transactions.

Although the U.S. government is not keen on carte blanche permission to export software or devices that use strong cryptography, advancements in the field continue, primarily within academia. If the government continued to have its way, the NSA would be the only user of strong cryptography, but the Clinton administration changed in the 1990s.

With the aid of supercomputers (massively parallel processors), communities of hackers who work together to crack the strongest cryptosystems, and the increasing sophistication of modern computer technology, cryptography is becoming more tried and true. It is evolving into a highly reliable process with well-established practices.

Basic Terms and Concepts

Cryptography is a domain loaded with new terms and concepts. Following are some of the more common terms and concepts you're likely to encounter when studying the field of cryptology:

- A cryptosystem disguises messages, allowing only selected people to see through the disguise.
- Cryptography is the science (or art) of designing, building, and using cryptosystems.
- Cryptanalysis is the science (or art) of breaking a cryptosystem.
- Cryptology is the umbrella study of cryptography and cryptanalysis.

■ Cryptographers rely on two basic methods of disguising messages: transposition, in which letters are rearranged into a different order, and substitution, in which letters are replaced by other letters and/or symbols.

Plain text is the message that is passed through an encryption algorithm, or cipher—it becomes ciphertext. When ciphertext is passed through a decryption algorithm, it becomes plain text again.

An understanding of these basic terms will help you as you move forward in this chapter.

FYI: Codebooks

Cryptography, the art and science of secret codes, has evolved dramatically over the centuries, especially since World War II. For most of their history, codes have relied on sharing secrets between small groups of people who needed to communicate safely and privately. For example, the shared secret might have been a codebook that translated important words and phrases into short, nonsense words. This not only concealed a message's meaning, but also shortened the message. Codebooks were popular among wealthy individuals and large companies during the days of the telegraph. Because the sender had to pay for each word in a telegram, a well-designed code could reduce telegraph costs. Private companies produced codebooks that they sold to anyone who asked for them. The most effective codebooks were custom made to be shared among a restricted group of business associates who maintained their privacy by keeping their codes secret.

In the days of the telegraph, business executives often had real worries about the secrecy of their telegrams. Unlike a telephone call, which travels automatically without human intervention, each telegram had to be keyed in by a telegraph operator at the sending office, transcribed by an operator at the receiving office, and occasionally transcribed by other operators along its route. Telegraph operators were not always paid well enough to resist bribery, so sensitive business information occasionally found its way into competitors' hands. Secret telegraph codes gave businessmen confidence that their private traffic remained private.

Secrecy doesn't always guarantee safety, however. Mary, Queen of Scots, learned this lesson more than 400 years ago when agents of Queen Elizabeth I unmasked a plot against her by Mary's supporters. Mary used a codebook to communicate with her associates, but Elizabeth's spies succeeded in deducing the codebook's contents. They read numerous coded messages, guessed their contents, and systematically tested the guesses by trying to decode other messages. Although Elizabeth's agents didn't break Mary's entire code, they figured out enough of it to identify and arrest the plotters. While in prison, the plotters revealed the rest of the code, and Mary's decoded letters helped convict her of high treason.

Mary's code was not sophisticated enough to resist a systematic attack, but its present-day analogues generally are. Modern codes, particularly those used in computers, generally consist of two separate parts: the coding procedure, called the algorithm, and the key, which tells the algorithm how to scramble a message. The algorithm might be public knowledge, but the key is always kept secret. In essence, the secrecy of encrypted data relies entirely on the secrecy of the key. Instead of worrying about how to keep the data confidential, you need only concern yourself with keeping the key itself secret.

Strength of Cryptosystems

A strong cryptosystem is considered strong only until it's been cracked. That might sound like common sense, but you can never *prove* that a cryptosystem is strong or unbreakable—you can simply ensure that certain properties are present within it. Each defeat of an attempt to crack a cryptosystem strengthens the belief in its ability to secure. Similar to monetary currency, a cryptosystem has value because its users believe in its worth. If that worth is proven to be unfounded, the cryptosystem collapses and no one relies on it anymore.

The most popular commercial cryptosystems found in software products have similar characteristics. Their algorithms are made readily available to the public (through published standards and public posting), and the strength of the algorithm rests in the keys used to encrypt and decrypt (in general, the longer the key, the better). The basic idea is to keep the keys, not the algorithm, secret. Many government cryptosystems are kept secret and are not intended for public or commercial use.

FYI: Random Number Requirements

Perfectly random numbers, thought to exist in nature, are impossible to achieve using deterministic devices such as computers. The best a computer can do is generate pseudo-random numbers. Cryptography demands far more pseudo-randomness than most other applications, such as computer games. For a string of bits to be considered cryptographically random, it must be computationally infeasible to predict what the nth random bit will be when given full knowledge of the algorithm and the values of the bits already generated. Because computers are deterministic, at some point, a random number generator becomes periodic (it begins to repeat). The challenge, then, is to build random number generators that won't predictably repeat values generated. Some of the pseudo-random number generators available today show randomness through 2^{256}, making them more suitable for use in cryptography than the kinds of random number generators built into programming languages, such as the random number generation function in C or C++ rnd().

Strong cryptosystems produce ciphertext that always appears random to standard statistical tests. They also resist all known attacks on cryptosystems and have been brutally tested to ensure their integrity. Cryptosystems that have not been subjected to brutal testing are considered suspect.

In Practice

A Simple Transposition Encryption Example

Although a firm grasp of the actual mechanics of cryptosystems is not directly required to understand how they are used in securing systems, some understanding of the complexities involved helps you appreciate what is going on behind the curtain.

Using the transposition technique with a symmetric key (shared secret), we can take a look at how encryption and decryption might operate manually.

Assume that this is the plain text message you want to encrypt:

`SECURITY BEGINS WITH YOU`

You choose the word `TEACUPS` as your keyword (secret key) and send it to your intended recipient using a secure channel other than the one you will use to send the message. This is for added security and to ensure that the recipient has the key when the ciphertext arrives.

Encrypt the message through the following steps:

1. Write the key horizontally as the heading for columns:

   ```
   T   E   A   C   U   P   S
   ```

2. Assign numerical values to each letter, based on the letter's order of appearance in the alphabet: A=1, C=2, and so on.

   ```
   T   E   A   C   U   P   S

   6   3   1   2   7   4   5
   ```

3. Align the plain-text message across each key/value column heading, skipping to the next line when you reach the last column of the matrix.

   ```
   T   E   A   C   U   P   S

   6   3   1   2   7   4   5

   S   E   C   U   R   I   T

   Y   B   E   G   I   N   S

   W   I   T   H   Y   O   U
   ```

4. Read down along each column according to the ordinal value of the column to produce the ciphertext (A-1 is the first column, C-2 is the second, and so forth):

   ```
   CET   UGH   EBI   INO   TSU   SYW   RIY
   ```

5. Send the ciphertext to the recipient using any channel desired. Because they already possess the shared secret, you don't need to worry about it getting into the wrong hands.

Upon receipt of the ciphertext, the recipient decrypts it through the following steps:

1. Write the key horizontally as the heading for columns:

   ```
   T   E   A   C   U   P   S
   ```

2. Assign numerical values to each letter, based on the letter's order of appearance in the alphabet.

   ```
   T   E   A   C   U   P   S

   6   3   1   2   7   4   5
   ```

3. Transpose the ciphertext, three letters at a time, using the ordinal value of each column to determine its placement. Because A is column value 1, the first group of letters, CET, is written vertically under A-1. Group 2 belongs under C-2, and so forth:

```
T   E   A   C   U   P   S

6   3   1   2   7   4   5

S   E   C   U   R   I   T

Y   B   E   G   I   N   S

W   I   T   H   Y   O   U
```

4. Read the message horizontally to reveal the plain-text message:

SECURITY BEGINS WITH YOU

If the message had been longer, such as

SECURITY BEGINS WITH EVERYONE AT HOME

the ciphertext groups would have consisted of four letters instead of three, growing with the length of the message. If this example had included the use of numbers or special characters, they would have been treated separately and would have agreed with their positional values in the alphabet; otherwise, the algorithm would not have worked.

Even with a simple example such as this, you can begin to see the protocol developed to make it work. Steps must be performed with some rules in mind:

- The steps must be performed in order.

- No steps can be skipped.

- Steps cannot be altered in any way.

Cryptosystems Answer the Needs of Today's E-Commerce

Before you move on to specific implementations of data encryption and secure networks, it's important to understand that different situations call for different levels of security.

A college student sending an email home to his parents for money is mainly concerned that the note reaches its intended destination and that no one tampers with the contents of the note. An internal corporate memo to all employees, on the other hand, might contain sensitive information that should not go beyond the company's intranet. The CEO assumes that when she sends the note, only the intended audience will read the note. Likewise, the employees assume that the note did indeed come from the president and no one else. No real authentication is performed because the company's email system relies on the notion of trust. Each employee must have an ID and password to access the email system, but beyond that, any guarantees of authenticity require implicit trust in the users of the system.

To ensure that electronic commerce is secure requires an *implicit distrust* in users of the Internet and public networks. Most users are law-abiding citizens who use the network for legitimate purchases. They are who they say they are, and they enjoy the convenience that Internet shopping and banking affords. However, the decentralized design of the Internet enhances the potential for an unscrupulous few to wreak havoc on the many. Electronic commerce can never be made too secure. And the bad press resulting from a security failure could destroy a business.

The Role of Keys in Cryptosystems

Keys (secrets) used for encryption and decryption come in two basic forms, symmetric and asymmetric. This simply means that either the same key is used to both encrypt and decrypt, or a pair of keys is needed.

When the same key is used to both encrypt and decrypt messages, it's called symmetric key or shared secret cryptography. When different keys are used, it's called asymmetric key cryptography. The Data Encryption Standard (DES) uses the former technique; RSA (named after its inventors, Rivest, Shamir, and Adelman) uses the latter technique. Pretty Good Privacy (PGP), discussed later in this chapter, is a public-domain cryptosystem that also uses asymmetric key cryptography.

In Practice

A Simple Substitution Example

An even easier method of cryptography is the substitution cipher. The Caesar cipher uses simple letter substitution. It originated with the Greeks long before Caesar's time and first appeared in one of the earliest works on military science, *On the Defense of Fortified Places*, by Aeneas the Tactician. As Julius Caesar claimed in his book *The Gallic Wars*, this cipher was only subsequently applied to Roman military strategy.

According to history, Caesar wrote to Cicero and others in a cipher in which the plain-text letters were replaced by letters standing three places or rotated three places further down the alphabet.

On the Internet, the most popular example of a Caesar cipher is called ROT13, from "rotate alphabet 13 places." You can find it in most Internet network news or Usenet (NNTP) groups. This cipher encloses the text in a wrapper that the reader must choose to open (for instance, to post things that might offend some readers).

This simple Caesar cipher encryption replaces each English letter with the one 13 places forward or back along the alphabet. With this encryption scheme, "The butler did it!" becomes "Gur ohgyre qvq vg!"

The following is an example of how to convert plain text to ciphertext using ROT13.

1. Write down the alphabet, splitting it across two rows in the middle:

A	B	C	D	E	F	G	H	I	J	K	L	M
N	O	P	Q	R	S	T	U	V	W	X	Y	Z

> **2.** With the plain-text message THE BUTLER DID IT, substitute the letter above or below each letter in the sentence to come up with the ciphertext. T becomes G, U becomes H, and so forth.
>
> One major advantage of ROT13 over other Caesar rotation values is that it is self-inverse, so the table shown works for encoding and decoding.
>
> Computer-based cryptography, though far more robust than anything that could be accomplished by hand, uses the same approaches, if not the same algorithms, as the ones illustrated here, but with far more complexity and processing requirements.

Symmetric Keys

When you use the same key to both encrypt and decrypt a message, it's called symmetric key cryptography. This is the method used in the previous example. The most common form of symmetric key cryptography is the Data Encryption Standard. DES was developed by IBM at the request of the U.S. government. It was adopted as a Federal Information Processing Standard (FIPS) in 1976 for use with unclassified government communications between agencies. It uses 64 bits of data (8 bytes) with a 56-bit (7 byte) key within it. Triple DES (3DES) is identical but uses a double-length key (128 bits) that encrypts, then encrypts, and then encrypts again (called "folding" in crypto-speak). Banks commonly use 3DES to protect your PIN number when you enter it at an ATM or on a point-of-sale keypad (where you swipe your credit or debit card at the cash register). The bank never stores your PIN as you know it: It's always stored in encrypted forms, to prevent its use in the event of theft. If the ATM enciphers your PIN exactly as your bank stores it, access is granted.

In early October 2000, the National Institute of Standards and Technology (NIST) announced the end of a 4-year search for a successor to the aging DES, used to protect nonclassified government information and systems. The successor became the Advanced Encryption System (AES), based on the Rijndael algorithm, which takes its name from its Belgium co-creators, Vincent Rijmen and Joan Daemon. The U.S. Department of Commerce adopted AES as the Federal Information Processing Standard (FIPS) in 2001. AES also found its way into current tools and technologies for encrypting sensitive corporate, e-commerce, and banking data.

One of the most significant challenges of symmetric key cryptography lies in sharing keys before they're needed. Asymmetric key cryptography can help with this task.

FYI: Cryptography Protects the Skies

To answer the question, "Who goes there?", military organizations have come up with a novel use of applied cryptography. The Identification Friend or Foe (IFF) System uses advanced symmetric key cryptography to help pilots and ships at sea to determine whether another vessel or aircraft is a "friend." The highest security level for IFF is Mode 4, and this is the only true IFF system. Mode 4, used on war planes, utilizes sophisticated encryption that includes a long challenge word with a preamble to inform the transponder that it is about to receive a secure message. If the plane's transponder is incapable of deciphering the challenge, it effectively identifies the aircraft as something other than a friend. Keys are periodically changed and reentered into transponders and interrogators, to help ensure the continued security of the codes. (Source: www.encyclopedia. com/topic/IFF.aspx)

Asymmetric Keys

With asymmetric key cryptography, two keys are needed. A message encrypted using one key can be decrypted only using the other, and vice versa. One key is called a public key, and the other is called a private key. Fundamental to operating properly, the private key must always remain private and must never be shared or copied from where it was generated.

Using asymmetric key cryptography, you share your public key with everyone you want to communicate with privately, but you keep your private key secret. Your private key essentially is your identity—when someone can successfully decrypt a message that you sent encrypted with your private key, they know that the message could have come from only you if the decryption using the public key succeeds. That's the basis of asymmetric key or public key infrastructures (PKI).

The two keys that comprise a key pair are mathematically related, but neither can be derived from the other. Typically, the keys used with strong asymmetric key cryptography are 1024 bits long (128 bytes) and are meant to foil a brute-force attack on messages that are signed and encrypted using standard PPK applications.

PPK cryptography enables you to communicate over any open channel with high degrees of confidence and permits you to trust in these ways:

- **Authentication:** Messages you receive came from their advertised source.
- **Privacy:** Messages you send can be read only by their intended receiver(s).
- **Message integrity:** All messages sent and received arrived intact.

Putting the Pieces to Work

Now that you've begun to understand the principles of public and private key pairs, it's time to examine how PPK systems are used for authentication, privacy, and message integrity. To start, you need to be familiar with a computer programming technique called hashing. A hash is a transformation of data into distilled forms that are unique to the data. This is a one-way function—it's easy to do and nearly impossible to undo. Think of how hamburger is made: Whole chunks of meat are run through a grinder (easy to do), but after the meat is ground up, it can never be reassembled into chunks of meat (hard to undo). With a computer program, a document is run through a one-way hashing formula to produce a small numeric value that's unique but easily repeatable for that exact stream of data. This process is also called digesting data or creating a message digest. The UNIX and Linux operating systems, among others, employs this principle for storing passwords in the `/etc/passwd` file.

Digesting Data

Several well-known digest-creation techniques, including the Secure Hashing Algorithm (SHA) and the Message Digest 5 (MD5) algorithm, are common. Using one of the variations of SHA, unique message digests (fingerprints) can be computed so that the chances of two different messages computing to the same digest values are 1 in 10^{48}. After computing the message digest for your message, you encrypt it using your private key and append (attach) the encrypted message digest to your original message. This process is called creating a digital signature or digitally signing a message.

At this point, if you send your message to your recipient (who already holds a copy of your public key), that person can test your signature to see if the message really came from you and arrived unaltered.

Here's how digital signing works: Because the digital signature can be decrypted only using your public key, your recipient knows that you created the digest because you never shared your private key with anyone else. Your recipient's software also uses the same hashing algorithm that you used to compute message digests, so he runs the message he received through it. His software then compares the newly calculated message digest to the one he successfully decrypted from you. If they match, he's now also assured that the message he received is the same message that you sent, without any alteration.

Think of digital signatures in a similar vein as notary public services. If you receive a notarized document, you have a high degree of assurance that the person who signed it is the person he or she claims to be—because we, as a society, trust notaries. Digital signatures enhance the process and security of communications. If I sent you a nine-page document bearing a notary seal, you'd know it came from me, but you wouldn't know whether the document had been altered after the notary attested to my signature. With a digital signature, if even a single byte of data changes, the message digest computes to a completely different value. If your recipient's comparison of the two digests doesn't match, the software indicates that the message should not be trusted and recommends that it be discarded.

FYI: What Is the Secure Hashing Algorithm (SHA)?

Described in Federal Information Processing Standards (FIPS) Standard 180-1, the Secure Hash Algorithm (SHA-1) is specified for creating a digest of a message or a data file. Modern, collision-resistant hash functions were designed to create small, fixed-size message digests so that a digest could act as a proxy for a possibly large variable-length message in a digital signature algorithm, such as RSA or Digital Signature Algorithm. These hash functions have since been widely used for many other applications, including hash-based message authentication codes, pseudo-random number generators, and key derivation functions. A series of related hash functions has been developed, including MD4, MD5, SHA-0, SHA–1, and the SHA–2 family (which includes 224-, 256-, 384-, and 512-bit variants). NIST began the standardization of the SHA hash functions in 1993, with a specification of SHA-0 in the Federal Information Processing Standards Publication (FIPS PUBS) 180, the Secure Hash Standard. Subsequent revisions of the FIPS have replaced SHA-0 with SHA-1 and added the SHA-2 family in FIPS 180-1 and FIPS 180-2. (Source: http://csrc.nist.gov/groups/ST/hash/documents/FR_Notice_Nov07.pdf)

SHA-3 Competition (2007-2012)

In 2007, NIST announced a public competition to develop a new cryptographic hash algorithm, called SHA-3, for standardization. The competition was NIST's response to advances made in the cryptanalysis of hash algorithms. NIST received 64 entries from cryptographers around the world by October 31, 2008. NIST selected 51 first-round candidates in December 2008, 14 second-round candidates in July 2009, and 5 finalists (BLAKE, Grøstl, JH, Keccak, and Skein) in December 2010 to advance to the final round of the competition. Throughout the competition, the cryptographic community has provided an enormous amount of feedback. Based on the public comments and internal review of the candidates, NIST announced Keccak as the winner of the SHA-3 Cryptographic Hash Algorithm Competition on October 2, 2012, ending the five-year competition. (Source: http://csrc.nist.gov/groups/ST/hash/sha-3/index.html)

As an example of using SHA, when the message `This is a unique message` is run through a SHA-1 calculator, the output is `fcc6a03cb4dbb02fcdaf842d1084a0e6dd1ea1de`.

When the message `This is a unique message too` is run through the calculator, the result is `f687b5becf5e48d739ea62a2c3f9c1815be2044a`, which is nothing like the first value calculated. You can play with a hashing calculator yourself at www.fileformat.info/tool/hash.htm.

With a single process, you can add sender authentication and message integrity to the otherwise untrusted communication channel called the Internet. But privacy still needs to be addressed.

In practice, you would never send a digitally signed message without further encryption. Because the digest is appended to the plain-text message, anyone who intercepted it en route could still read the message. Instead, you need to put the message and its digest into a safe and secure envelope before you send it on its way. To accomplish this, you use your recipient's public key (you already have a copy of this or know where to find it) to encrypt both the message and the digest, creating what's called a digital envelope. Because no one else has the private key from your recipient's key pair, you're assured that no one else can "open" the envelope. Now you have all the elements you want: sender authentication, privacy, and message integrity.

Figure 11.1 takes a graphical look at the digital signing process. Figure 11.2 illustrates the process of creating digital envelopes.

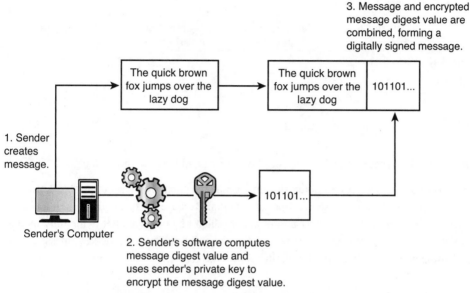

FIGURE 11.1   Using public-private key pairs to create a digital signature.

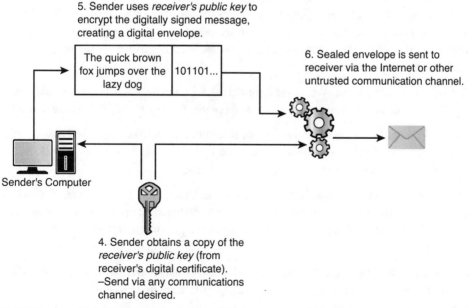

FIGURE 11.2   Using public-private key pairs to create a digital envelope.

In summary, Table 11.1 shows the purposes and uses of public and private keys to secure electronic communications.

TABLE 11.1   Public/Private Key Uses

	Create Digital Signature	Verify Digital Signature	Create Digital Envelope	Open Digital Envelope
Sender's private key	X			
Sender's public key		X		
Receiver's public key			X	
Receiver's private key				X

With all the keys needed for security, where do they come from and how are they managed?

You cannot rely on the users of a computer system to manage their own cryptographic keys and provide the amount of trust needed for secure implementation. Because of the need for high levels of trust, businesses require a predictable infrastructure under which key management is the only theme. Because e-commerce is an environment of trusted relationships, it requires a public key infrastructure (PKI) for establishing and maintaining trusted digital certificates.

Digital Certificates

Digital certificates behave in the online world the same way driver's licenses, passports, and other trusted documents behave beyond the online world. Digital certificates use the basic PPK cryptography principles discussed previously to offer the security people demand for private communications and electronic commerce. The digital certificate standard X.509 governs how certificates are constructed and used between communicating parties.

When used for signing electronic messages (creating digital signatures), the private key associated with the public key in the digital certificate creates the unforgeable fingerprint (digest) for the message.

For PPKs to operate successfully, the principles dictate that public-private key pairs be obtained in a manner that's impervious to attack. The primary assumption is that a person's private key will always remain private. Digital certificates help to implement this principle.

In 1988, X.509 became an International Telecommunications Union (ITU) recommended standard and has since become a de facto industry standard for user authentication on open systems, such as the Internet. X.509 certificates are similar to notary seals—they bind a person's identity to a pair (or pairs) of cryptographic keys.

Digital certificates are issued by a trusted party, called a certificate authority, or CA. These CAs operate on behalf of those who want to operate a public key infrastructure (PKI) using X.509 recommended standards.

Figure 11.3 illustrates the structure and contents of a typical X.509 public key certificate.

Certificate Format Version
Certificate Serial Number
CA Signature Algorithm Identifier
CA X.500 Name
Validity Period (Beginning/Ending Dates/Times)
Subject's X.500 Name (Distinguished Name)
Subject's Public Key Information (Algorithm Identifier and Public Key Value)
Issuer's Unique Certificate ID Number
Other Issuer's Unique Number(s)
Certificate Extension(s) Extension Type/Critical or Noncritical/Value
CA Digital Signature on Entire Certificate's Values

FIGURE 11.3   An X.509 public key certificate's structure.

Certificates often contain extensions (see the bottom of Figure 11.3) that describe how the certificate may be used and under which conditions. For example, a certificate that's used to access network resources cannot be used to access bank accounts. Each certificate is issued for specific uses and with guidelines described within the certificate's extensions. Extensions can be labeled as critical, mandatory, or optional, depending on the issuer's requirements.

CAs maintain a tree of trust that's checked each time a certificate is presented as proof of one's identity. When the tree of trust is successfully traversed, the recipient can ascertain proof of identity and proof of a person's right to use the key.

Many of the higher-order e-commerce protocols, such as Secure Sockets Layer (SSL), use a robust set of digital certificates to authenticate people and resources, to ensure that all parties possess the rights needed to transact. A corporation might issue digital certificates to its employees as an alternative to IDs and passwords for access to network services, mainframe applications, and other locations of secure data. These certificates normally are stored in software that resides on the user's PC within a web browser. Certificates also can be stored on smart cards (see Chapter 10, "Access Control Systems and Methodology") to permit access.

Using digital certificates offers system users high degrees of security along several dimensions of communications. Because of the cryptography used to process messages, anyone receiving a signed message, along with the public key in the sender's digital certificate, can be confident that the message came from the specific person (user authentication) and that the message itself arrived intact (integrity).

PKIs are often challenging to develop. Not only do they require extremely tight security measures to protect CA private keys, but they're also difficult to transition from electronic forms to the real world.

Now that you are armed with a basic understanding of the principles of modern cryptography, the next sections examine some common implementations that are mixed and matched to produce useful work in effectively securing digital resources and data.

Examining Digital Cryptography

Several types of cryptosystems have come into the mainstream over the years. The most significant categories follow:

- Hashing functions (SHA-1 and SHA-3)

- Block ciphers (DES, 3DES, and AES)

- Implementations of RSA Public-Private Key (PPK)

Each of these categories is discussed in greater detail in the following sections.

Hashing Functions

Thus far, you've seen some of the most common hashing functions to create the message digest for digitally signed messages. Hashing-type functions can also be used with symmetric key cryptography; the result of the operation is called a message authentication code, or MAC. When you hear the term *hash*, think of digital signatures, and when you hear the term *MAC*, think of shared secret cryptography operations.

Hashing is a powerful mechanism for protecting user passwords. If a system requires IDs and passwords for any reason, it is best to store the passwords people create in the form of a hash value. That way, even if hackers steal the security database records, they won't be able to use the data to impersonate customers directly. Instead, they'll need to use additional resources and time to attempt to find out what passwords are associated with which user IDs. UNIX and Linux operating systems implemented this technique right from the start. Many Microsoft Windows implementations are similar but are considered weaker because of backward-compatibility issues to older versions of Microsoft operating systems.

The Secure Hashing Algorithm (SHA) variants are the most common forms of hashing functions you'll encounter with most commercial software.

Block Ciphers

Earlier, you read about DES, Triple-DES, and AES as the most common forms of symmetric key block cipher cryptosystems. DES uses a 56-bit (7 bytes plus a checksum byte) key, which is considered weak today. Triple DES uses a 112-bit (14 bytes plus 2 checksum bytes) key, and AES uses a variable-length key (256 bits, 512 bits, and so on).

Block ciphers are important for encrypting/decrypting data in bulk, such as files or batches of data. They're also useful for encrypting data in storage systems to prevent unauthorized access. Block ciphers can be used to encrypt data fields (attributes) in records and tables, entire records of data, or entire files or database tables.

Besides DES, 3DES, and AES, plenty of other block cipher algorithms exist, and many of them have already been subjected to brutal cryptanalysis attacks.

Implementations of PPK Cryptography

Public-private key cryptography has found its way into numerous implementations intended to better secure Internet communications and prove identities, including these systems:

- Secure Sockets Layer (SSL)
- Transport Layer Security (TLS)
- Pretty Good Privacy (PGP)
- Secure Multipurpose Internet Mail Extensions (S/MIME)
- Secure Electronic Transactions (SET)

Each one is explained in greater detail in the following sections.

The Secure Sockets Layer Protocol

Secure Sockets Layer (SSL) is the most popular form of PPK and has become the de facto standard for transporting private information across the Internet. People have not only grown more comfortable with entering their payment card information into SSL-protected sessions, but they demand it and even expect it.

SSL addresses some of the concerns of transporting confidential data via the Internet. The goals of SSL are to ensure the privacy of the connection, to authenticate a peer's identity, and to establish a reliable transport mechanism for the message using integrity checks and hashing functions.

SSL was designed for client/server applications, to prevent the unwanted tampering of data transmission, whether eavesdropping, data alteration, or message forgery. It's intended to ensure the privacy and reliability of communications between two applications. When you shop online, you're already likely using SSL, whether you know it or not. Consider two signs that SSL is active during an Internet session:

- The URL begins with `https//` instead of `http://`.
- A little padlock appears on the status bar of the browser.

The Transport Layer Security Protocol

The Transport Layer Security (TLS) protocol is designed to provide communications privacy over the Internet. The protocol allows client/server applications to communicate in ways that are designed to prevent eavesdropping, tampering, or message forgery. The goals of TLS protocols are to provide the following:

- **Cryptographic security:** TLS should be used to establish a secure connection between two parties.

- **Interoperability:** Independent programmers should be able to develop applications using TLS that can then successfully exchange cryptographic parameters without knowing one another's code.

- **Extensibility:** TLS seeks to provide a framework into which new public key and bulk encryption methods can be incorporated as necessary. This also accomplishes two subgoals: It prevents the need to create a new protocol, which would risk the introduction of possible new weaknesses, and it avoids the need to implement an entire new security library.

- **Relative efficiency:** Cryptographic operations, particularly public key operations, tend to be highly CPU intensive. For this reason, the TLS protocol has incorporated an optional session caching scheme to reduce the number of connections that need to be established from scratch. Additionally, care has been taken to reduce network activity.

The Pretty Good Privacy Protocol

Pretty Good Privacy (PGP) is a distributed key-management approach that does not rely on certificate authorities. Users can sign one another's public keys, adding some degree of confidence to a key's validity. Someone who signs someone else's public key acts as an introducer for that person to someone else, with the idea that if someone trusts the introducer, that person should also trust the person who's being introduced.

PGP was written by Phil Zimmerman in the mid-1980s and remains popular because of its ability primarily to encrypt electronic mail. Zimmerman distributed his first version of PGP over the Internet as freeware and then ran into legal problems because he didn't realize he had given away the rights to public key cryptography patents (most notably, the patent that was issued to protect the RSA Cryptosystem). Legal matters were eventually straightened out in 1993 when ViaCrypt, a company with a valid license for the RSA patent, worked out a deal with Zimmerman to distribute a commercial version of PGP.

PGP is often used to encrypt documents that can be shared via email over the open Internet. Users of PGP password-protect the file, the password is used in the process of encryption, and, upon arrival, the password is requested. Only at the point the exact password is entered can the file be decrypted. Users share the password "out of band" by sending it in a separate message or leaving the recipient a voice message with the password to use.

The Secure/Multipurpose Internet Mail Extensions Protocol

Based on technology from RSA Data Security, Secure/Multipurpose Internet Mail Extensions (S/MIME) offers another standard for electronic mail encryption and digital signatures. S/MIME, along with a version of PGP called Open PGP, were implemented in the original Netscape Communications Corporation web browsers. Unfortunately, the dual electronic mail encryption standards created problems with users.

S/MIME and Open PGP use proprietary encryption techniques and handle digital signatures differently. Simply put, if Person A uses a web browser that supports S/MIME and tries to communicate with Person B, who uses a different browser supported by PGP, the two individuals most likely will not be able to communicate successfully.

The Secure Electronic Transactions Protocol

Secure Electronic Transactions (SET) was designed to address most of the consumer demands for privacy when using a credit card to shop online. SET uses are specific to the payment acceptance phases of the shopping experience. This protocol covers the steps from the point a particular payment card is selected for use through the point the merchant completes the transaction and settles the batch with the acquirer bank or processor.

SET was designed to use a robust set of strictly controlled digital certificates to identify cardholders, merchants, and acquiring payment gateways, to ensure the security of messages passing through open channels such as the Internet. It also uses multiple forms of symmetric key cryptography (such as DES) to provide confidentiality of payment card and transaction data.

SET never really caught on in the commercial world because of a number of factors, including costs beyond what an immature sales channel would bear to implement the system within banks, merchants, and credit processors; a lack of any mandate from the banks to implement the protocol; and incompatibilities in software implementations of SET that sometimes prevented end-to-end communications. Lessons learned from SET have influenced other activities in the financial services industry to protect online credit card payments (for example, Verified by Visa, 3D SSL, and 3D Secure).

Summary

Computer applications need cryptography to implement the privacy and security that users demand.

Cryptography is commonly found in security systems and security mechanisms. It's useful as a tool to protect confidential information and to verify the identity of people who send electronic messages and conduct electronic transactions.

The strength of a cryptosystem rests in the size and means used to protect cryptographic keys—in general, the longer the key, the harder it is to break the encryption. With symmetric keys, the same key can be used to both encrypt and decrypt information; with asymmetric keys, different keys are used for encryption and decryption.

Cryptography relies on two basic methods: transposition and substitution. With transposition, ciphertext is created by scrambling a message based on a shared secret key. In substitution, letters are exchanged with other letters based on a substitution pattern known to both sender and receiver.

Digital signatures are used in asymmetric key cryptography to protect a message's content from disclosure, prove the integrity of a message upon receipt, and verify that the sender of the message is indeed who he or she claims to be. Digital signature technology relies on a public key infrastructure for implementation and is at the heart of many commercial products used in modern electronic commerce.

Test Your Skills

MULTIPLE-CHOICE QUESTIONS

1. Which of the following represents the two types of ciphers?

    A. Transposition and permutation

    B. Transposition and shift

    C. Transposition and substitution

    D. Substitution and replacement

2. Which of the following terms best describes the substitution cipher that shifts the alphabet by 13 places?

    A. Caesar cipher

    B. Polyalphabetic cipher

    C. ROT13 cipher

    D. Transposition cipher

3. The DES, 3DES, and AES algorithms are examples of which type of cryptography?

   A. Symmetric key

   B. Two-key

   C. Asymmetric key

   D. Public key

4. Which of the following statements best describes a digital signature?

   A. A digital signature is a method used to encrypt confidential data.

   B. A digital signature is the art of transferring handwritten signatures to electronic media.

   C. A digital signature allows the recipient of data to prove the source and integrity of data.

   D. A digital signature can be used as a signature system and a cryptosystem.

5. A message is said to be digitally signed if it's sent with which of the following?

   A. A message digest

   B. A message digest encrypted with the sender's public key

   C. A message digest encrypted with the sender's private key

   D. A message and the sender's digital certificate

6. Why does a digital signature contain a message digest?

   A. To detect any alteration of the message

   B. To indicate the encryption algorithm

   C. To confirm the identity of the sender

   D. To enable transmission in a digital format

7. Which of the following terms best describes a mathematical encryption operation that cannot be reversed?

   A. One-way hash

   B. DES

   C. Transposition

   D. Substitution

8. Which of the following statements related to a private key cryptosystem is false?

   A. The encryption key should be secure.

   B. Data Encryption Standard (DES) is a typical private key cryptosystem.

   C. The key used for decryption is known to the sender.

   D. Two different keys are used for the encryption and decryption.

9. Which of the following standards applies to digital certificates?

   A. X.400

   B. X.25

   C. X.509

   D. X.75

10. Which of the following offers confidentiality to an email message?

    A. The sender encrypting it with its private key

    B. The sender encrypting it with its public key

    C. The sender encrypting it with the receiver's public key

    D. The sender encrypting it with the receiver's private key

11. Which of the following attributes is included in an X.509 (digital) certificate?

    A. The secret key of the issuing CA

    B. The distinguished name of the subject

    C. The key pair of the certificate holder

    D. The telephone number of the department

12. Which of the following statements is true?

    A. The Secure Hash Algorithm (SHA) creates a fixed-length message digest from a fixed-length input message.

    B. The Secure Hash Algorithm (SHA) creates a variable-length message digest from a variable-length input message.

    C. The Secure Hash Algorithm (SHA) creates a fixed-length message digest from a variable-length input message.

    D. The Secure Hash Algorithm (SHA) creates a variable-length message digest from a fixed-length input message.

13. Which of the following statements best describes the primary purpose for using one-way encryption of user passwords within a system?

    A. It prevents an unauthorized person from trying multiple passwords in one log-on attempt.

    B. It prevents an unauthorized person from reading or modifying the password list.

    C. It minimizes the amount of storage required for user passwords.

    D. It minimizes the amount of processing time used for encrypting passwords.

14. Which of the following statements is true?

    A. The most secure email message authenticity and confidentiality is provided by signing the message using the sender's public key and encrypting the message using the receiver's private key.

B. The most secure email message authenticity and confidentiality is provided by signing the message using the sender's private key and encrypting the message using the receiver's public key.

C. The most secure email message authenticity and confidentiality is provided by signing the message using the receiver's private key and encrypting the message using the sender's public key.

D. The most secure email message authenticity and confidentiality is provided by signing the message using the receiver's public key and encrypting the message using the sender's private key.

15. Which of the following terms best describes the encryption algorithm selected by NIST for the new Advanced Encryption Standard?

  A. RSA

  B. DES

  C. RC6

  D. Rijndael

16. Which of the following algorithms is used today for encryption in PGP?

  A. RSA

  B. DES

  C. SHA-1

  D. RC5

17. Which of the following mail standards relies on a web of trust?

  A. Secure Multipurpose Internet Mail Extensions (S/MIME)

  B. Pretty Good Privacy (PGP)

  C. MIME Object Security Services (MOSS)

  D. Privacy Enhanced Mail (PEM)

18. Which of the following was developed in 1997 as a means of preventing fraud during electronic payments?

  A. Secure Electronic Transaction (SET)

  B. MONDEX

  C. Secure Shell (SSH-2)

  D. Secure Hypertext Transfer Protocol (S-HTTP)

EXERCISES

EXERCISE 11.1: **Practicing Encryption Using Transposition**

1. Encrypt the following message using the keyword CAUTION and the transposition method:

   MARCH FORWARD INTO THE NIGHT TUESDAY NEXT

2. What result did you get?

EXERCISE 11.2: **More Practicing of Encryption Using Transposition**

1. Using the shared secret PRIVACY, encrypt the following message with the transposition method:

   ANYONE CAN HIDE MESSAGES

2. What result did you get?

EXERCISE 11.3: **Practicing Decryption Using Transposition**

1. Decrypt the following message using the keyword CAUTION and the transposition method:

   RAU CRM TYF GSN OIU PHH YPC

2. What result did you get?

EXERCISE 11.4: **More Practicing of Decryption Using Transposition**

1. Decrypt the following message using the keyword CAUTION and the transposition method:

   OYES NTRE ECMG UNMS BAYE NUDA OOAS

2. What result did you get?

EXERCISE 11.5: **Practicing Encryption Using Substitution**

1. Encrypt the following using the substitution method with a rotate value of 13:

   ALL GOOD MEN SHOULD COME TO THE AID OF THEIR COUNTRY

2. What result did you get?

EXERCISE 11.6: **More Practicing of Decryption Using Substitution**

1. Decrypt the following using the substitution method with a rotate value of 13:

   PELCGBTENCUL VF SHA

2. What result did you get?

PROJECTS

PROJECT 11.1: Researching the RSA Cryptosystem

1. Visit the RSA Security website (www.rsa.com) to begin your research.

2. Search online for commercial products that implement the RSA Cryptosystem to protect electronic commerce transactions and communications.

3. Up to this point, how aware were you of when you were using the RSA system?

4. As you continue using the Internet, what signs will you look for to verify that the RSA system is active?

PROJECT 11.2: Researching Desktop Encryption Products

Laptop theft has become rampant, and companies are becoming concerned about the loss or theft of business confidential data. As such, they are adopting desktop encryption products at a rapid pace.

1. Search online for products that perform PC desktop encryption to protect locally stored files.

2. What differences do you find in how they implement and manage the cryptography?

3. How do these different approaches offer different types of protection (file encryption, disk encryption, and so forth)?

4. Which product would you recommend to management for use throughout the organization?

5. Which product would you consider adopting for yourself?

PROJECT 11.3: Exploring the Issues Behind the SHA-3 Competition

MD5 and SHA-1 have come under fire since 2004 because of research findings demonstrating that these algorithms might not be as secure as previously thought.

1. Search online for the problems researchers cite with MD5.

2. Find out what problems researchers cite with SHA-1.

3. Determine whether the problems cited are a vulnerability that should be addressed immediately or whether they are theoretical issues that would cause problems only in extremely rare circumstances.

4. What are researchers and experts recommending to commercial users about these findings?

5. What would you recommend to your managers if you were asked what your organization should do?

Chapter | **12**

Telecommunications, Network, and Internet Security

Chapter Objectives

After reading this chapter and completing the exercises, you will be able to do the following:

- Classify the International Organization for Standardization /Open Systems Interconnection (ISO/OSI) layers and characteristics

- Summarize the fundamentals of communications and network security and their vulnerabilities

- Analyze the Transmission Control Protocol/Internet Protocol (TCP/IP)

- Distinguish among wide area networks (WANs), local area networks (LANs), and the Internet, intranets, and extranets

- Outline the roles of packet-filtering routers, firewalls, and intrusion detection/prevention technology in network perimeter security

- Classify the various configurations and architectures for firewalls

- Illustrate the elements of IP security (IPSec) and how virtual private networks implement IPSec

Introduction

The Internet has grown faster than any telecommunications system in history, including the telephone system. It continues to grow as wireless broadband spans more continents and becomes more ubiquitous.

Still, typical users of the Internet fail to realize that Internet-attached corporate and internal networks are attractive targets for intruders who seek out massive collections of credit card information, personally identifiable information (PII), and corporate secrets.

New Internet sites, in particular, are often prime targets for malicious activity, including break-ins, file tampering, vandalism, and service disruptions. Not only is this activity difficult to discover and correct, but it also is highly embarrassing to the organization and is costly in terms of lost productivity and damage to data, company reputation, and customer goodwill.

Information security practitioners must be vigilant about the risks of computer security incidents from the Internet and the steps they can take to secure public and private sites. This chapter discusses management and technical concerns related to telecommunications and network security.

The chapter contains some of the most technical and challenging information that security professionals must understand in detail. Designing a secure network is rigorous but interesting and fulfilling work. Many people depend on the network engineers and security specialists to design, implement, and maintain the networks that keep businesses humming while simultaneously protecting them from ever-present threats to corporate computing resources.

An Overview of Network and Telecommunications Security

Telecommunications, Network, and Internet Security is one of the largest of the domains in the Common Body of Knowledge (in terms of content) and one of the most essential areas of focus.

Topics in this domain include the following:

- The Open Systems Interconnection (OSI) reference model to promote interoperability for disparate network communications

- TCP/IP, the Transmission Control Protocol/Internet Protocol, developed by the U.S. Department of Defense in the 1970s and widely used on the Internet

- Security services to protect networks from attack: authentication, access control, data confidentiality, data integrity, nonrepudiation, and logging

- Data network types, including local area networks (LAN), wide area networks (WAN), and the Internet, intranets, and extranets

- Devices for network security: routers, firewalls, and intrusion detection and prevention systems (IDSs/IPSs)

- Virtual private networks, or VPNs, a kind of private "tunnel" through the Internet that use IP security (IPSec) to perform encryption and authentication to address the lack of security on IP-based networks

Using the building blocks of network security (the bricks) along with the objectives and principles (the mortar) for protecting networks from unauthorized access and unauthorized changes, you can mix and match technologies, architectures, and processes to meet any security requirements you'll encounter in the real world.

Network Security in Context

Information security (IS) practitioners must never lose sight of the security mantra of confidentiality, integrity, and availability (CIA), explained in Chapter 2, "Information Security Principles of Success." Nowhere are the principles of defense in depth more prevalent than in the Network and Telecommunications Security Domain. In fact, starting with the DiD Principle, you'll gain the best context for understanding the why's and how-to's for security information system networks.

We refer to these principles again to remind you that, to an IS specialist, any security-related discussion about network architecture is done not in and for itself, but in the context of CIA. Will the network architecture guarantee the confidentiality, reliability, integrity, resilience, and accessibility of the data?

Confidentiality touches on the topics of network authentication and data encryption. Integrity protects the data from unauthorized or accidental modification through the use of firewalls, cryptography, and intrusion detection tools. As you saw in Chapter 6, "Business Continuity Planning and Disaster Recovery Planning," availability involves sound disaster recovery planning procedures based on an accepted business continuity plan.

The Open Systems Interconnection Reference Model

Any discussion of network and Internet security necessarily begins with an overview of the Open Systems Interconnection (OSI) reference model, the model for network communications. The International Organization for Standardization (ISO) developed OSI in the early 1980s to promote interoperability of network devices. Think of OSI as the translation service at the United Nations that allows speakers from different nations to communicate with each other, and imagine what the Internet would be like today had the ISO not promoted such a standard.

This section looks at the seven layers of the data flow stack, as it is called, and follows up with a discussion of the OSI security services.

The Protocol Stack

When the ISO developed the Open Systems Interconnection reference model, it realized that it had to define a standard set of communication protocols. These protocols would allow dissimilar networks and equipment from different manufacturers to communicate with each other. The OSI reference model is exactly what it says: a reference to help people understand highly complex activities by using an abstract description. As an organizing framework for humans, it does not exist exactly as specified in the computing and networking industry. Its usefulness is in the "seams" between the layers that describe the specifications on how one layer interacts or interfaces with another layer. This means that an implementation of a layer written by one manufacturer that follows the specifications can operate with an implementation of another layer (above or below) written by another manufacturer.

The seven layers create a top-down hierarchy of protocol services on the client side of the model. Protocols are the rules and standards that enable communication between computers over the Internet. This hierarchy works in reverse order on the server side of the model. The hierarchy in no way represents levels of importance; it simply represents a series of different protocols with different tasks to perform.

Figure 12.1 shows the seven layers of the OSI protocol stack. This model defines the standard by which two computers share data over the network. A quick look at this illustration shows how data moves from the Application Layer on the client or "application" side of the model down through several other layers until it reaches the bottom of the stack, the Physical Layer. The data then crosses the network to the server (or application services) side of the model and climbs back up the ladder of the protocol stack. Each layer in the stack performs a specific set of tasks and can communicate with adjacent layers. For example, the Network Layer communicates with the level above it (the Transport Layer) and the layer beneath (the Data Link Layer). Another reason ISO developed the standard was to help computer scientists break the protocols into a structured representation and facilitate a discussion of how the model works.

Layer No.	Layer Name	Description
7	Application	Consists of standard communication services and applications that everyone can use.
6	Presentation	Ensures that information is delivered to the receiving machine in a form that it can understand.
5	Session	Manages the connections and terminations between cooperating computers.
4	Transport	Manages the transfer of data and assures that received and transmitted data are identical.
3	Network	Manages data addressing and delivery between networks.
2	Data Link	Handles the transfer of data across the network media.
1	Physical	Defines the characteristics of the network hardware.

FIGURE 12.1   The OSI data flow reference model.

The following discussion examines the layers on a superficial level. You need not understand the mechanics of how the protocols work—you do need to understand the general purpose of each layer. A discussion of the OSI security services then follows. A handy way to remember the OSI Layers and their order is to use the mnemonic "All People Seem To Need Data Processing (or Dominos Pizza)," starting with the Application Layer and ending with the Physical Layer.

Application Layer (Layer 7)

The Application Layer, the highest layer in the stack, is the one most directly related to the computer user. It provides several application services, such as file transfer, resource allocation, and the identification and verification of computer availability. For example, your program might be trying to obtain resources on a network server that currently are unavailable. Programs no doubt familiar to you at this level include these:

- Email

- Discussion groups

- World Wide Web

Each time you send an email, you are invoking protocols at the Application Layer level.

Presentation Layer (Layer 6)

As its name indicates, this layer translates or "presents" data to the Application Layer. Data encryption and decryption occur in this layer along with data translation. Whenever you view a photograph in JPEG (a compressed photo storage standard) format on the Internet, watch a video someone has sent you in MPEG format (a compressed movie storage format), or listen to an MP3 file (a compressed audio storage format), you are interacting with OSI Presentation Layer protocol services.

Session Layer (Layer 5)

Now the water begins to get a little deeper and murkier. The protocols at this level establish, maintain, and manage sessions between computers. When you request information about your checking account balance from your bank's web application, the Session Layer makes the initial contact with the host computer, formats the data you are sending for transmission, establishes the necessary communication links, and handles recovery and restart functions. If you have selected various options from drop-down lists to obtain information from a website on the network (for example, looking for a home with certain characteristics in a specific price range and location or entering an artist name for a song search), you have used data formatting routines at the OSI Session Layer level.

Transport Layer (Layer 4)

Protocols at this level provide the point-to-point integrity of data transmissions. They determine how to address the other computer, establish communication links, handle the networking of messages, and generally control the session. The Transmission Control Protocol (TCP) operates at this level. TCP allows two computers to connect with each other and exchange streams of data while guaranteeing delivery of the data and maintaining it in the same order. Although the context of communications works at the higher layers of the protocol stack, the transport of this context over the network occurs at Layer 4.

Network Layer (Layer 3)

The Network Layer decides how small bundles, or packets, of data route between destination systems on the same network or interconnected networks. A packet (sometimes called a protocol data unit, or PDU) is a bundle of data organized for transmission that contains control information (destination, length, origin, and so forth), the data itself (payload), and error detection and correction bits. Packets traverse packet switching networks that divide messages into standard-sized packets for greater efficiency of routing and transport.

Unlike the Transport Layer, the Network Layer doesn't know the destination to deliver your data—it only knows how to address the data and drop the packet onto the network for the Transport Layer to route.

Data Link Layer (Layer 2)

Now the water is extremely deep and dark. The Data Link Layer transfers units of information to the other end of the physical link. Protocols at this level establish communication links between devices over a physical link or channel, converting data into bit streams for delivery to the lowest layer, the Physical Layer. 802.11 wireless LANs operate at Layer 2 and Layer 1 (covered next).

Physical Layer (Layer 1)

Finally, protocols at the Physical Layer transmit bit streams on a physical medium. They manage the interfaces of physical devices with physical transmission media, such as coax cable. This layer has the fewest tasks to perform. It sends bit streams across the network to another device and receives a bit stream response in return. The High Speed Serial Interface (HSSI) is one example of a standard interface working at the Physical Layer level.

Assuming that every layer does its job correctly, when you send a request from an application down through the layers of the protocol stack, your data traverses the network to the Physical Layer of the receiving device and winds its way back up the stack to the receiving application on the other side. Data (email, financial transactions, MP3 downloads, and so on) streams back and forth in this way at millions of bits per second from myriad users, all because the ISO and other dedicated computer scientists established common routines for the transmission and receipt of data.

The OSI Reference Model and TCP/IP

As mentioned earlier, the OSI seven-layer model is commonly used as a reference model to help people organize their thinking about abstract layers of networking. A real-world implementation, the Transmission Control Protocol/Internet Protocol (TCP/IP), described shortly, is an implementation of a more compact network protocol that roughly maps to the seven layers of the OSI model (see Figure 12.2).

Referring to activities of the seven-layer model is useful even though they don't actually exist as distinct clear-cut layers in the TCP/IP world. By using the principle of defense in depth (see Chapter 2), the principle by which each system on the network is protected to the greatest degree possible, you can gain clarity of thought when deciding how to secure communications at all levels of the protocol.

TCP/IP is the collection of protocols the U.S. Department of Defense used in the 1970s to build the predecessor of the Internet, called ARPANET, or the Advanced Research Projects Network. Among other duties, TCP/IP provides universal connectivity across the Internet using a reliable delivery mechanism. It handles data in bundles, called packets, keeping them from getting lost, damaged, or disordered.

OSI Ref. Layer No.	OSI Layer Equivalent	TCP/IP Layer	TCP/IP Protocol Examples
5, 6, 7	Application, Session, Presentation	Application	NFS, NIS +, DNS, Telnet, FTP, "r" commands ("r" commands include rlogin, rsh, and rcp), RIP, RDISC, SNMP, others
4	Transport	Transport	TCP, UDP
3	Network	Network	IP, ARP, ICMP
2	Data Link	Data Link	PPP, IEEE 802.2
1	Physical	Physical Network	Ethernet (IEEE 802.3) Token Ring, RS-232, others

FIGURE 12.2   TCP/IP mapped to the OSI model.

The primary protocols in TCP/IP are bundled in each layer and briefly described next:

■ Transport Layer (host-to-host) protocols

The Transport Layer consists of two elements:

   ■ **Transmission Control Protocol:** TCP is a reliable service that maintains the proper sequence of incoming packets and acknowledges receipt to the user.

   ■ **User Datagram Protocol (UDP):** UDP is a less robust version of TCP. It does not acknowledge receipt of packets and is a connectionless and less reliable service. Its advantage over TCP is its faster speed and lower overhead.

■ Network (Internet) Layer protocols

The Network Layer is responsible for these services and protocols:

   ■ **Internet Protocol:** The protocol of protocols, IP addresses are assigned by the Internet Assigned Numbers Authority (www.iana.org/) to each host computer on the network. This serves as a logical ID. The IP address assists with the routing of information across the Internet. Outgoing data packets have the originator's IP address and the IP address of the recipient.

   ■ **Address Resolution Protocol (ARP):** ARP matches an IP address to an Ethernet address, which is a physical device (network adapter) that has a unique media access control (MAC) address assigned by the manufacturer of the device. MAC addresses are much longer numbers than IP addresses, and humans tend to work better with IP addresses than with MAC addresses. Thus, ARP and RARP (covered next) exist to help with network addressing tasks.

   ■ **Reverse Address Resolution Protocol (RARP):** If ARP translates an IP address to a MAC address, then RARP translates hardware interface (MAC) addresses to IP protocol addresses.

- **Internet Control Message Protocol (ICMP):** The ICMP is tightly integrated with the IP protocol. Some of its functions include announcing network errors and congestion, troubleshooting, and reporting timeouts. ICMP is the management protocol for TCP/IP and is often the source of security issues; network hackers use it to select targets and determine network level information about these targets. For example, the common `ping` command, used to determine whether an IP or host name is online, is an ICMP command.

The following are the primary applications using TCP/IP:

- **File Transfer Protocol (FTP):** FTP is one of the oldest Internet protocols. It facilitates the transfer of data files (such as customer purchase information from a mainframe to a data warehouse) between two similar or dissimilar FTP devices. FTP can also perform certain directory functions.

- **Remote login (Telnet):** First published in 1983, Telnet was originally designed to facilitate remote logins to a computer via the Internet for terminal (interactive) sessions. A user running a local Telnet program (client) can execute a login session on a remote computer (for example, to access a university library) using a Telnet server program for communication. Because of security issues using Telnet (clear-text IDs and passwords, lack of encryption for session data), its use has fallen out of favor and is most often replaced with Secure Shell, or SSH.

- **Electronic Mail or Simple Mail Transfer Protocol (SMTP):** This is the protocol used to send email via the Internet in a host-to-host configuration that relays messages from source to destination through as many intermediate relay systems exist along the route.

You can think of these application programs running at the Application Layer of the OSI model, along with all other network-based services that require external connectivity. Because TCP/IP was built for resilience in the face of nuclear war, the designers did not consider security of the network an issue to consider at the time.

The OSI Model and Security

Now that you have seen the complexity of the OSI protocol stack and its relationship to the real-world TCP/IP, you can begin to think of the layers as interdependent links in a chain. Each link is subject to security attacks and, in keeping with the old saying about a chain and its weakest link, the OSI had to address security services and the mechanisms needed to keep the chain strong.

ISO Security Services

ISO has identified six security services to protect networks from attack:

- **Authentication:** Access to documents can be restricted in one of two ways: by asking for a username and password or by using the hostname of the browser. The former, referred to as user authentication, requires creating a file of user IDs and passwords (an access control list— see Chapter 5, "Security Architecture and Design") and defining critical resources (such as files and documents) to the server.

- **Access control:** Unlike authentication, which is security based on the user's identity, restricting access based on something other than identity is called access control. "Allow and deny" directives allow or deny access to network services based on hostname or address (see Chapter 5).

- **Data confidentiality:** This service protects data against unauthorized disclosure and has two components: content confidentiality and message flow confidentiality. The former protects the plain-text message from unauthorized disclosure; the latter allows the originating network to conceal the path or route that the message followed on its way to the recipient. Message flow confidentiality is useful in preventing an attacker from obtaining information from observing the message.

- **Data integrity:** The goal is to protect data from accidental or malicious modification, whether during data transfer, during data storage, or from an operation performed on it, and to preserve it for its intended use.

- **Nonrepudiation:** This service guarantees that the sender of a message cannot deny having sent the message and the receiver cannot deny having received the message.

- **Logging and monitoring:** These services allow IS specialists to observe system activity during and after the fact by using monitoring and logging tools. These include operating system logs, server records, application log errors, warnings, and observation of network switch and router traffic between network segments.

The OSI model additionally identifies eight security mechanisms that implement the aforementioned security services:

- **Encipherment:** The conversion of plain-text messages into ciphers or encoded messages that only the person with the cipher key can unlock.

- **Digital signature:** In general, the use of public and private key encryption that allows the sender to encrypt a message and the intended recipient to decrypt the message.

- **Access control:** See the earlier description.

- **Data integrity:** See the earlier description.

- **Authentication:** See the earlier description.

- **Traffic padding:** The technique by which spurious data is generated to disguise the amount of real data being sent, thus making data analysis or decryption more difficult for the attacker.

- **Routing control:** The Internet has routes between networks. When a network drops, the routing control processor determines in real time the optimal path, to reduce downtime.

- **Notarization:** Digital notarizations, the counterpart to the paper notary, prove that electronic files have not been altered after they were digitally notarized. (See Chapter 11, "Cryptography," for more information on digital signatures.)

Data Network Types

Now that you have an understanding of the OSI protocol stack and some of the services and mechanisms used to protect it, this section steps back to look at basic network configurations. The various types of data networks are listed here:

- Local area networks (LANs)
- Wide area networks (WANs)
- Internet, intranet, and extranets

Local Area Networks

A local area network, or LAN, is a network configuration designed for a limited space or geographic area, such as a series of offices in the same building (for example, a university administration building). LANs share network services such as databases, email, and application services by connecting workstations and servers through a set of LAN protocols and access methods. Two common types of LANs are the campus area network (CAN), used to connect buildings through a network backbone, and the metropolitan area network (MAN), used to connect branches of an organization using wireless (satellite or cellular) devices over a long distance between branches. A MAN can cover an area of 5 to 50 kilometers, roughly the size of a city. Most of today's LANs rely on wireless or Wi-Fi networks that use radio signals to transport TCP/IP packets over a confined distance (depending on the Wi-Fi router in use). Appendix C, "Sample Policies," includes a basic wireless LAN security standard to help in configuring an access point for an acceptable level of security for typical uses.

Wide Area Networks

A group of smaller LANs connected logically or physically is referred to as a wide area network, or WAN. As you might suspect, the WAN covers a larger geographic area than a LAN (technically, a network that covers an area larger than a single building). A WAN can span an entire nation or even the globe using satellites. A WAN is inherently more complex than a LAN because of its size and use of multiple network protocols and configuration. WANs can combine other subnetworks, such as intranets, extranets, and virtual private networks (VPNs), to provide enhanced network capabilities.

Internet

Sometimes referred to as a network of networks, the Internet is an interconnection of different-sized networks (LANs) around the world. Evolving from the U.S. military's ARPANET in the late 1960s and early 1970s, the Internet uses the TCP/IP protocols (covered shortly) in a scheme decentralized by design. Each host computer on the Internet is independent; its operators can choose the Internet services and local services they want to offer.

FYI: What Makes the Internet Tick?

The Internet is a store-and-forward network, meaning that TCP/IP packets can be sent to (and stored on) any number of computers along the way to their destination. If a direct network link exists between two host computers—that is, if a physical cable is linking them—the packets can fly right through. Most of the time, however, no direct link exists. In this case, the sending computer (host) sends the packets to one that's a little closer to the destination. That machine moves the packets further down the line, and so on, until the packets reach their destination. It's not uncommon for a cross-country trip to make 20 or 30 hops on different routers along the way. Hop count refers to the intermediate devices (such as routers) through which data must pass from the source to the destination. Most of the time, this happens very, very quickly (at the speed of electricity—roughly the speed of light).

Intranet

An intranet is a local or wide area network based on TCP/IP, but with fences (firewalls) that limit the network's access to the Internet. Intranets use the standard software and protocols you find on the Internet, but they are for private use and are not accessible to the public via the Internet. Companies can use low-cost Internet software such as browsers to build internal sites, such as human resources and internal job postings. An intranet is more secure than the Internet because it has a restricted user community and local control.

Extranet

An extranet is an intranet that allows select users outside the firewalls to access the site. For example, a company might give vendors and suppliers limited access to the intranet while excluding the general public.

Protecting TCP/IP Networks

Protecting computer networks is a challenging job and is best approached by applying the principle of defense in depth. The following sections begin to examine the pieces of the security puzzle to see how to best fit them together for effective defenses and coverage. We explore several types of security approaches that are usually present wherever the Internet and corporate networks intersect. These include the use of these components:

- Routers
- Firewalls
- Intrusion detection systems (IDSs)
- Intrusion prevention systems (IPSs)

Basic Security Infrastructures

Figure 12.3 illustrates the basic design for network security. As you see, the infrastructure relies on layers of devices (think defense in depth) that serve specific purposes and provide multiple barriers of security that protect, detect, and respond to network attacks, often in real time.

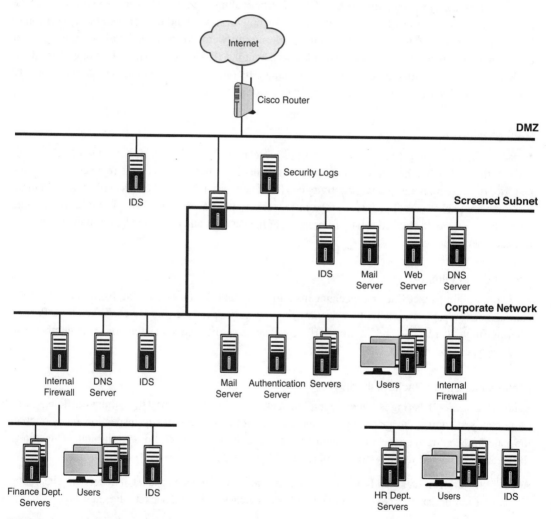

FIGURE 12.3   A basic network security model.

The following sections focus on the individual building blocks needed to complete the network security picture.

Routers

A router is a network traffic management device that operates in between subnetworks (LANs) and routes traffic intended for or leaving the network segments to which it's attached. Because of their special role in network management, routers are sensible places to implement packet-filtering rules, based on the security policies already developed for the routing of network traffic . You can think of the placement of routers as creating a subnetwork segment. Devices behind the perimeter or border router for that segment have unique IP addresses that the router forwards to the subnetwork when traffic over the entire network passes to the router that knows about the IP addresses behind it. Network Address Translation (NAT) is often used on perimeter routers. Its purpose is to the hide the internal device IP addresses from Internet users, to help secure the network.

Packet Filtering

A packet filter is a simple and effective form of protection. It matches all packets against a series of rules. If the packet matches a rule, an action is performed; the packet is accepted, rejected, logged, and so forth. Because malicious network activity can harm network users, and because all network communications are packet based, packets can be inspected as they traverse the network; those that contain commands that are disallowed can be filtered out of the network and discarded before they cause harm or unauthorized activity.

Basic Packet Filtering

Basic or straight packet-filtering mechanisms allow communication originating from one side of the communication path. To enable two-way traffic, you must specify a rule for each direction. Packet-filtering firewalls identify and control traffic by examining the source, destination, port number, and protocol types (for example, UDP or TCP).

Stateful Inspection Packet Filtering

Stateful inspection filtering is a more complex packet-filtering technology that filters traffic based on more than just source, destination, port number, and protocol type. Stateful inspection keeps track of the state of the current connection to help ensure that only desired traffic passes through. This allows the creation of one-way rules—for example, inside to outside.

A packet-filtering router yields a permit or deny decision for each packet it receives. The router examines each IP datagram to determine whether it matches one of its packet-filtering rules.

Benefits of Packet-Filtering Routers

A number of Internet firewall systems are deployed using only a packet-filtering router. Other than the time spent planning the filters and configuring the router, implementing packet filtering involves little or no cost because the feature is included as part of standard router software releases. Because a WAN interface usually provides Internet access, there is little impact on router performance if traffic loads are moderate and few filters are defined. Packet-filtering routers are generally transparent to users and applications, eliminating the need for specialized user training or specific software on each connected host system.

Limitations of Packet-Filtering Routers

Defining packet filters can be a complex task because network administrators need to have a detailed understanding of the various Internet services, packet header formats (packets typically have header and trailer records marking the beginning and end of the data packet), and specific values they expect to find in each field. If complex filtering requirements must be supported, the filtering rule set can become robust and complicated, increasing in difficulty to manage and comprehend. Finally, few testing facilities exist to verify the correctness of the filtering rules after they are configured on the router. This can potentially leave a site open to untested vulnerabilities.

Any packet that passes directly through a router could potentially be used to launch a data-driven attack. Data-driven attacks occur when the router forwards seemingly harmless data to an internal host. The data might contain hidden instructions that cause the host to modify access control and security-related files, making it easier for the intruder to gain access to the system.

Generally, the packet throughput of a router decreases as the number of filters increase. Routers are optimized to extract the destination IP address from each packet, make a relatively simple routing table lookup, and then forward the packet to the proper interface for transmission. If filtering is enabled, the router must not only make a forwarding decision for each packet, but also apply all the filter rules to each packet.

IP packet filters might not be capable of providing enough control over traffic. A packet-filtering router can permit or deny a particular service, but it cannot understand the context/data of a particular service. For example, a network administrator might need to filter traffic at the Application Layer to limit access to a subset of the available FTP or SSH commands or to block the import of mail or newsgroups concerning specific topics. This type of control is best performed at a higher layer by application-level gateways often called firewalls.

Firewalls

Firewalls insulate a private network from a public network using carefully established controls on the type of requests they'll route to the private network for processing and fulfillment. For example, an HTTP request for a public web page will be honored, whereas an FTP request to a host behind the firewall might be dishonored.

Firewalls typically run monitoring software to detect and thwart external attacks on the site and protect the internal corporate network. When you install a firewall, you essentially break the network so that no communications can occur until the rules for permissible communications are established and implemented. Firewalls are an essential device for network security, and many of the architectures needed for security rely on one or more firewalls within an intelligent design.

Several firewall architecture models are used to protect the perimeter of a network and control the flow of permitted communications. Nonpermitted traffic (requests for services that are not authorized) is discarded by the firewall before entering the protected network or network segment. The following sections describe two of the most common firewall building block architectures: application-level gateways and bastion hosts.

> ## Home Sweet Home
>
> Homing, in firewall-speak, refers to the number of network interfaces that are available to the firewall. A single-homed firewall, for example, attaches to a network segment and determines what types of traffic can enter or exit (ingress and egress) that segment. Multihomed firewalls reside on multiple network segments at their edge and can move traffic from one segment to another based on the rules established for that traffic (for example, connection to an Internet router on one segment and to a DMZ on another segment). Using multihomed firewalls is an effective method to control network traffic based on explicit policies related to what types of traffic are allowed and where.

Application-Level Gateway Firewall

An application-level gateway enables the network administrator to implement stricter security policies than packet-filtering routers can manage. Instead of relying on a generic packet-filtering tool to manage the flow of Internet services through the firewall, special-purpose code (a proxy service) is installed on the gateway for each desired application. If the network administrator does not install the proxy code for a particular application, the service is not supported and cannot be forwarded across the firewall. In addition, the proxy code can be configured to support only the specific features of an application that the network administrator considers acceptable, while denying all other features.

This enhanced security comes with increased costs in these areas:

- Purchase of the dedicated gateway hardware
- Configuration of the proxy service applications
- Time, knowledge, and skills required to configure the gateway system
- Degradation in the level of service provided to users because of the overhead of firewall operation
- Lack of transparency for remote users, resulting in a less user-friendly system

Note that users are permitted access to the proxy services, but they are never permitted to log in to the application-level gateway itself. If users are permitted to log in to the firewall system, the security of the firewall is threatened because an intruder could potentially perform some activity that compromises the effectiveness of the firewall. To that end, the firewall software you purchase must be operated exclusively on a hardened server (a server whose software has been modified to make it more difficult to attack), with all unnecessary services eliminated from the host.

Additionally, each proxy service might require its own authentication before granting user access. The following are characteristics of the proxy server:

- Each proxy is configured to support only a subset of the standard application's command set. If the proxy application does not support a standard command, it is simply not available to the authenticated user.

- Each proxy is configured to allow access only to specific host systems. This means that the limited command/feature set can be applied only to a subset of systems on the protected network.

- Each proxy maintains detailed audit information by logging all traffic, each connection, and the duration of each connection. Audit logs are essential tools for discovering and terminating intruder attacks. Each proxy is a small and uncomplicated program specifically designed for network security.

- Each proxy is independent of all other proxies on the bastion host. If a problem occurs with the operation of any proxy or if a future vulnerability is discovered, it can be uninstalled without affecting the operation of the other proxy applications.

- Each proxy runs as a nonprivileged user in a private and secured directory on the bastion host. If users require support for new services, the network administrator can easily install the required proxies on the bastion host. A proxy generally performs no disk access other than to read its initial configuration file. This makes it difficult for an intruder to install Trojan horse sniffers or other dangerous files on the bastion host.

Bastion Hosts

An application-level gateway is often referred to as a bastion host because it is a designated system that is specifically armored and protected against attacks. Unlike packet-filtering routers, which allow the direct flow of packets between inside systems and outside systems, application-level gateways allow information to flow between systems but do not allow the direct exchange of data. The primary risk of allowing packet exchange between inside systems and outside systems is that the host applications residing on the protected network's systems must be secured against any threat posed by the allowed services. Figure 12.4 illustrates the application-level gateway firewall configuration.

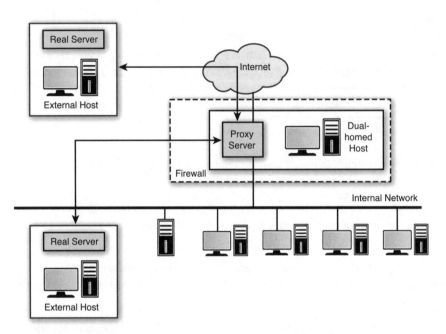

FIGURE 12.4   Application-level gateway firewall configuration.

Several design features provide security for a bastion host. The bastion host hardware platform operates a secure (hardened) version of its operating system. For example, if the bastion host is a UNIX platform, it executes a secure version of the UNIX operating system that is specifically designed to protect against operating system vulnerabilities and ensure firewall integrity.

Network administrators install only services they consider essential on the bastion host. An uninstalled service is not vulnerable to attack. Generally, a limited set of proxy applications, such as SSH, DNS, FTP, SMTP, and user authentication, is installed on a bastion host. The bastion host might be configured to require additional authentication before a user is allowed access to the proxy services.

Benefits of Application-Level Gateways

Application-level gateways have many benefits. They give the network manager complete control over each service because the proxy application limits the command set and determines which internal hosts the service can access. In addition, the network manager has complete control over permitted services because the absence of a proxy for a particular service means that the service is completely blocked. Application-level gateways also have the capability to support strong user authentication and provide detailed logging information. Finally, the filtering rules for an application-level gateway are much easier to configure and test than for a packet-filtering router.

Limitations of Application-Level Gateways

The greatest limitation of an application-level gateway is that it requires either modified user behavior or specialized software installed on each system that accesses proxy services. For example, Telnet access via an application-level gateway requires two user steps to make the connection instead of a single step.

FYI: The Rise of Network Security Appliances

Vendors of modern firewalls and network filters (such as spam filters) are increasingly delivering products as appliances that resemble pizza boxes. These devices are deliberately sealed and meant to use as plug-and-play protection. Essentially, appliances are servers that come prehardened and operate *only* for their specific use (as opposed to general-purpose servers). You can implement these devices alongside other networking gear and then configure them for their specific use on your specific network.

Firewall Implementation Examples

The following are a few examples of common implementations using firewall technologies.

Packet-Filtering Router

The most common Internet firewall system consists of nothing more than a packet-filtering router deployed between the private network and the Internet. Figure 12.5 shows this configuration.

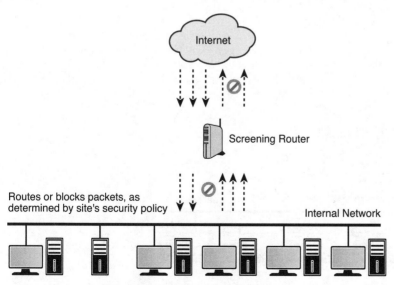

FIGURE 12.5   Packet-filtering router firewall.

A packet-filtering router performs the typical routing functions of forwarding traffic between networks, as well as using packet-filtering rules to permit or deny traffic. Typically, the filter rules are defined so that hosts on the private network have direct access to the Internet, while hosts on the Internet have limited access to systems on the private network. The external posture of this type of firewall system dictates that all traffic that is not specifically permitted be denied.

Although this firewall system has the benefit of being inexpensive and transparent to users, it possesses all the limitations of a packet-filtering router, such as exposure to attacks from improperly configured filters and attacks that are tunneled over permitted services. Because the direct exchange of packets is permitted between outside systems and inside systems, the potential extent of an attack is determined by the total number of hosts and services to which the packet-filtering router permits traffic. This means that each host directly accessible from the Internet needs to support sophisticated user authentication, and the network administrator needs to examine each host for signs of an attack. Also, if the single packet-filtering router is penetrated, every system on the private network could be compromised.

Screened Host Firewalls

The second firewall example employs both a packet-filtering router and a bastion host, as in Figure 12.6. This firewall system provides higher levels of security than the previous example because it implements both Network Layer security (packet-filtering) and Application Layer security (proxy services). In addition, an intruder has to penetrate two separate systems to compromise the security of the private network.

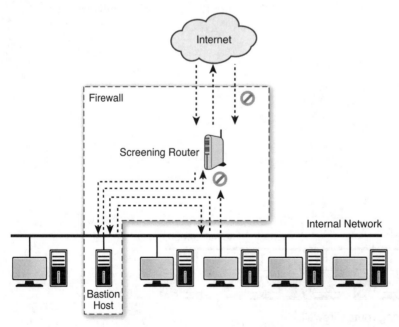

FIGURE 12.6   Screened host firewall system (single-homed bastion host).

For this firewall system, the bastion host is configured on the private network with a packet-filtering router between the Internet and the bastion host. The filtering rules on the exposed router are configured so that outside systems can access only the bastion host; traffic addressed to all other internal systems is blocked. Because the inside hosts reside on the same network as the bastion host, the security policy of the organization determines whether inside systems are permitted direct access to the Internet or whether they are required to use the proxy services on the bastion host. Inside users can be forced to use the proxy services by configuring the router's filter rules to accept only internal traffic originating from the bastion host.

One benefit of this firewall system is that a public information server providing web and FTP services can be placed on the segment shared by the packet-filtering router and the bastion host. If the strongest security is required, the bastion host can run proxy services that require both internal and external users to access the bastion host before communicating with the information server. If a lower level of security is adequate, the router can be configured to grant outside users direct access to the public information server.

An even more secure firewall system can be constructed using a dual-homed bastion host system, such as the one illustrated in Figure 12.7. A dual-homed bastion host has two network interfaces, but the host's capability to directly forward traffic between the two interfaces bypassing the proxy services is disabled. The physical topology forces all traffic destined for the private network through the bastion host and provides additional security if outside users are granted direct access to the information server.

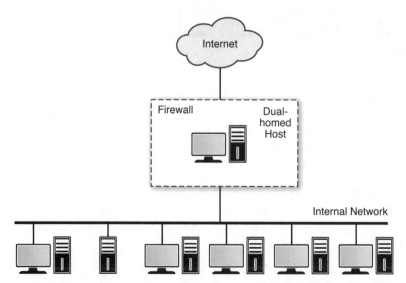

FIGURE 12.7   Screened host firewall system (dual-homed bastion host).

Demilitarized Zone or Screened-Subnet Firewall

The final firewall example employs two packet-filtering routers and a bastion host, as in Figure 12.8. This firewall system creates the most secure firewall system because it supports both Network Layer and Application Layer security while defining a demilitarized zone (DMZ) network. The network administrator places the bastion host, information servers, modem pools, and other public servers on the DMZ network. The DMZ network functions as a small, isolated network positioned between the Internet and the private network. Typically, the DMZ is configured so that systems on the Internet and systems on the private network can access only a limited number of systems on the DMZ network, but the direct transmission of traffic across the DMZ network is prohibited.

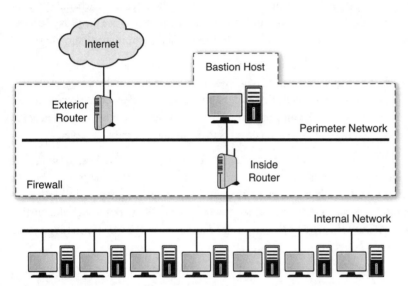

FIGURE 12.8   Screened-subnet firewall system.

For incoming traffic, the outside router protects against the standard external attacks (source IP address spoofing, source routing attacks, and so forth) and manages Internet access to the DMZ network. It permits external systems to access only the bastion host (and possibly the information server). The inside router provides a second line of defense, managing DMZ access to the private network by accepting only traffic originating from the bastion host.

For Internet-bound traffic, the inside router manages private network access to the DMZ network. It permits internal systems to access only the bastion host (and possibly the information server). The filtering rules on the outside router require use of the proxy services by accepting only Internet-bound traffic from the bastion host.

The deployment of a screened-subnet firewall system delivers several key benefits:

- An intruder must crack three separate devices without detection (see the next section of this chapter) to infiltrate the private network: the outside router, the bastion host, and the inside router.

- Because the outside router advertises the DMZ network only to the Internet, systems on the Internet do not have routes to the protected private network. This allows the network manager to ensure that the private network is "invisible" and that only selected systems on the DMZ are known to the Internet via routing table and DNS information exchanges.

■ Because the inside router advertises the DMZ network only to the private network, systems on the private network do not have direct routes to the Internet. This guarantees that inside users must access the Internet via the proxy services residing on the bastion host. Packet-filtering routers direct traffic to specific systems on the DMZ network, eliminating the need for the bastion host to be dual-homed. The inside router supports greater packet throughput than a dual-homed bastion host when it functions as the final firewall system between the private network and the Internet. Because the DMZ network is a different network than the private network, a NAT can be installed on the bastion host to eliminate the need to renumber or resubnet the private network.

Why Is NAT Important to Network Security?

NAT is designed to conserve IP addresses when using IPv4. NAT permits private IP networks that use unregistered IP addresses to connect to the Internet. NAT operates on a perimeter router, usually connecting two networks, and translates the private (not globally unique) addresses in the internal network into legal addresses before packets are forwarded to another network.

A feature of NAT is that it can be configured to advertise only one address for the entire network to the outside world. This provides additional security by effectively hiding the entire internal network behind that address. NAT offers the dual functions of security and address conservation and is typically implemented in remote-access environments. (Source: www.cisco.com/c/en/us/support/docs/ip/network-address-translation-nat/26704-nat-faq-00.html)

Choose Wisely!

In considering the deployment of an Internet firewall, there is no single answer or any one correct design. Decisions on how to build firewall architecture are influenced by many different factors related to corporate security policies, technical background of the staff, costs, and the perceived threat level. However, because the benefits of connecting to the Internet are certain to exceed the related costs to implement and maintain a secure connection, network managers can design a level of safety commensurate with the needs, resources, and risk tolerance of a client. A network can be made as safe as need be if the proper precautions are taken.

By adding one other element to the building blocks for secure networks—intrusion detection systems and/or intrusion prevention systems—you can keep an eye out for problems before they get out of hand. An IDS and IPS work in conjunction with routers and firewalls by monitoring and standing as a sentry on guard to protect your networks against attacks.

Intrusion Detection Systems

An intrusion detection system (IDS) attempts to detect an intruder breaking into your system or an authorized user misusing system resources. The IDS operates constantly on your system, working in the background, and notifies you only when it detects something it considers suspicious or illegal.

Potential intruders fall into two major classifications:

- Outside intruders
- Inside intruders

IDSs are needed to detect both types of intrusions: break-in attempts from the outside and knowledgeable insider attacks. Effective intrusion detection systems detect both.

As you have seen all along, security policies define what's permitted and what's denied on your computer systems. The two basic philosophical options in designing policy follow:

- Prohibit everything that is not expressly permitted (restrictive posture).
- Permit everything that is not expressly denied (permissive posture).

Generally, people more concerned about security exercise the first option. Policies are put in place to describe exactly what operations are allowed on a system. Any operation that is not detailed in the policy will be considered banned on the system.

Others who operate their systems under the spirit of cooperative computing typically adopt the second philosophy. Unfortunately, this philosophy does not work well in today's hostile computing environments.

What Kind of Intrusions?

Before discussing the detection or prevention of intrusions, it is important to understand what is meant by an intrusion. Intrusions are defined relative to a security policy. Unless you decide what is and what is not allowed on your system, trying to detect intrusions is pointless.

An intrusion is defined as any set of actions that attempt to compromise the integrity, confidentiality, or availability of a resource. Intrusions can be categorized into two main classes:

- Misuse intrusions are well-defined attacks on known weak points within a system. They can be detected by watching for certain actions being performed on certain objects.
- Anomaly intrusions are based on observations of deviations from normal system usage patterns. They are detected by building up a profile of the system in question and detecting significant deviations from this profile.

Because misuse intrusions follow well-defined patterns, they can be detected by doing pattern matching on audit trail information. Anomalous intrusions are detected by observing significant deviations from normal behavior. An anomaly could be a symptom of a possible intrusion. Given a set of metrics that can define normal system usage, abnormal patterns of system usage can detect security violations.

Anomaly detection can also use other mechanisms, such as neural networks (networks that learn with experience and can remember patterns of behavior that it witnesses), machine learning classification techniques (pattern matching), and even efforts to mimic biological immune systems (such as antivirus and cell repair).

Anomalous intrusions are harder to detect. No fixed patterns can be monitored here, so a more complex approach is needed. Ideally, a system that combines humanlike pattern-matching capabilities with the vigilance of a computer program could eliminate most problems.

Many intrusion detection systems base their operations on analysis of operating system audit trail data. This data forms a footprint of system usage over time. Audit trails are convenient sources of data and are readily available on most systems. Using audit trail observations, the IDS can compute metrics about a computer network's overall state and decide whether an intrusion is occurring.

Characteristics of Good Intrusion Detection Systems

An intrusion detection system should address the following issues, regardless of what mechanism it uses:

- It must run continually without human supervision. The system should be reliable enough to run autonomously in the background of the system being observed.

- It must be fault tolerant. It must survive a system crash without requiring the rebuilding of the IDS's knowledge base each time the system is restarted.

- It must resist subversion. The system should monitor itself to ensure that it has not been subverted.

- It must impose minimal overhead on the attached network.

- It must observe deviations from normal behavior.

- It must be easily tailored to the network in question. Every system has different usage patterns, and the defense mechanisms should adapt easily to these patterns.

- It must cope with changing system behavior over time as new applications are being added. The system profile will change over time, and the IDS must be capable of adapting.

False Positives, False Negatives, and Subversion Attacks

IDS processing errors are categorized as false positives, false negatives, or subversion errors. A false positive occurs when the system classifies an action as anomalous (a possible intrusion) when it is a legitimate action. A false negative occurs when an actual intrusive action has occurred, but the system allows it to pass as nonintrusive behavior. A subversion error occurs when an intruder modifies the operation of the intrusion detector to force false negatives to occur.

False positive errors lead users of the intrusion detection system to ignore its output because it classifies legitimate actions as intrusions. This type of error should be minimized (completely eliminating it might not be possible), to provide useful information to the operators. If too many false positives are generated, the operators will come to ignore the output of the system over time, which could lead to an actual intrusion being detected but ignored.

A false negative error occurs when an action proceeds even though it is an intrusion. False negative errors are more serious than false positive errors because they give a misleading sense of security. If these actions are allowed to proceed, a suspicious action will not be brought to the attention of the operator. The intrusion detection system then is a liability because the security of the system is less than it was before the intrusion detector was installed.

Subversion errors are more complex and tie in with false negative errors. An intruder could use knowledge about the internals of an intrusion detection system to alter its operation, possibly allowing anomalous behavior to proceed. The intruder could then violate the system's operational security constraints. A human operator examining the logs from the intrusion detector might discover it, but the intrusion detection system would still appear to be working correctly.

Another form of subversion error is fooling the system over time. Because the detection system is observing behavior on the system over time, it might be possible to carry out operations that pose no threat individually but form a threat to system integrity in aggregate. How would this happen? As mentioned previously, the detection system is continually updating its notion of normal system usage. As time goes by, a change in system usage patterns is expected, and the detection system must cope with this. But if an intruder could perform actions over time that are just slightly outside normal system usage patterns, the actions could be accepted as legitimate even though they form part of an intrusion attempt. The detection system would come to accept each of the individual actions as slightly suspicious, but not a threat to the system. It would not recognize the combination of these actions as a serious threat to the system.

Intrusion Prevention Systems

Using the concepts of intrusion detection, intrusion prevention systems (IPSs) go one step further. The IPS typically sits directly behind the firewall, in line with network traffic, and performs an additional layer for the analysis of traffic. Unlike an IDS, which behaves as a passive system that scans traffic and reports back on threats, the IPS actively analyzes and performs actions on all traffic flows that enter the network, including these:

- Sending an alarm to the administrator (such as an IDS)
- Blocking traffic from the source address
- Resetting the connection

As an in-line security component, the IPS must work efficiently to avoid degrading network performance. It must also work fast because exploits can happen in near real time. In addition, the IPS must detect and respond accurately, to eliminate threats and false positives (legitimate packets misread as threats). The IPS has a number of detection methods for finding exploits, but signature-based detection and statistical anomaly–based detection (described earlier) are the two prevailing mechanisms.

With packet-filtering routers, firewalls, proxies, and intrusion detection and/or prevention systems in place, network managers can protect their networks from both internal and external threats while still keeping the channels of communications open for customers and employees on the outside.

Virtual Private Networks

A virtual private network, or VPN, is a network technology that makes it possible to establish private "tunnels" over the public Internet, reducing the cost of dedicated private network connections such as leased lines and dial-up networks. The three primary uses for VPNs are for employee remote access to corporate networks, extranet connections with business partners and suppliers, and branch office networks. All that is needed for a VPN is a specialized firewall, client, or server software (to initiate and maintain a connection) and an Internet service provider (ISP) connection for Internet connectivity.

The original and most popular version is IP version 4, or IPv4. The next generation of IP, called IP version 6, or IPv6, is intended to eventually replace IPv4, which still carried the vast majority of Internet traffic as of 2013. As of September 2013, the percentage of users reaching Google services over IPv6 surpassed 2 percent for the first time. IPv6 mandates the use of a new set of security features that are optionally available for IPv4. These features, called IP security, or IPSec, operate at both the Network Layer and the Session Layer of the TCP/IP protocol stack.

To answer some of the enhanced security requirements that are mandatory as Internet demand increases, certain vendors of networking systems are responding with both proprietary (customized for a manufacturer, not based on industry standards) and nonproprietary (standardized) solutions that tunnel private traffic over public networks such as the Internet.

IPSec

The Internet Engineering Task Force (IETF) developed IPSec as RFC 1825-9, based on the work conducted in the Automotive Network exchange (ANX) project (now run by ANXeBusiness Corp.) by the Big 3 automakers. IPSec performs both encryption and authentication to address the inherent lack of security on IP-based networks. Its design supports most of the security goals: sender authentication, message integrity, and data confidentiality. IPSec operates by encapsulating an IP packet within another packet that surrounds it and then encrypts the result. IPSec provides security without requiring organizations to modify user applications.

Just as TCP/IP networks operate using a series of layers, security processing can occur at one or more layers of the protocol stack. IPSec is designed to operate at the Network Layer of TCP/IP, enabling applications operating at higher layers (such as public key cryptography) to enhance the security that an IPSec-compliant network already provides.

Communication using computer networks can be deemed secure only when it meets three characteristics:

- Sender authentication, to prove that messages originate from their advertised source
- Message integrity, to ensure that messages arrive intact and unaltered
- Confidentiality, to ensure that only the intended receiver can successfully read private messages that are sent

IPSec meets these requirements using two security mechanisms:

- Authentication header (AH)
- Encapsulating Security Protocol (ESP)

The authentication header modifies IP datagrams by adding an attribute field that enables receivers to check the authenticity of the data within the datagram.

AH provides connectionless data integrity, data authentication, and protection against replay attacks.

FYI: Replay Attack

A replay attack is a repeat transmission of a valid data transmission that was already conducted, typically a malicious action meant to cover the perpetrator's fraudulent intent, such as replaying a log-in activity that was recorded when the legitimate user first logged in. These attacks can occur when a man in the middle of a conversation stream collects and stores the communication and then goes back through the stream looking for authentication credentials or session initiation messages.

The added block of data on IPSec packets is called an integrity value check (IVC). It is generally used to carry a message authentication code (MAC) or a digital signature (a message digest signed using the sender's private key—see Chapter 11). Protection against replay attacks is provided by adding a sequence number to the packet to prevent reprocessing if it's received multiple times. IPSec can be operated in one of two basic modes:

- Transport mode, in which protection is applied to upper-layer protocols (TCP or UDP)
- Tunnel mode, in which an entire IP packet is wrapped inside a new IP packet and attached with a new IP header before it's transmitted through the public network

The destination address contained in the new header is an IPSec-capable host that unwraps the packet and sends it to its ultimate destination. A benefit of tunneling is the capability to hide source and destination addresses before data is sent, thus increasing communications security.

Because IPSec defines the framework for using IP securely, it does not mandate specific cryptographic algorithms. Instead, it's written to permit the uses of a variety of cryptosystems for MAC and/or digital signatures.

Encapsulating Security Protocol

The Encapsulating Security Protocol (ESP) provides one or more of these security services:

- Confidentiality (in IPSec tunnel mode)
- Connectionless data integrity
- Data origin authentication
- Protection against replay attacks

Unlike AH, ESP operates under the principle of encapsulation; encrypted data is sandwiched between an ESP header and an ESP trailer.

Again, IPSec does not mandate the use of any specific cryptosystem for confidentiality or sender authentication, but it supports a number of cryptographic algorithms.

Security Association

AH and ESP require certain parameters that both senders and receivers must agree on before communication can take place. To manage these parameters, IPSec uses the concept of a security association (SA).

A security association is a secure "connection" between two endpoints that applies a security policy and keys to protect information. You can think of an SA as the set of data that describes how a given communication will be secured. An SA is uniquely identified by the combination of these three fields:

- IP destination address
- Security protocol identifier (AH or ESP)
- Security parameter index (SPI)

IPSec stores these security associations in a database called the security association database (SAD). The database stores all the parameters used for a specific SA and is consulted each time a packet is sent or received.

SAs contain the actual keys used for encrypting data or signing message authentication codes or message digests. Because key exchange is normally performed out-of-band to the communication that will use these keys to communicate, IPSec provides a separate protocol for exchanging security associations. Using this approach, IPSec separates its key-management mechanisms from other security mechanisms, enabling the substitution of key-management protocols without affecting the implementation of the security mechanism (see Chapter 11).

The protocol to negotiate security associations under IPSec is called Internet Security Association and Key Management Protocol (ISAKMP).

> **FYI: Out-of-Band Communications**
>
> Out-of-band communications occur when a secondary mode of communications is established to share information needed to communicate successfully in the primary channel. An example is sharing a secret key to encode or decode messages using postal mail and then applying the secret key to Internet-based communications.
>
> Imagine that you and your friend want to encrypt your email to one another, but you don't want to share the key that you use for encryption and decryption using email. You can send your friend the key using FedEx, and she can load it into her email program so that she can encrypt the messages she sends you and can decrypt the messages that you send to her.

Internet Security Association and Key Management Protocol

Internet Security Association and Key Management Protocol (ISAKMP) is not usable on its own because it defines a general framework or structure to use one of any number of possible key exchange protocols. To make ISAKMP useful, IPSec associates it with other session key exchange and establishment mechanisms. The Oakley Key Determination Protocol is one such mechanism. Together, ISAKMP and Oakley result in a new protocol, called Internet Key Exchange (IKE).

Oakley Key Determination Protocol

Oakley uses a hybrid Diffie-Hellman key exchange protocol to exchange session keys on Internet hosts and routers. (The Diffie-Hellman protocol enables two users to exchange a key over an insecure medium without any prior association or set of steps.) Oakley optionally provides the security property called perfect forward secrecy (PFS). In addition to providing traditional key exchange under Diffie-Hellman, Oakley can be used to derive new keys from old keys or to distribute keys by encrypting them with a different shared secret key. Oakley consists of three components:

- Cookies exchange for stateless connections (such as the Internet)

- Diffie-Hellman public key values exchange mechanism

- Authentication mechanism with the options of anonymity, perfect forward secrecy on the identities, and/or nonrepudiation

Security Policies

IPSec protects traffic based on the policy choices defined in the security policy database (SPD). The SPD is used for decision making on each packet of traffic. Information in the SPD is consulted to determine whether a packet will undergo IPSec transformation, be discarded, or be allowed to bypass IPSec. The database contains an ordered list of rules that define which IP packets within the network will be affected by the rule and enforces the scrutiny or transformation by the IPSec gateway server(s). SPD rules correspond to SAs in the SA database. The SPD, which the network administrator configures, is consulted with each receipt or transmission of IPSec (AH or ESP) packets and refers to entries within the SAD.

IPSec Key Management

As you've seen, IPSec requires generating and sharing multiple keys to carry out its security features. Following are three of the most common methods used for key exchanges:

- Manual key exchange
- Simple Key Interchange Protocol (SKIP)
- ISAKMP/Oakley

The simplest and most widely used method for key exchange is the manual key exchange, defined in Internet Engineering Task Force RFC 1825. Using the manual exchange, a person manually configures each system with its own keys and those needed to communicate with other VPNs. Keys generated and managed under this approach are manually entered into the security association database.

Simple Key Exchange Protocol is a key-management standard proposed by Sun Microsystems. SKIP is based on generating a shared secret using Diffie-Hellman, with already authenticated public key values.

The IETF selected ISAKMP as the key-management protocol for IPSec in September 1996. ISAKMP is used to negotiate security associations using the parameters (keys, protocols, and so forth) related to any security mechanism. ISAKMP is needed to negotiate, establish, modify, and delete security associations and their corresponding data.

Applied VPNs

With the advent of modern application of VPN technology, branch office networks and extranets (partner-attached networks) are typically based on IPSec, whereas remote access networks for employees working at remote locations or from home (telecommuting) are typically based on SSL.

SSL VPNs have an advantage related to implementation because they require no end-user software for establishment and operation. Connections originate from an Internet-accessible URL that the company gives its authorized users and, most often, a second-factor authentication token (such as RSA's SecureID Token). After authentication, users have access to the corporate network as though they're attached to it via a wire-line connection while in the office.

IPSec-based VPNs are usually found for establishing networks that create an extension of the internal network to other branch offices for the company, reducing the need for dedicated network connections (such as Frame Relay) and also reducing the costs of network maintenance.

Extranets are similar but come with additional restrictions on what can be accessed on the Internal network. Suppliers, partners, and others who need to regularly exchange information can be set up with an extranet using IPSec. These types of connections could be to services for purchasing, sales force management, and so on.

Cloud Computing

No discussion of computer networks is complete without cloud computing. Cloud computing has expanded to offer virtually any computer service via the cloud. You will use Software as a Service (SaaS), Platform as a Service (PaaS), Infrastructure as a Service (IaaS), and Network as a Service (NaaS). With the advent, rise, and increasing sophistication of virtual machines (VMs), computing power is at an all-time high and companies want to capitalize on their investments by offering expanded processing power by subscribing to their service. Assembling your own server farms, adding network capabilities, and building new data centers for backup and recovery from disasters once was quite expensive, but cloud computing has made these activities almost trivial.

Some of the more popular cloud services that have sprung up over the last decade include DropBox, for personal or business storage of documents that provides ubiquity wherever there's Internet access; large providers such as Amazon.com, which can deliver amazing amounts of bandwidth rapidly (such as when streaming movies to home TVs), and Salesforce.com, which serves as a global sales, customer relationship management, and marketing management platform for companies. At the time of publication, we've just begun to see how cloud computing is taking over.

Cloud computing raises as many information security questions as it answers. Concerns about security in the cloud remain pervasive but are being addressed little by little. The Cloud Security Alliance (https://cloudsecurityalliance.org/) is leading the effort to address security in the cloud.

Summary

The content of the Telecommunications, Network, and Internet Security domain is broad, deep, and complex. This domain is one of the most important areas for security practitioners to understand well because modern computing is highly reliant on communication for success.

After you have gained a level of comfort in how network communications operate with the aid of the OSI model, you can begin to determine where malicious activity threatens the network; then you can begin to mix and match the building blocks of network security tools and techniques to implement defense in depth to preserve confidentiality, integrity, and availability.

It's not essential to memorize all the various firewall architectures or how VPNs operate under the covers, but it is important to know how to find this information and how to decide which architecture is most appropriate for a given situation. No cookbooks or recipes work for all conditions, but the principles of network security will guide you to the right solutions at the right time.

Test Your Skills

MULTIPLE-CHOICE QUESTIONS

1. Which of the following ISO/OSI layers defines how to address the physical devices on the network?

   A. Session Layer

   B. Data Link Layer

   C. Application Layer

   D. Transport Layer

2. ISO/OSI Layer 6 is which of the following?

   A. Application Layer

   B. Presentation Layer

   C. Data Link Layer

   D. Network Layer

3. Which of the following statements best describes an extranet?

   A. An extranet is an intranet on steroids.

   B. An extranet is an intranet that provides extra services.

   C. An extranet is an intranet that allows specific users outside the network to access its services.

   D. None of the above.

4. Intrusion detection has which of the following sets of characteristics?

   A. It is adaptive rather than preventative.

   B. It is administrative rather than preventative.

   C. It is disruptive rather than preventative.

   D. It is detective rather than preventative.

5. Which of the following statements best describes a firewall?

   A. A firewall is a pass-through device that allows only certain traffic in and out.

   B. A firewall is a network segment off the firewall in which you put systems that require different levels of access than other network components.

   C. A firewall is an external DNS server.

   D. A firewall is a mail relay.

6. Which of the following statements best describes application-level firewalls?

   A. Application-level firewalls operate at OSI protocol Layer 7, the Application Layer.

   B. Application-level firewalls operate at OSI protocol Layer 6, the Presentation Layer.

   C. Application-level firewalls operate at OSI protocol Layer 5, the Session Layer.

   D. Application-level firewalls operate at OSI protocol Layer 4, the Transport Layer.

7. Which of the following is the simplest type of firewall to implement?

   A. A stateful packet-filtering firewall

   B. A packet-filtering firewall

   C. A dual-homed host firewall

   D. An application gateway

8. The Telecommunications, Network, and Internet Security domain of information security is also concerned with the prevention and detection of the misuse or abuse of systems, which poses a threat to the tenets of _____.

   A. Confidentiality, integrity, and entity (CIE)

   B. Confidentiality, integrity, and authenticity (CIA)

   C. Confidentiality, integrity, and availability (CIA)

   D. Confidentiality, integrity, and liability (CIL)

9. Which of the following is most affected by denial-of-service (DoS) attacks?

   A. Confidentiality

   B. Integrity

   C. Accountability

   D. Availability

10. Which of the following protocols does the Internet use?

   A. NAT

   B. ISO

   C. TCP/IP

   D. SSH

11. Which of the following statements best describes the location of a DMZ?

   A. A DMZ is located immediately behind your first Internet firewall.

   B. A DMZ is located immediately in front of your first Internet firewall.

   C. A DMZ is located immediately behind your first network active firewall.

   D. A DMZ is located immediately behind your first network passive Internet HTTP firewall.

12. Which protocol of the TCP/IP suite addresses reliable data transport?

   A. Transmission Control Protocol (TCP)

   B. User Datagram Protocol (UDP)

   C. Internet Protocol (IP)

   D. Internet Control Message Protocol (ICMP)

13. Which of the following terms is another name for a VPN?

   A. Tunnel

   B. One-time password

   C. Pipeline

   D. Bypass

14. Which of the following advantages does a VPN offer?

   A. A VPN reduces the need for dedicated network connections (such as Frame Relay) and reduces the costs associated with network maintenance.

   B. A VPN is generally more secure than shared network services.

   C. A VPN allows employees and business partners access to the organization's network in a secure manner.

   D. All of the above.

15. Which of the following statements is true of IPSec?

   A. IPSec performs encryption and authentication.

   B. IPSec provides redundant security for IP-based networks.

   C. IPSec is an acronym for International Policy on Security Enforcement Committee.

   D. IPSec existed before the birth of the Internet.

EXERCISES

EXERCISE 12.1: Researching the International Organization for Standardization (ISO)

1. Visit the ISO website at www.iso.org/iso/home/about.htm.

2. Describe how the ISO is organized.

3. Describe how the ISO functions.

4. What services does the ISO provide in addition to the standardization of computer networks?

EXERCISE 12.2: Investigating a Layer of the OSI

1. Review the OSI seven-layer model.

2. Choose one of the several layers of the OSI protocol stack to research in detail.

3. Write a paper on what you've discovered. Describe how that layer is used to transform or provide context to the data in the lower level just below it and how it prepares data for the level above it.

EXERCISE 12.3: Researching a Security Mechanism

1. Investigate in greater detail one of the eight security mechanisms defined by the ISO for network security (digital signatures, traffic padding, access control, or others).

2. Write a paper describing where and how the mechanism is implemented in some computer networks.

EXERCISE 12.4: Comparing the Three Major Data Network Types

1. Describe the form and function of a LAN.

2. Describe the form and function of a WAN.

3. Describe the form and function of an intranet.

PROJECTS

PROJECT 12.1: Building a Home Computer Network

Home computer systems are becoming increasingly sophisticated as the availability of tools at a reasonable price improves.

1. Research articles on the Internet about building a home computer network complete with firewalls and Internet access using Wi-Fi.

2. Describe the basic configuration.

3. How would you configure the firewall? What document would you need to prepare? (See Chapter 4, if needed.)

4. What commercial tools are available to secure your home network? (You might want to go to the following site to begin your research: http://compnetworking.about.com/cs/homenetworking/a/homenetguide.htm.)

5. How would you verify that the security of your network is working as intended?

PROJECT 12.2: Interviewing a Network Administrator

1. Interview a network administrator at your company or school to learn about the type of security controls in place on your network.

2. What types of firewalls are used? For what purposes?

3. Are intrusion detection and/or intrusion prevention systems present? Who monitors them?

4. Ask the network manager what different methods are used to protect the networks that operate the school's record-keeping systems versus the network that's open for student educational uses.

5. Which security posture is adopted on which network segments?

PROJECT 12.3: Researching Intrusion Detection Systems

1. Visit the distributed intrusion detection system called DShield at www.dshield.org/ within the Internet Storm Center.

2. Which types of attacks were most prevalent at the time of your visit to the site?

3. Where is the origin of most of the attacks?

4. What is the status of the Internet Storm Center at the time of your visit?

PROJECT 12.4: Researching Cloud Computing Security

1. Visit the Cloud Security Alliance at https://cloudsecurityalliance.org/.

2. Describe the security standards that have been developed to secure cloud implementations.

3. Describe the CSA STAR program.

4. What types of training does CSA provide to security professionals and cloud providers?

Chapter 13

Software Development Security

Chapter Objectives

After reading this chapter and completing the exercises, you will be able to do the following:

- Describe the importance of security activities throughout the system development life cycle (SDLC) to implement secure systems
- Describe the tasks and activities within each phase of the SDLC needed for an overall secure software program
- Understand the major industry models for measuring the maturity of a secure software development program

Introduction

This chapter, like many of the other domains of the Common Body of Knowledge, deals with the process, people, and technical controls needed to help people develop high-quality software that's secure and capable of long-term use in the face of constant threats from malicious users on the Internet.

If we have learned nothing else from more than 60 years of software development, it's that secure, high-quality code does not happen naturally. National governments have long understood that quality and security must be specified, designed, and implemented from soup to nuts throughout the software development lifecycle (SDLC). Governments go to great lengths to ensure that only provably secure software is used to protect national secrets. Unfortunately, this philosophy has never spilled over into the commercial world, and what we're left with is a precarious branch filled with brittle applications of questionable reliability.

This chapter introduces you to the concepts of securing software throughout its development life cycle. In the early days of computing using mainframe computers and dumb terminals that could communicate only with the mainframe, application developers had little concern for the security of their programs as they were running in the "Glass House," as mainframe data centers were called. As computer systems became increasingly available and computing power moved out of the Glass House and into server rooms and user desktops, the concomitant risk of malicious computer use rose. As you shall see, threats to computer systems have forced the software industry to anticipate and defend against malicious users instead of reacting after an attack.

The Practice of Software Engineering

Software is useful for what it does. People purchase software because it fulfills their need to perform some function. These functions (or features) can be as simple as allowing a user to type a letter or as complex as calculating the fuel consumption for a rocket trip to the moon. Functions and features are the reasons people purchase software, and it's in these terms that people think about software.

People also (erroneously) assume that the software they purchase is written with some degree of quality. When you purchase a software package, you just assume that it will operate as advertised, and you never really think about how well the program does its job—just as long as it works.

The sad truth is that most software is flawed straight out of the box, and these flaws can threaten the security and safety of the very systems on which they operate. These flaws are present not just in the traditional computers we use every day, but also in critical devices, such as our cellphones and medical devices (think pacemakers and cars), and national infrastructures, such as banking and finance, energy, and telecommunications.

Programmers are taught to write code—they are not taught how to write *good code*.

Web applications especially are inherently flawed with certain types of vulnerabilities (such as cross-site scripting, XSS) unless the developer has made a *conscious effort* to prevent it. If the developer fails to include appropriate input validation routines and output encoding routines, the application will most certainly be vulnerable by default to XSS.

To a developer, the software might work just as intended, but the developer never tested it to see how it behaves when it's being fed malicious input or is under direct attack.

Writing software, like driving a car, is a habit. Until someone teaches us how to drive safely, we don't personally know the dangers of driving and the skills needed to prevent or avoid accidents. Cars often have safety mechanisms built into them, but as drivers, we have to consciously use our own safe driving skills. Experience teaches us that we are better off instilling safe driving skills before we let people loose on the roads—their first accident could be their last.

Software Development Life Cycles

What is an SDLC? Some people call it a methodology, others a religion, and still others a set of hand-cuffs that restricts their creative energies. To some degree, everyone who has an opinion on the subject is right. Software engineers have followed a number of different software engineering processes over the years, beginning with no process at all (a.k.a., "spaghetti code" for its resemblance to a disorganized mess and need to use a "code and fix" methodology without any ability to repeat successes from one project to the next), moving on to higher levels of maturity and structure, and, finally, arriving at the more recent agile techniques and languages. Regardless of the process, software engineers undoubtedly perform the same fundamental tasks to build information technology systems:

- Understand the requirements of the system

- Analyze the requirements in detail until the detailed business model is complete

- Determine the appropriate technology for the system based on its purpose and use

- Identify and design program functions

- Code the programs

- Test the programs individually and collectively

- Install the system into a secure "production" environment

FYI: Agile and Scrum Methodology

Agile software development was a direct response to the dominant project management paradigm, the waterfall model, and it borrows many principles from lean manufacturing. When agile development is adopted within an organization, usually one subset of the methodology is chosen. Subsets include Crystal Clear, Extreme Programming (XP), Feature Driven Development, Dynamic Systems Development Method (DSDM), and Scrum. Of the agile methodologies, Scrum has become the most popular and is rooted in the idea of empirical process control. Scrum uses the real-world progress of a project, not a best guess or an uninformed forecast, to plan and schedule releases. In Scrum, projects are divided into explicit work cycles, known as sprints, that typically last one week, two weeks, or three weeks. At the end of each sprint, stakeholders and team members meet to assess the progress of a project and plan its next steps. This allows a project's direction to be adjusted or reoriented based on completed work, not on speculation or predictions. To learn more about agile development and Scrum, visit The Scrum Alliance at www.scrumalliance.org/. (Source: Scrum Methodology, http://scrummethodology.com/)

If you are an aspiring or practicing software engineer, you are most likely familiar with one or more of these methodologies: the simple SDLC, the waterfall model, and the Scrum model. These approaches differ less in their content than in the weighting and ordering of specific tasks within the SDLC. One approach might be more data driven; for example, the data model takes precedence over all else (as in data flow diagramming). Another approach might focus more on user interaction with the system (as with Rational Unified Process/use cases). Regardless, all methodologies fall short in security for their systems. Security risks must be considered and mitigated in all phases of the SDLC.

Table 13.1 shows the security components related to the stages of the SDLC. Consider these a roadmap of security concerns as you traverse the system life cycle process.

TABLE 13.1   SDLC Phases and Associated Security Activities.

SDLC Phase	Security Components and Activities
Phase zero (project inception)	Business stakeholders and project team members should refer to company information security policies and review any overarching legal or regulatory issues that might become risks to the project. For example, the Health Insurance Portability and Accountability Act (HIPAA) would be a concern for a system that will process confidential medical information. In financial services, the Payment Card Industry Data Security Standard (PCI-DSS) dictates how credit card holder data must be secured in processing, transit, and storage. This phase is required to identify which security policies are applicable for the software under development.
System requirements	Project team members should consider threats to the application and potential vulnerabilities as part of the system design. What level of protection is needed for the system data? Who should have access to the data? At what level? Will the data be available for external users? If so, how broad will the user community be? What kind of testing will be required to test system security? Security personnel should be included as part of the requirements-gathering activity to ensure that corporate security requirements are included.
System design	At the design level, security measures/controls needed to meet system security requirements must be identified. These include all legal and regulatory requirements and audit trails to ensure user accountability and responsibility. Is data encryption required? If so, how robust must the encryption be? What kind of security testing is needed at the module (program) level? What about at the subsystem (collection of programs) level or the operating system level? Which security application programming interfaces (APIs) must be used and test plans specified in this phase?
Development	Individual modules must adhere to the security specification requirements. Code scanning and code walkthroughs validate that security features are present. Test plans are adjusted as needed.
Test	Subsystem, module, and full system testing is done to eliminate coding vulnerabilities, errors, bugs, and undesirable behavior, as well as to measure results against the test plans.
Deployment	All testing steps are complete, remediation plans are in place and have been accepted by management, and a response plan is ready for operations to install and launch the application into production.

Don't Bolt Security On—Build It In

Software flaws appear in software because, somewhere along the specification, development, and testing conveyor belt, requirements that mandate secure software fell on the floor and were neglected. Software is secure only when it's designed for security; most attempts at bolting on security after the fact yield more problems than when security is considered from the beginning of a development effort.

To actually make progress in software security, security must be built into the development life cycle itself. This begins with a management-sponsored secure coding initiative to fundamentally improve how an organization thinks about and develops software for public use, in-house use, and sale to others.

Any secure coding initiative must deal with all stages of a program's life cycle. Secure programs are secure by design, during development, and by default. As with any significant change initiative, education plays a key role. Education is the cornerstone to any effective intervention to improve software quality and must not be treated as optional. Before relying on the people involved in software development for secure code, it's essential to administer training in secure design and coding to help the analysts, designers, and developers better understand how incomplete analysis, poor design decisions, and poor coding practices contribute to application and system vulnerabilities.

Once educated, SDLC participants begin behaving differently and start to serve as an internal checks-and-balances mechanism that catches problems earlier in the SDLC and leads to lower costs of development and higher-quality systems.

Education needs to prepare personnel in the basics of web application flaws, familiarize them with the hacking tools of the trade intended to break application software, and prepare them to carry out their craft with new skills and techniques.

Catch Problems Sooner Rather Than Later

From the earliest days of software development, studies have shown that the cost of remediating vulnerabilities or flaws in design is far lower when problems are caught and fixed during the early requirements/design phases than after launching the software into production. Therefore, the earlier you integrate security processes into the development life cycle, the cheaper software development becomes in the long haul.

These security processes are often just common-sense improvements, and any organization can and should adopt them into their existing environment. No one right way of implementing these processes exists—each organization must fine-tune and customize them for its specific development and operating environments. These process improvements add more accountability and structure into the system, too. Several well-accepted secure software development methodologies, including Microsoft's Secure Development Lifecycle (SDL) and Cigital's Touchpoints, are workable options.

Regardless of which software development methodology an organization follows (waterfall, agile, Extreme Programming [XP], and so on), these security processes must be present in some form. Even though the development life cycle explained shortly fits more into custom software development, security-related processes must be included in all life cycle models meant for product development or line-of-business applications within an enterprise's software development practices.

Figure 13.1 provides a high-level overview of the fundamental security and resilience processes that should be integrated into the various SDLC phases, from requirements gathering to deployment and beyond. Each process yields its own findings, and recommendations are prepared to make appropriate changes to design, architecture, source code, use of third-party components, deployment configurations, and other considerations, to help understand and reduce risk to an acceptable level. The following section provides guidance on practices to consider implementing for each phase of development:

- Requirements gathering and analysis

- Systems design and detail designs

- Software coding and reviews

- Testing steps

- Deployment steps

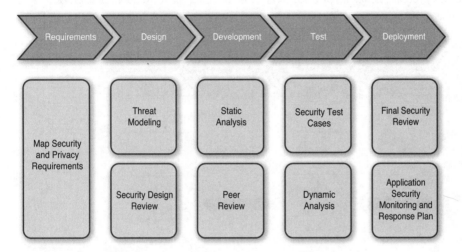

FIGURE 13.1   Security and the SDLC

Requirements Gathering and Analysis

The key activities during the requirements gathering and analysis phase are intended to map out and document the nonfunctional requirements (NFRs) for the system under development. Having these ready before the translation of business requirements into technical requirements begins is vital; designers need to understand the constraints they are expected to face and be prepared to answer the call for security and resilience, as well as other NFRs. To be effective, business systems analysts and systems designers should be sure they are very familiar with the environment in which they are operating by reviewing and maintaining their knowledge in these areas:

- Organizational security policies and standards

- Organizational privacy policy (which might have varying requirements in different places)

- Regulatory requirements (Sarbanes-Oxley, HIPAA, and so on)

- Relevant other industry standards (PCI DSS, ANSI-X9 for banks, and so on)

The NFRs are then mapped against these critical security and resilience goals:

- Confidentiality and privacy

- Integrity

- Availability

- Nonrepudiation

- Auditing

Finally, these security requirements are prioritized and documented for subsequent phases. See Figure 13.2 for an example of this type of mapping.

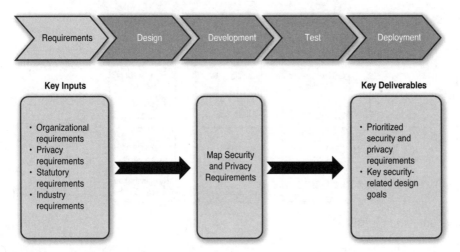

FIGURE 13.2   Requirements phase

Systems Design and Detailed Design

Threat modeling and design reviews are the two major processes commonly found during the design phase. Two classes of vulnerabilities exist: design-related and implementation-related vulnerabilities. The latter are easy to find; the former are expensive and time-consuming to locate and fix if they are not detected early in the SDLC. Security subject matter experts should be deeply involved with the project during this phase to ensure that no bad design issues creep into the design and architecture of the software or the system.

Detailed threat modeling is an excellent way to determine the technical security posture of an application to be developed or under development. It consists of four key steps:

1. Functional decomposition

2. Categorizing threats

3. Ranking threats

4. Mitigation planning

Functional Decomposition

Functional decomposition is typically performed using data flow diagrams. The key aspect of this step is to understand the boundaries of untrusted and trusted components, for a better understanding of the *attack surface* of an application that an attacker might want to exploit.

FYI: What Is an Attack Surface?

The *attack surface* is a highly useful concept to help identify, assess, and mitigate risks in today's software systems. A simple definition of an attack surface is all possible entry points that an attacker can use to attack the application or system under consideration. It is the area within the network or application that is visible to an attacker and can potentially be attacked. The largest contributors to the attack surface, however, are web applications. Whereas a firewall can effectively block typical services such as Telnet and FTP, web applications running on Port 80 (HTTP) and Port 443 (HTTPS) are open to the Internet and anyone wanting to exploit problems.

Categorizing Threats

Even though attackers' goals vary, understanding the different types of threat agents and their potential impacts on an organization is important.

Ranking Threats

Ranking potential threats for a software system requires a fair amount of subjective judgment. The level of damage a successful exploit can cause varies significantly, depending on various factors.

Mitigation Planning

With a list of ranked threats, you can document a high-level mitigation plan by mapping them to the potential vulnerabilities in the software system.

Design Reviews

The next activity in this phase is the security design review. A security subject matter expert (not a member of the core development team) usually carries out the design review, with the key objective of ensuring that the design is "secure from the start." These reviews are typically iterative in nature. They start with the high-level design review and then dive deeply into each component or module of the software.

Threat modeling and design reviews can leverage commercial off-the-shelf tools, custom in-house software, or even simple checklists. Personnel must use their best judgment based on the environment, the organizational structure, and existing processes and practices. See Figure 13.3 for the major steps in the design phase.

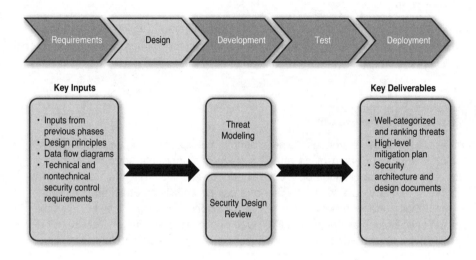

FIGURE 13.3   Design Phase

What Software Threats and Vulnerabilities Must Be Addressed?

The Open Web Application Security Project (OWASP) maintains the OWASP Top 10 as a current list of the 10 most severe web security issues.

The OWASP Top Ten provides a powerful awareness document for web application security. The OWASP Top Ten represents a broad consensus about what the most critical web application security flaws are. You can find the current version of the OWASP Top Ten at https://www.owasp.org/index.php/Category:OWASP_Top_Ten_Project.

Development (Coding) Phase

Activities in the development phase often generate implementation-related vulnerabilities. Static analysis and peer review are two key processes to mitigate or minimize these vulnerabilities.

Static Analysis

Static analysis involves using automated tools to find issues within the source code itself:

- Bug finding (quality perspective)
- Style checks
- Type checks
- Security vulnerability review

Automated security review tools tend to have a high percentage of false positives, but they are very efficient at catching the low-hanging vulnerabilities that plague most application software (lack of input validation, SQL injection, and so on). However, static analysis cannot detect all types of vulnerabilities or security policy violations—manual peer review becomes important at that point.

Peer Review

A peer review process is far more time-consuming than automated analysis, but it is an excellent control mechanism to ensure the quality and security of the code base. Developers review each others' code and provide feedback to the owners (original coders) of the different modules so they can make appropriate changes. Developers can accomplish this with or without specialized tools.

Unit Testing

Unit testing is another key process that many organizations fail to perform regularly but that is important from a security and resilience perspective. Unit testing helps prevent bugs and flaws from reaching the testing phase. Developers can validate certain boundary conditions and prevent vulnerabilities such as buffer overflows and integer over- or underflows within a module or submodule of an application. See Figure 13.4 for a diagram of the security activities in the development phase.

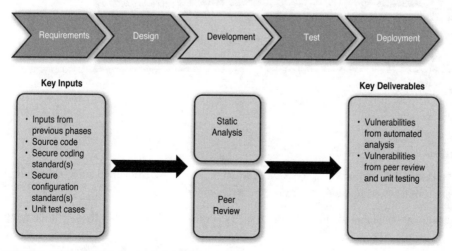

FIGURE 13.4   Development phase

Testing

The test phase is critical for discovering vulnerabilities that were not discovered and fixed earlier. If not already performed in the analysis or design phases, the first step in the test process is to build security test cases. A key input to this process is the systems requirements documentation. The (security) test team uses all the assumptions and business processes captured to create several security test cases. Security testers then use these test cases during dynamic analysis of the application. The software is loaded and operated in the test environment and tested against each of the test cases. A specialized penetration testing team is often deployed during this process. These manual security reviews are effective in discovering business logic flaws in the application.

Dynamic analysis also consists of using automated tools to test for security vulnerabilities. Similar to static analysis tools, these tools are very efficient in ensuring "code complete" scanning coverage and catching high-risk vulnerabilities such as cross-site scripting and SQL injection.

These tests are iterative in nature and result in a list of vulnerabilities that are then ranked for risk and prioritized. The development team fixes these errors and sends the remediated code back for regression testing. See Figure 13.5 for a diagram of the security steps in the test phase of the SDLC.

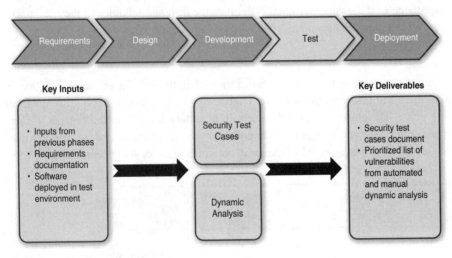

FIGURE 13.5   Test phase

Deployment

The deployment phase is the final phase of the SDLC, when the software is installed and configured in the production environment and made ready for use by its intended audience.

A key part of managing changes is to employ a change advisory board (CAB—see the accompanying FYI).

During the deployment phase, security subject matter experts who might or might not be part of the change advisory board perform a final security review to ensure that the security risks identified during all the previous phases have been fixed or have a mitigation plan in place. During this phase, the development team coordinates with the release management and production support teams to create an application security monitoring and response plan. The production support team, in conjunction with the network/security operation center, uses this plan during the operation of the application to manage security incidents and engage the appropriate teams for response and remediation.

The ongoing monitoring of the application also includes periodic security testing of the application in production, using manual and automated testing techniques to help ensure that new threats and vulnerabilities do not affect the security and resilience of the application because of changes in supporting software or reliant systems. See Figure 13.6 for the security activities in the deployment phase of the SDLC.

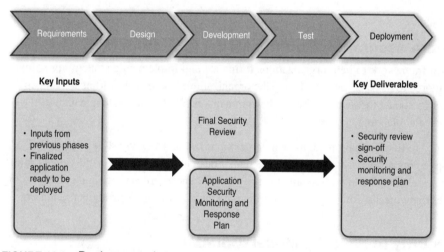

FIGURE 13.6   Deployment phase

FYI: What Is a Change Advisory Board (CAB)?

A change advisory board (CAB) offers the multiple perspectives necessary to ensure good decision making. A CAB is an integral part of a risk management process that is designed to balance the need for change with the need to minimize inherent risks. For example, the CAB is responsible for overseeing the changes in the production environment.

Security Training

Training might not seem to fit directly into any particular SDLC phase, but it plays an important role in improving the overall security and resilience of developed software. Training should be a prerequisite for anyone who has a role anywhere in the software development environment. All developers and other technical members of the software design/development/test teams should undergo security training that explains the responsibilities of their role, establishes the expectations for their part for security and resilience, and provides best practices and guidance for developing high-quality software.

Measuring the Secure Development Program

This section examines two leading software security maturity measurement models, OWASP's Open Software Assurance Maturity Model (OpenSAMM) and the Building Security in Maturity Model (BSIMM).

Open Software Assurance Maturity Model (OpenSAMM)

SAMM is an open framework to help organizations formulate and implement a strategy for software security that is tailored to the specific risks facing the organization. OpenSAMM offers a roadmap and well-defined maturity model for secure software development and deployment, along with useful tools for self-assessment and planning.

SAMM was defined to fit any small, medium, and large organization using any style of an SDLC. The model can be applied organization-wide, for a single line of business, or even on an individual project. OpenSAMM comes as a PDF file with detailed descriptions of each core activity and corresponding security processes that you can download for free from the OpenSAMM website at opensamm.org.

Building Security in Maturity Model (BSIMM)

BSIMM is designed to help you understand, measure, and plan a software security initiative. It was created through a process of understanding and analyzing real-world data from nine leading software security initiatives; it was then validated and adjusted with data from 21 additional leading software security initiatives.

When properly used, BSIMM can help you determine where your organization stands with respect to real-world software security initiatives and what steps can be taken to make your approach more effective.

To help you get started with BSIMM, seek out some free resources on the BSIMM website for collecting information in MS Excel and developing a project implementation plan in MS Project. To find out more about BSIMM, visit bsimm.com.

Summary

In this chapter, you learned about the importance of building security into all phases of the software development life cycle, and you identified which activities are often found in each phase. You also learned about maturity models for measuring the progress and the maturity of the software security program and its role within the overall SDLC.

Secure applications do not come about by accident—only though careful planning and deliberate actions can high-quality software emerge from the software development life cycle. Every phase of the SDLC is rife with iterative activities and steps that require dedicated time and effort explicitly for security and software quality.

Test Your Skills

MULTIPLE-CHOICE QUESTIONS

1. Which of the following statements best describes the process of software development?

   A. The process of software development has remained fundamentally the same over the past several decades.

   B. The process of software development has changed from a passive to an active acceptance of security needs.

   C. The process of software development has outgrown the need for methodology because of increased maturity of development models.

   D. The process of software development has had a diminishing importance since the threat of terrorism has increased.

2. Which of the following statements best defines the SDLC?

   A. The SDLC is a task force committed to promoting consistent software development methodologies across operating platforms.

   B. The SDLC is a branch of the Department of Homeland Security.

   C. The SDLC is a learning center for software design.

   D. The SDLC is a series of activities describing the process of building computer systems.

3. Which of the following statements is true?

   A. Most computer industry experts view security in software as a requirement.

   B. Most computer industry experts view security in software as a nice-to-have feature.

   C. Most computer industry experts view security in software as an elective.

   D. Most computer industry experts view security in software as a foolproof mechanism to thwart computer attacks.

4. The information security staff's participation in which of the following system development life cycle phases provides maximum benefit to the organization?

   A. In parallel with every phase throughout the project

   B. System design specifications phase

   C. Project initiation and planning phase

   D. Development and documentation phase

5. Which of the following statements best defines OWASP?

   A. OWASP is a private consortium of concerned parties working to solve web application security issues.

   B. OWASP is a an open community dedicated to enabling organizations to develop, purchase, and maintain applications that can be trusted.

   C. OWASP is a government-sponsored initiative to improve the security of commercial off-the-shelf software applications.

   D. OWASP is sponsored by software security evaluation vendors and service organizations.

6. The security activity in the Requirements Gathering phase of the SDLC is needed to do which of the following?

   A. Map security and privacy needs

   B. Develop the software that implements security controls

   C. Perform a risk analysis on the intended application

   D. Perform peer reviews of the documentation

7. Which of the following phases of a system development life cycle is most concerned with establishing a sound policy as the foundation for design?

   A. Development/acquisition

   B. Implementation

   C. Initiation

   D. Maintenance

8. The industry standard that mandates everyone who touches credit card information use secure systems is known as which of the following?

   A. ISO/IEC 27002

   B. Federal Information Systems Management Act (FISMA)

   C. Payment Card Industry Data Security Standard

   D. Federal Information Processing Standard (FIPS) 201

9. Which of the following statements best describes BSIMM?

   A. BSIMM is used to measure the maturity of a software assurance program by looking for evidence of security best practices in the SDLC.

   B. BSIMM is used to measure the maturity of a software assurance program by looking for evidence of security procedures in the SDLC.

   C. BSIMM is used to measure the maturity of a software assurance program by looking for evidence of security activities in the SDLC.

   D. BSIMM is used to measure the maturity of a software assurance program by looking for evidence of security requirements in the SDLC.

10. Which of the following statements best describes risk reduction in a system development life cycle?

    A. Risk reduction in a system development life cycle should be applied mostly to the initiation phase.

    B. Risk reduction in a system development life cycle should be applied mostly to the development phase.

    C. Risk reduction in a system development life cycle should be applied mostly to the disposal phase.

    D. Risk reduction in a system development life cycle should be applied equally to all phases.

11. At which of the following stages of the applications development process should the security department become involved?

    A. Before the implementation

    B. Before systems testing

    C. During unit testing

    D. During requirements development

12. Which of the following statements is true?

    A. When considering an IT system development life cycle, security should be mostly considered during the initiation phase.

    B. When considering an IT system development life cycle, security should be mostly considered during the development phase.

    C. When considering an IT system development life cycle, security should be treated as an integral part of the overall system design.

    D. When considering an IT system development life cycle, security should be added after the design is completed.

13. Which of the following statements best defines BSIMM?

    A. BSIMM is designed to help organizations understand, measure, and plan a software security initiative.

    B. BSIMM is a predefined set of process elements that can be integrated into any software development process.

    C. BSIMM is a method to collect and document security requirements.

    D. BSIMM is a method to maintain software assurance results and evidence.

14. The peer review activity is found in which of the following phases of the SDLC?

    A. Design phase

    B. Deployment phase

    C. Development phase

    D. Requirements phase

15. Dynamic analysis is found in which of the following Secure SDLC phases?

    A. Project initiation

    B. Testing phase

    C. Design phase

    D. Development phase

EXERCISES

EXERCISE 13.1: Understanding Security in Application Development

1. Why is application development security important?

2. What elements of application development should security professionals be most concerned with?

3. How can application developers stay current on threats to application software?

EXERCISE 13.2: Researching a "Buffer Overflow" Condition

1. Conduct an Internet search for "buffer overflow or buffer overrun."

2. Read through a number of the sites that appear, and try to find what causes this condition in software.

3. What can developers do to discover buffer overflow problems, as well as other unvalidated input problems in their own software, and eliminate them before releasing the program to users?

EXERCISE 13.3: **Investigating the Importance of the "Sandbox"**

1. Conduct an Internet search of "Java sandbox."

2. Why are Java applications less susceptible to buffer overflow problems?

3. What are the security benefits of the sandbox?

EXERCISE 13.4: **Educating Stakeholders**

Since education and awareness are the cornerstones for a successful secure software development lifecycle:

1. Where would you begin to educate those who are charged with designing and developing custom software for your organization?

2. Who should be trained?

3. What kind of training should they receive?

PROJECTS

PROJECT 13.1: **Researching Efforts to Address Software Security**

1. Find some of the industry and public efforts in the marketplace to address software security.

2. Document in a paper each issue separately:

   Security testing for commercial software

   Software liability issues

   Developer education and awareness

PROJECT 13.2: **Evaluating Offshore Software Development Security**

Increasingly, U.S. organizations are outsourcing software development activities to countries such as India, Pakistan, and China, to gain the benefits of reduced costs and faster turnaround times. But these efforts come at a price.

1. What security issues does overseas development of software raise in commercial and custom systems intended for use in the United States?

2. What privacy issues are raised?

3. How are these issues being addressed?

4. What trends can you determine on the future of offshore development?

5. What is the IT security industry doing to counter the threats from offshore development?

PROJECT 13.3: **Understanding SDLC and Government Regulations**

1. Review the provisions of the Security Rule for the Health Insurance Privacy and Accountability Act (HIPAA) as it relates to software development activities (see www.hrsa.gov/healthit/toolbox/HealthITAdoptiontoolbox/PrivacyandSecurity/hipaarules.html).

2. Review the provisions of Section 404 of the Sarbanes-Oxley Act as it relates to software development activities (see http://msdn.microsoft.com/en-us/library/aa480484.aspx).

3. What role does the SDLC play in compliance with these regulations?

4. What should software security specialists do to help their organizations comply?

5. How can software security specialists help IT auditors better understand what controls are necessary and operating as intended?

Chapter 14

Securing the Future

After reading this chapter and completing the exercises, you will be able to do the following:

- Follow the evolution of increased cybercrimes and efforts to reduce cybercrime
- Discuss the future of information technology (IT) software security developments and the outlook for InfoSec professionals
- Discuss the trends that drive the growth of the industry, technology, and regulations

Introduction

Each chapter from Chapters 4–13 discussed key concepts within the ten domains of the Common Body of Knowledge, or CBK. Students with a solid grounding in these subject areas will be well on the way to earning the professional certification of their choosing. If this is not your intent and you simply want to understand the importance of information security as part of a larger computer science curriculum, you now have a good grasp of the basic principles of this discipline. If you are an information technology (IT) business manager or even a consumer worried about the computer attacks and threats you read about in the news—and, perhaps more important, threats you do not hear about—you have become more mindful of the importance of the subject. Regardless of your goal, this text has given you additional guidance in case you want to investigate a specific topic in greater depth.

With this understanding of IT security in the context of modern business, you can begin to map solutions to problems that you'll encounter in both personal and organizational security issues. In this chapter, we wrap up with a view into trends in cybersecurity and steps being taken to secure the future and protect the networks that modern-day lives depend on.

Operation Eligible Receiver

In 1997, Operation Eligible Receiver demonstrated the potential vulnerabil
ment's information systems. The National Security Agency (NSA) hired 35
lated attacks on the national information structure. The hackers obtained root access (the highest level
of control) in 36 of the government's 40,000 networks. If the exercise had been real, the attackers
would have been able to create power outages across Los Angeles, Chicago, Washington, and New
York. They could have disrupted the U.S. Department of Defense's communication systems (taking
out most of the Pacific Command) and gained access to computer systems aboard U.S. Navy vessels.

It was such a disturbing exercise that several top White House officials at the time spoke of the possibility of an "electronic Pearl Harbor" attack on the U.S. mainland. Added to these vulnerabilities is the
fact that most Americans have no sense of how information warfare would affect them. Worse still, the
attackers discovered that 80 to 90 percent of the nation's critical infrastructure rests in private hands
that the government cannot manage, control, or repair.

The exercise also set a decades-long trajectory for national and international initiatives called Critical
Infrastructure Protection, or CIP. In 1998, President Clinton signed Presidential Decision Directive
(PDD) Number 63 to establish the program.

Take a look at this excerpt the White House Fact Sheet dated May 22, 1998:

> This Presidential Directive builds on the recommendations of the President's Commission on
> Critical Infrastructure Protection. In October 1997, the Commission issued its report calling for
> a national effort to assure the security of the United States' increasingly vulnerable and inter-
> connected infrastructures, such as telecommunications, banking and finance, energy, transpor-
> tation, and essential government services.

Today, most of the U.S. government activity that began from PDD63 has continued and is a comprehensive function of the U.S. Department of Homeland Security. DHS helps deter, prevent, and
mitigate acts of terrorism by assessing vulnerabilities in the context of continuously changing threats.
DHS strengthens the nation's protective posture and disseminates timely and accurate information to
federal, state, local, private, and international partners.

Information Sharing and Analysis Centers (ISACs), the mechanism to inculcate public–private information exchange, have been expanded from the original 8 sectors to 15 sectors, with varying degrees
of participation and maturity. Many of these follow the model established for the banking and finance
sector, called the Financial Services ISAC, or the FS-ISAC (www.fsisac.com). The National Council
of ISACs (NCI; www.isaccouncil.org/home.html) formerly called the ISAC Council, was formed
in 2003 to meet monthly for developing trusted relationships among the CIP sectors and to address
common issues and concerns. Their activities include these:

- Running drills and exercises

- Hosting a private sector liaison at the Department of Homeland Security (DHS)

- Setting up a National Infrastructure Coordinating Center (NICC) during incidents of national
  significance, for emergency classified briefings, and for real-time sector threat-level reporting

⊿ Hosting an annual Critical Infrastructure Protection (CIP) Congress to bring together the critical infrastructure community for networking, learning, and addressing issues of concern to CIKR stakeholders

Carders, Account Takeover, and Identity Theft

The back alleys of the Internet are a dark and murky place where lots of unsavory people find increasingly effective methods to separate you from your money.

Networks upon networks are thriving in the exchange of credit card numbers, PINs, Social Security numbers, credentials for accessing online bank accounts, mother's maiden names, dates of birth, full addresses, and on and on. These sites, usually called Carder sites, are open to a select number of people who prove they're one of them by trading in stolen information.

Credit cards are traded from a few dollars per account to hundreds of dollars, depending on several factors (issuer of the card, proof that it's active and usable, and so on). The sources of this card data include phishing drop sites, databases stolen over the Internet from vulnerable web applications (from SQL injection or other means), and old-fashioned physical dumpster diving activity.

Some Definitions

Often, people lump together all types of financial crimes into a general bucket of identity theft. However, these crimes have their own unique attributes. These definitions should help clear things up:

■ When stolen credit card data is used to transact, it's called credit card fraud.

■ When stolen log-in credentials are used to access a private bank or credit card account, it's called account takeover.

■ When stolen personally identifiable information (PII) is used to open new lines of credit unbeknownst to the victim, it's called identity theft.

These crimes require different degrees of intervention to investigate and *try* to resolve them.

Financial crimes are on the rise and have become more difficult to detect and stop as the sophistication of the carder network and their tools grows.

ZeuS Banking Trojan

Viruses, Trojan horse programs, and malware of all shapes and forms remain with us, but one example deserves special attention, primarily because of its effectiveness, sophistication, and global reach.

The ZeuS Banking Trojan, written for the MS Windows Operating System, was first detected in July 2007 when it was used to attack the U.S. Department of Transportation. Since 2007, ZeuS has morphed into new forms and gained functionality and use. ZeuS steals data from infected computers via web browsers and protected storage. When it's infected, the computer sends the stolen data to a bot command and control (C&C) server, where the data is stored. ZeuS is sold in the criminal underground as a kit for around $3,000 to $4,000 (as of early 2014) and is likely the malware most utilized by criminals specializing in financial fraud. ZeuS has evolved over time and includes a full arsenal of information-stealing capabilities (see www.secureworks.com/cyber-threat-intelligence/threats/zeus/):

- Steals data submitted in HTTP forms

- Steals account credentials stored in Windows Protected Storage

- Steals client-side X.509 public key infrastructure (PKI) certificates

- Steals FTP and POP account credentials

- Steals/deletes HTTP and Flash cookies

- Modifies the HTML pages of target websites for information-stealing purposes

- Redirects victims from target web pages to attacker-controlled ones

- Takes screenshots and scrapes HTML from target sites

- Searches for and uploads files from the infected computer

- Modifies the local hosts file (`%systemroot%\system32\drivers\etc\hosts`)

- Downloads and executes arbitrary programs

- Deletes crucial Registry keys, rendering the computer incapable of booting into Windows

Phishing and Spear Phishing

So how does ZeuS wind up on millions of computers all over the world? Typically, it does so by way of the "drive-by download" and phishing attacks.

If a criminal can somehow convince you to visit a different website than the one you think you're visiting, your browser and computer can be infected with whatever malware the attacker wants you to have. Keystroke recorders, Trojan horse programs (such as ZeuS), and countless others are downloaded to your PC, most often without your knowledge or consent. After your computer installs the programs for them, your PC is what they call "PWNED" (OWNED) in the hacker vernacular. This ownership comes at your expense when you suddenly find your savings account diminished or you see charges on your credit card that you don't recognize.

Spear phishing is even more insidious. It's phishing with a personal touch. It's crafted to target specific people so meticulously that even the most overly cautious person is convinced. Spear phishing is carried out on the criminal's favored targets: users who manage company bank accounts, especially small businesses with commercial banking relationships. Often, companies are unaware of any attacks until the checks begin bouncing. By then, the money is long gone.

Other Trends in Internet (In)Security

The physical world and the cyber world collided when one of the most sophisticated pieces of software was used to take over the control of Iranian nuclear enrichment facilities.

Security research company Kaspersky discovered the Stuxnet worm in 2010. Kaspersky Lab confirmed that Stuxnet is a one-of-a-kind, sophisticated malware attack backed by a well-funded, highly skilled attack team with intimate knowledge of supervisory control and data acquisition (SCADA) technology.

"I think that this is the turning point, this is the time when we got to a really new world, because in the past, there were just cybercriminals, [but] now I am afraid it is the time of cyberterrorism, cyber-weapons, and cyberwars," says Eugene Kaspersky, cofounder and chief executive officer of Kaspersky Lab. "This malicious program was not designed to steal money, send spam, grab personal data—no, this piece of malware was designed to sabotage plants, to damage industrial systems."

Stuxnet's ultimate aim was to access SIMATIC WinCC SCADA, used as industrial control systems that monitor and control industrial, infrastructure, or facility-based processes. Similar systems are widely used in oil pipelines, power plants, large communication systems, airports, ships, and even military installations across the globe.

Kaspersky Lab believes that Stuxnet is a working—and fearsome—prototype of a cyberweapon that will lead to the creation of a new arms race in the world. This time, it will be a cyber arms race. (See www.kaspersky.com/about/news/virus/2010/Kaspersky_Lab_provides_its_insights_on_Stuxnet_worm for more on this interview.)

The Year (Decade?) of the Breach

Annually, at least since 2010, journalists have pondered whether the previous year was the "Year of the Breach." Year after year, breach statistics grow in frequency and size, with no seeming end in sight. The largest breach in U.S. history was a security breach at TJX Corporation (owner of TJ Maxx, Home Goods, and Marshalls), which eclipsed the next-largest breach of 2005 when 40 million debit and credit card numbers were stolen from CardSystems Solutions, a payment card processor. TJX lost 45.6 million credit and debit card numbers over 18 months to an unknown number of intruders. At the time, TJX said it believed the intrusion took place in May 2006 but wasn't discovered until mid-December, 7 months later. A few weeks later, the company revised those dates and said that an investigation by IBM and General Dynamics, two companies it hired in the wake of the breach discovery, believed the intrusion might have taken place in July 2005 (see www.computerworld.com/s/article/9014782/TJX_data_breach_At_45.6M_card_numbers_it_s_the_biggest_ever).

The Christmas shopping season of 2013 started off with a bang at Target Corporation when 40 million credit and debit cards were stolen between November 27 and December 15. A week after Target reported the breach, the company added that encrypted PIN numbers were also stolen from the systems—but said the public should not be worried.

Credit and debit card fraud has nearly quadrupled since the early 2000s. It reached $11.3 billion in losses worldwide in 2013, according to the Nilson Report, a publication for card and mobile payment executives (www.nilsonreport.com).

To keep up with the trends and current happenings related to financial crimes and the tools and techniques these criminals use, regularly visit the site Krebs on Security, hosted by Brian Krebs, a former journalist for *The Washington Post* (www.krebsonsecurity.com). Krebs writes extensively on the topic and shares his insights and investigations with his readership.

The Rosy Future for InfoSec Specialists

Dealing with some of the previously described problems (and they are only the tip of the iceberg!) has motivated companies and other organizations to turn to highly trained information security professionals for answers and solutions. It's only a matter of time before the spirit of self-regulation is undone with increasingly stringent regulations and certifications for companies to remain in business. Companies understand that they need to hire the right professionals with the right expertise. Otherwise, the potential negative impact on their business could be enormous.

Demand for information security experts in the United States is outstripping the available supply by a widening margin, according to a pair of reports from 2012 and 2013. Burning Glass Technologies, which develops technology to match people with jobs, conducted a report based on a study of job postings for cybersecurity professionals placed by U.S. businesses and government agencies. The report shows that demand for cybersecurity professionals over the past 5 years grew 3.5 times faster than demand for other IT jobs and about 12 times faster than for *all* other jobs.

Julie Peeler, director of the (ISC)^2 Foundation, the developer of the CISSP program, says soaring demand is undoubtedly exacerbating an already difficult demand-and-supply situation for security experts. In 2014, Peeler estimated a need for 330,000 more IT security professionals worldwide. A recent foundation survey of some 12,000 information security professionals worldwide found that a shortage of talent has had a dramatic impact on the capability of organizations to defend against or recover from a cyberattack. More than half of the respondents to the (ISC)^2 survey said the shortage affects the capability of their organizations to defend against cyberthreats. This growing shortage has meant better salaries for information security professionals compared to many other IT jobs (see www.computerworld.com/s/article/9237394/Demand_for_IT_security_experts_outstrips_supply).

Although these numbers bode well for someone considering a career in InfoSec, what do they mean for the industry in general? Does an increase in the numbers of the local police force mean that the town is getting serious about fighting crime or that the crime rate is out of control?

Should we take an increase in the number of InfoSec professionals as a preventative measure on the part of organizations or as a type of damage control? No one knows for sure, partly because organizations that have been hacked are reluctant to make this generally known. However, with heightened interest in Internet security from the consumer and increased pressure from governments to make systems safer, we can safely surmise that those who specialize in this field will be highly sought-after individuals in IT for many years to come.

Summary

The Common Body of Knowledge (CBK) consists of ten areas of study and discipline, ranging from security management practices to laws, investigations, and ethics. Although the future direction of information security is as uncertain as the technology it protects, experts indicate that constant vigilance and monitoring are critical to keeping systems safe and secure.

Security experts must improve their ability to predict, not just react to, the future. Cybercrime is increasing annually, and the efforts to reduce these problems must also increase. Colleges need to improve their information security curriculum, and the industry as a whole must do a better job of educating the public about the importance of information security.

Improved technologies such as intelligent agents, improved preventative measures, and applied defensive programming are needed to ensure the security design of new applications. Creating a culture of information security specialists who are motivated, skilled, prepared, and available as needed is critical for the future of society.

Are you ready to join?

Test Your Skills

MULTIPLE-CHOICE QUESTIONS

1. Encryption/decryption belongs to which of the following CBK domains?

   A. Security Architecture and Design

   B. Cryptography

   C. Business Continuity Planning and Disaster Recovery Planning

   D. Operations Security

2. Risk assessment belongs to which of the following CBK domains?

   A. Physical (Environmental) Security

   B. Legal, Regulations, Investigations, and Compliance

   C. Telecommunications and Network Security

   D. Information Security Governance and Risk Management

3. Virtual private networks (VPNs) belong to which of the following CBK domains?

   A. Telecommunications and Network Security

   B. Physical (Environmental) Security

   C. Information Security Governance and Risk Management

   D. Access Control

4. Perimeter alarm systems belong to which of the following CBK domains?

   A. Access Control

   B. Operations Security

   C. Information Security Governance and Risk Management

   D. Physical (Environmental) Security

5. Software copyrighting belongs to which of the following CBK domains?

   A. Cryptography

   B. Telecommunications and Network Security

   C. Legal, Regulations, Investigations, and Compliance

   D. Business Continuity and Disaster Recovery Planning

6. The OSI Model belongs to which of the following CBK domains?

   A. Security Architecture and Design

   B. Software Development Security

   C. Access Control

   D. Network and Telecommunications Security

7. Retina scanning belongs to which of the following CBK domains?

   A. Physical (Environmental) Security

   B. Access Control

   C. Operations Security

   D. Legal, Regulations, Investigations, and Compliance

8. Intrusion detection belongs to which of the following CBK domains?

   A. Physical (Environmental) Security

   B. Cryptography

   C. Network and Telecommunications Security

   D. Access Control

9. Cold-site facility belongs to which of the following CBK domains?

   A. Business Continuity Planning and Disaster Recovery Planning

   B. Security Architecture and Design

   C. Information Security Governance and Risk Management

   D. Physical (Environmental) Security

10. CGI scripting belongs to which of the following CBK domains?

    A. Software Development Security

    B. Telecommunications and Network Security

    C. Operations Security

    D. Access Control

11. Which of the following best defines carders?

    A. An underground hacker network for the trafficking of stolen credit and debit cards

    B. Identity thieves

    C. Hackers who extricate data from government databases

    D. Germ-warfare agents

12. Which of the following factors might account for an increasing need for information security specialists?

    A. Increased government regulation

    B. Heightened public awareness

    C. Growth of Internet technologies

    D. All of the above

13. What was the purpose of Operation Eligible Receiver?

    A. To test the readiness of the NFL's computer systems

    B. To detect the robustness of Iraqi computer systems

    C. To test the security strength of our national computer systems

    D. To determine whether hackers were compromising the National Security Agency's email system

14. Which of the following statements best describes the President's 1998 Commission on Critical Infrastructure Protection?

    A. It was the result of Presidential Decision Directive 63, signed by President Clinton in 1998.

    B. It was a national effort to secure critical U.S. infrastructures.

    C. It was an interagency effort to recommend a holistic framework for solving problems with critical systems such as finance, energy, and communications.

    D. All of the above.

15. Which of the following statements best describes Stuxnet?

    A. Stuxnet is a network of security professionals.

    B. Stuxnet is a network that disseminates timely information about security threats to federal, state, and local agencies.

    C. Stuxnet is a piece of sophisticated malware that bridges and threatens the cyber and physical world.

    D. Stuxnet is a network that trades in stolen banking information.

EXERCISES

EXERCISE 14.1: Researching Hacking

1. Using your favorite Internet search engine, find some stories about white-hat hackers.

2. How do white-hat hackers differ from gray-hat hackers?

3. How do white-hat hackers differ from black-hat hackers?

EXERCISE 14.2: Understanding Presidential Decision Directive 63

1. Download and read the Fact Sheet for Presidential Decision Directive 63 (www.fas.org/irp/offdocs/pdd-63.htm).

2. What are the main points of the directive?

3. In what ways has this directive impacted information security?

EXERCISE 14.3: Comparing Private Sector Careers to Public Sector Careers in IT Security

1. Investigate the pros and cons of pursuing a career in information security in the private and public sectors.

2. What are some of the advantages and disadvantages in working for industry versus working for the government?

EXERCISE 14.4: Assessing Attitudes in Security

1. Describe some ways your personal attitude toward information security has changed as a result of this course.

2. Can you imagine that your behavior when using computers will change as a result of this course? What will you do differently?

PROJECTS

PROJECT 14.1: Staying Current in the Field

1. From the (ISC)² website, view a copy of the Resource Guide for Today's Information Security Professional (see https://resourceguide.isc2.org/).

2. Scroll through the guide and look for resources and publications to help practitioners remain current in the field.

3. Why do you think dozens of security conferences and events are held during the year throughout the world?

4. What value can security professionals gain from attending and participating in these conferences and seminars?

PROJECT 14.2: Comparing U.S. Government Roles in National Security

1. Visit the website of the National Security Agency (NSA; www.nsa.gov) to determine its mission in protecting the national interest in computer use.

2. Visit the website of the U.S. Department of Homeland Security (DHS; www.dhs.gov) to determine its mission in protecting the national interest in cybersecurity.

3. Visit the website of the U.S. Department of Commerce NIST Computer Security Resource Center (http://csrc.nist.gov) to determine its mission in protecting the national interest in cybersecurity.

4. How are these agencies alike, and what are some of the overlapping elements of their mission statements?

5. How are these agencies different, and how is their work compatible or complementary?

PROJECT 14.3: Understanding the High Price of Cybercrime

Four Russians and one Ukrainian have been charged with masterminding a massive hacking spree that was responsible for stealing more than 160 million bank card numbers from companies in the U.S. over a 7-year period. The alleged hackers were behind some of the most notorious breaches. One of them, notorious hacker Albert Gonzalez, was convicted in 2010 and is currently serving multiple 20-year sentences simultaneously.

1. What was Albert Gonzalez charged with?

2. How was he convicted?

3. Do you believe his sentence was too severe or too lenient?

4. How has his arrest affected financial crimes?

PROJECT 14.4: **Understanding Careers in Information Security**

1. Visit the website of the U.S. Department of Labor's Outlook for Computer Support Specialists (www.bls.gov/ooh/computer-and-information-technology/computer-support-specialists.htm).

2. Prepare a want ad for an information security specialist. Include in your position announcement the nature of the work, working conditions, qualifications, work environment, salary information, and so forth.

3. Prepare a list of criteria and questions you would ask a prospective employee for the position.

4. What (if any) certifications would you seek in a candidate?

5. Would a certified prospective employee have an advantage over an equally skilled but not certified candidate? Why or why not?

Appendix **A**

Common Body of Knowledge

The (ISC)² Common Body of Knowledge (CBK) is an organization and collection of topics relevant to information security professionals. The CBK establishes a common framework of information security terms and principles collected to assist worldwide information security professionals with discussions, debates, and help in resolving matters within a common understanding. The 10 domains of the CBK, along with the major topics and major subject areas, follow. You can find this information in the Candidate Information Bulletin (January 2012).

Access Control

Key areas of knowledge:

- Control access by applying the following concepts, methodologies, and techniques:
    - Policies
    - Types of controls (preventive, detective, corrective, and so on)
    - Techniques (nondiscretionary, discretionary, mandatory, and so on)
    - Identification and authentication
    - Decentralized/distributed access control techniques
    - Authorization mechanisms
    - Logging and monitoring

- Understand access control attacks
    - Threat modeling
    - Asset valuation

- Vulnerability analysis
- Access aggregation

- Assess effectiveness of access controls
  - User entitlements
  - Access review and audit

- Identity and access provisioning life cycle (provisioning, review, revocation, and so on)

Telecommunications and Network Security

Key areas of knowledge:

- Understand secure network architecture and design (for example, IP and non-IP protocols and segmentation)
  - OSI and TCP/IP models
  - IP networking
  - Implications of multilayer protocols

- Secure network components
  - Hardware (modems, switches, routers, wireless APs, and so on)
  - Transmission media (wired, wireless, fiber, and so on)
  - Network access control devices (such as firewalls and proxies)
  - Endpoint security

- Establish secure communication channels (for example, VPN, TLS/SSL, and VLANs)
  - Voice (POTS, PBX, and VoIP)
  - Multimedia collaboration (such as remote meeting technology and instant messaging)
  - Remote access (such as screen scraper and virtual application/desktop telecommuting)
  - Data communications

- Understand network attacks (such as DDoS and spoofing)

Information Security Governance and Risk Management

Key areas of knowledge:

- Understand and align security function to goals, mission, and objectives of the organization
- Understand and align security governance
    - Organizational processes (for example, acquisitions, divestitures, and governance committees)
    - Security roles and responsibilities
    - Legislative and regulatory compliance
    - Privacy requirements compliance
    - Control frameworks
    - Due care
    - Due diligence

- Understand and apply concepts of confidentiality, integrity, and availability
- Develop and implement security policy
    - Security policies
    - Standards/baselines
    - Procedures
    - Guidelines
    - Documentation

- Manage the information life cycle (for example, classification, categorization, and ownership)
- Manage third-party governance (on-site assessment, document exchange and review, process/ policy review, and so on)
- Understand and apply risk management concepts
    - Threat and vulnerability identification
    - Risk assessment/analysis (qualitative, quantitative, and hybrid)
    - Risk assignment/assessment
    - Countermeasure selection
    - Tangible and intangible asset valuation

- Manage personnel security

    - Employment candidate screening (reference checks, education verification, and so on)

    - Employment agreements and policies

    - Employee termination processes

    - Vendor, consultant, and contractor controls

- Develop and manage security education, training, and awareness
- Manage the security function

    - Budget

    - Metrics

    - Resources

    - Information security strategies

    - Assessment of the completeness and effectiveness of the security program

Software Development Security

Key areas of knowledge:

- Understand and apply security in the software development life cycle

    - Development life cycle

    - Maturity models

    - Operation and maintenance

    - Change management

- Understand the environment and security controls

    - Security of the software environment

    - Security issues of programming languages

    - Security issues in source code (buffer overflow, escalation of privilege, back doors, and more)

    - Configuration management

- Assess the effectiveness of software security
    - Certification and accreditation (system authorization)
    - Auditing and logging
    - Risk analysis and mitigation

Cryptography

Key areas of knowledge:

- Understand the application and use of cryptography
    - Data at rest (such as the hard drive)
    - Data in transit (such as on the wire)

- Understand the cryptographic life cycle (cryptographic limitations, algorithm/protocol governance, and so on)
- Understand encryption concepts
    - Foundational concepts
    - Symmetric cryptography
    - Asymmetric cryptography
    - Hybrid cryptography
    - Message digests
    - Hashing

- Understand key management processes
    - Creation/distribution
    - Storage/destruction
    - Recovery
    - Key escrow

- Understand digital signatures
- Understand nonrepudiation
- Understand methods of cryptanalytic attacks

- Chosen plain text

- Social engineering for key discovery

- Brute force (rainbow tables, specialized/scalable architecture, and so on)

- Cipher text only

- Known plain text

- Frequency analysis

- Chosen cipher text

- Implementation attacks

- Use cryptography to maintain network security

- Use cryptography to maintain application security

- Understand the public key infrastructure (PKI)

- Understand certificate-related issues

- Understand information hiding alternatives (steganography, watermarking, and so on)

Security Architecture and Design

Key areas of knowledge:

- Understand the fundamental concepts of security models (confidentiality, integrity, multilevel models, and so on)

- Understand the components of information systems security evaluation models

  - Product evaluation models (such as common criteria)

  - Industry and international security implementation guidelines (including PCI-DSS and ISO)

- Understand the security capabilities of information systems (memory protection, virtualization, trusted platform module, and so on)

- Understand the vulnerabilities of security architectures

  - System (such as covert channels, state attacks, and emanations)

  - Technology and process integration (for example, single point of failure and service-oriented architecture)

- Understand software and system vulnerabilities and threats

    - Web based (XML, SAML, OWASP, and so on)

    - Client based (for example, applets)

    - Server based (for example, data flow control)

    - Database security (interference, aggregation, data mining, warehousing, and so on)

    - Distributed systems (cloud computing, grid computing, peer to peer, and so on)

- Understand countermeasure principles (for example, defense in depth)

Operations Security

Key areas of knowledge:

- Understand security operations concepts

    - Need to know/least privilege

    - Separation of duties and responsibilities

    - Monitoring of special privileges (for example, operators and administrators)

    - Job rotation

    - Marking, handling, storage, and destruction of sensitive information

    - Record retention

- Employ resource protection

    - Media management

    - Asset management (for example, equipment life cycle and software licensing)

- Manage incident response

    - Detection

    - Response

    - Reporting

    - Recovery

    - Remediation and review (for example, root cause analysis)

- Implement preventive measures against attacks (malicious code, zero-day exploits, denial of service, and so on)

- Implement and support patch and vulnerability management

- Understand change and configuration management (for example, versioning and baselining)

- Understand system resilience and fault tolerant requirements

Business Continuity and Disaster Recovery Planning

Key areas of knowledge:

- Understand business continuity requirements

    - Develop and document project scope and plan

- Conduct business impact analysis

    - Identify and prioritize critical business functions

    - Determine maximum tolerable downtime and other criteria

    - Assess exposure to outages (local, regional, and global)

    - Define recovery objectives

- Develop a recovery strategy

    - Implement a backup storage strategy (offsite storage, electronic vaulting, tape rotation, and so on)

    - Recovery site strategies

- Understand the disaster recovery process

    - Response

    - Personnel

    - Communications

    - Assessment

    - Restoration

    - Training

- Exercise, assess, and maintain the plan (version control, distribution, and so on)

Legal Regulations, Investigations, and Compliance

Key areas of knowledge:

- Understand legal issues that pertain to information security internationally
    - Computer crime
    - Licensing and intellectual property (copyright, trademark, and so on)
    - Import/export
    - Transborder data flows
    - Privacy

- Understand professional ethics
    - (ISC)² Code of Professional Ethics
    - Support for the organization's code of ethics

- Understand and support investigations
    - Policy, roles, and responsibilities (rules of engagement, authorization, scope, and so on)
    - Incident handling and response
    - Evidence collection and handling (for example, chain of custody and interviewing)
    - Reporting and documentation

- Understand forensic procedures
    - Media analysis
    - Network analysis
    - Software analysis
    - Hardware/embedded device analysis

- Understand compliance requirements and procedures
    - Regulatory environment
    - Audits
    - Reporting

- Ensure security in contractual agreements and procurement processes (cloud computing, outsourcing, vendor governance, and so on)

Physical (Environmental) Security

Key Areas of Knowledge

- Understand site and facility design considerations
- Support the implementation and operation of perimeter security (physical access control and monitoring, audit trails/access logs, and so on)
- Support the implementation and operation of internal security (escort requirements/visitor control, keys and locks, and so on)
- Support the implementation and operations of facilities security (for example, technology convergence)
    - Communications and server rooms
    - Restricted and work area security
    - Data center security
    - Utilities and heating, ventilation, and air conditioning (HVAC) considerations
    - Water issues (such as leakage and flooding)
    - Fire prevention, detection, and suppression
- Support the protection and securing of equipment
- Understand personnel privacy and safety (such as duress, travel, and monitoring)

Appendix **B**

Security Policy and Standards Taxonomy

A complete Policy and Standards Library is essential to a comprehensive security programme (see Chapter 4, "Governance and Risk Management"). This appendix provides a minimum outline of the policies and standards you can expect to see—it is derived from ISO/IEC 27002:2005, "Code of Practice for Information Security Management." The first level (bolded) indicates where a policy would be expected; the second level (italicized) indicates where a control standard would be expected. Baseline standards, documented security procedures, and guidelines/guidance documents can be tied to the control standards they support. For example, system hardening baseline standards can be tied to Section 6.1.

Topics can be combined into fewer documents, but be sure to cover every topic to comply with the international standard.

1. **Security Policy**

   1.1 Information Security Program (note that this section can be a single document or web page containing the organization's overall policies related to the treatment of information security as a program)

2. **Organization of Information Security**

   2.1 Internal Organization

   2.2 External Parties

3. **Asset Management**

   3.1 Responsibility for Assets

   3.2 Information Classification

4. Human Resources Security

4.1 Prior to Employment

4.2 Termination or Change of Employment

5. Physical and Environmental Security

5.1 Secure Areas

5.2 Equipment Security

6. Communications and Operations Management

6.1 Operational Procedures and Responsibilities

6.2 System Planning and Acceptance

6.3 Protection Against Malicious and Mobile Code

6.4 Backup

6.5 Network Security Management

6.6 Media Handling

6.7 Exchange of Information

6.8 Electronic Commerce Services

6.9 Monitoring

7. Access Control

7.1 Business Requirements for Access Control

7.2 User Access Management

7.3 User Responsibilities

7.4 Network Access Control

7.5 Operating System Access Control

7.6 Application and Information Access Control

8. **Information Systems Acquisition, Development, and Maintenance**

   8.1 Security Requirements of Information Systems

   8.2 Correct Processing in Applications

   8.3 Cryptographic Controls

   8.4 Security of System Files

   8.5 Security in Development and Support Processes

   8.6 Technical Vulnerability Management

9. **Information Security Incident Management**

   9.1 Reporting Information Security Events and Weaknesses

   9.2 Management of Information Security Incidents and Improvements

10. **Business Continuity Management**

   10.1 Information Security Aspects of Business Continuity Management

11. **Compliance**

   11.1 Compliance with Legal Requirements

   11.2 Compliance with Security Policies and Standards, and Technical Compliance

   11.3 Information Systems Audit Considerations

Appendix | C

Sample Policies

This appendix provides real-world examples of security policies you're likely to find in use in a typical security programme (see Chapter 4, "Governance and Risk Management"). These standards illustrate the types of security documentation you can find at the SANS Security Policy Project; boilerplate documentation is available there, to reduce the need to reinvent the wheel each time a new policy is required. You can find the Security Policy Project at www.sans.org/resources/policies/.

Sample Computer Acceptable Use Policy

1.0.0 Acceptable Use Policy

1.1.0 Overview

<Company Name Here>'s intentions for publishing an Acceptable Use Policy are not to impose restrictions that are contrary to <Company Name Here>'s established culture of openness, trust, and integrity. <Company Name Here> is committed to protecting <Company Name Here> employees, partners, and the company from illegal or damaging actions by individuals, either knowingly or unknowingly. Internet/intranet/extranet-related systems, including but not limited to computer equipment, software, operating systems, storage media, network accounts providing electronic mail, WWW browsing, and FTP, are the property of <Company Name Here>. These systems are to be used for business purposes in serving the interests of the company, and of our clients and customers in the course of normal operations. Please review Human Resources policies for further details. Effective security is a team effort involving the participation and support of every <Company Name Here> employee and affiliate who deals with information and/or information systems. It is the responsibility of every computer user to know these guidelines and to conduct activities accordingly.

1.2.0 Purpose

The purpose of this policy is to outline the acceptable use of computer equipment at <Company Name Here>. These rules are in place to protect the employee and <Company Name Here>. Inappropriate use exposes <Company Name Here> to risks including virus attacks, compromise of network systems and services, and legal issues.

1.3.0 Scope

This policy applies to employees, contractors, consultants, temporaries, and other workers at <Company Name Here>, including all personnel affiliated with third parties. This policy applies to all equipment that is owned or leased by <Company Name Here>.

1.4.0 Policy

1.4.1 General Use and Ownership

- While <Company Name Here> network administration desires to provide a reasonable level of privacy, users should be aware that the data they create on the corporate systems remains the property of <Company Name Here>. Because of the need to protect <Company Name Here> network, management cannot guarantee the confidentiality of information stored on any network device belonging to <Company Name Here>.

- Employees are responsible for exercising good judgment regarding the reasonableness of personal use. Individual departments are responsible for creating guidelines concerning personal use of Internet/intranet/extranet systems. In the absence of such policies, employees should be guided by departmental policies on personal use; if there is any uncertainty, employees should consult their supervisor or manager.

- <Company Name Here> recommends that any information users consider sensitive or vulnerable be encrypted.

- For security and network maintenance purposes, authorized individuals within <Company Name Here> may monitor equipment, systems, and network traffic at any time, per the <Company Name Here> Audit Policy.

- <Company Name Here> reserves the right to audit networks and systems on a periodic basis to ensure compliance with this policy.

1.4.2 Security and Proprietary Information

- The user interface for information contained on Internet/intranet/extranet-related systems should be classified as either confidential or not confidential, as defined by corporate confidentiality guidelines, details of which can be found in Human Resources policies. Examples of confidential information include, but are not limited to, company private, corporate strategies, competitor sensitive, trade secrets, specifications, customer lists, and research data. Employees should take all necessary steps to prevent unauthorized access to this information.

■ Keep passwords secure and do not share accounts. Authorized users are responsible for the security of their passwords and accounts. Both system-level and user-level passwords should be changed quarterly.

■ All PCs, laptops, and workstations should be either secured with a password-protected screen-saver with the automatic activation feature set to 10 minutes or less, or secured by logging off (Control+Alt+Delete for Win2K users) when the host will be unattended.

■ Use encryption of information in compliance with <Company Name Here>'s Acceptable Encryption Use policy.

■ Because information contained on portable computers is especially vulnerable, special care should be exercised.

■ Postings by employees from a <Company Name Here> email address to newsgroups should contain a disclaimer stating that the opinions expressed are strictly their own and not necessarily those of <Company Name Here>, unless posting is in the course of business duties.

■ All hosts used by the employee that are connected to the <Company Name Here> Internet/intranet/extranet, whether owned by the employee or <Company Name Here>, shall be continually executing approved virus-scanning software with a current virus database, unless overridden by departmental or group policy.

■ Employees must use extreme caution when opening email attachments received from unknown senders, which may contain viruses, email bombs, or Trojan horse code.

1.4.3 Unacceptable Use

The following activities are, in general, prohibited. Employees may be exempted from these restrictions during the course of their legitimate job responsibilities (for example, systems administration staff may need to disable the network access of a host if that host is disrupting production services). Under no circumstances is an employee of <Company Name Here> authorized to engage in any activity that is illegal under local, state, federal, or international law while utilizing <Company Name Here> -owned resources.

The following lists are by no means exhaustive, but they attempt to provide a framework for activities that fall into the category of unacceptable use.

1.4.3.1 System and Network Activities

The following activities are strictly prohibited, with no exceptions:

■ Violations of the rights of any person or company protected by copyright, trade secret, patent or other intellectual property, or similar laws or regulations, including, but not limited to, the installation or distribution of "pirated" or other software products that are not appropriately licensed for use by <Company Name Here>.

- Unauthorized copying of copyrighted material, including, but not limited to, digitization and distribution of photographs from magazines, books, or other copyrighted sources; copyrighted music; and the installation of any copyrighted software for which <Company Name Here> or the end user does not have an active license.

- Exporting software, technical information, encryption software, or technology in violation of international or regional export control laws. Appropriate management should be consulted prior to export of any material that is in question.

- Introduction of malicious programs into the network or server (viruses, worms, Trojan horses, email bombs, and so on).

- Revelation of account passwords to others and allowed use of individual accounts by others. This includes family and other household members when work is being done at home.

- Use of a <Company Name Here> computing asset to actively engage in procuring or trans- mitting material that is in violation of sexual harassment or hostile workplace laws in the user's local jurisdiction.

- Fraudulent offers of products, items, or services originating from any <Company Name Here> account.

- Statements about warranty, expressly or implied, unless as a part of normal job duties.

- Security breaches or disruptions of network communication. Security breaches include, but are not limited to, accessing data for which the employee is not an intended recipient or logging into a server or account that the employee is not expressly authorized to access, unless these activities are within the scope of regular duties. For purposes of this section, "disruption" includes, but is not limited to, network sniffing, pinged floods, packet spoofing, denial of service, and forged routing information for malicious purposes.

- Port scanning or security scanning, unless prior notification to <Company Name Here> is made.

- Any form of network monitoring that will intercept data not intended for the employee's host, unless this activity is a part of the employee's normal job or duty.

- Circumvention of user authentication or security for any host, network, or account.

- Interference with or denial of service to any user other than the employee's host (for example, a denial of service attack).

- Use of any program/script/command, or the sending of messages of any kind, with the intent to interfere with or disable a user's terminal session via any means, locally or using the Internet/ intranet/extranet.

- Information about or lists of <Company Name Here> employees provided to parties outside <Company Name Here>.

1.4.3.2 Email and Communications Activities

The following activities are strictly prohibited, with no exceptions:

- Sending of unsolicited email messages, including "junk mail" and other advertising material, to individuals who did not specifically request such material (email spam).

- Any form of harassment via email, telephone, or paging, whether through language, frequency, or size of messages.

- Unauthorized use or forgery of email header information.

- Solicitation of email for any other email address, other than that of the poster's account, with the intent to harass or to collect replies.

- Creation or forwarding of "chain letters," "Ponzi" schemes, or other "pyramid" schemes of any type.

- Use of unsolicited email originating from within <Company Name Here> networks of other Internet/intranet/extranet service providers on behalf of or to advertise any service hosted by <Company Name Here> or connected via <Company Name Here> network.

- Posting of the same or similar non-business-related messages to large numbers of Usenet newsgroups (newsgroup spam).

1.5.0 Enforcement

Any employee found to have violated this policy may be subject to disciplinary action, up to and including termination of employment.

1.6.0 Definitions

Spam is unauthorized and/or unsolicited electronic mass mailings.

1.7.0 Revision History

7/24/2004: Initial Section Creation.

Sample Email Use Policy

1.0.0 Email Use Policy

1.1.0 Purpose

The purpose of this policy is to prevent tarnishing the public image of <Company Name Here>. When email goes out from <Company Name Here>, the general public will tend to view that message as an official policy statement from <Company Name Here>.

1.2.0 Scope

This policy covers appropriate use of any email sent from a <Company Name Here> email address and applies to all employees, vendors, and agents operating on behalf of <Company Name Here>.

1.3.0 Policy

1.3.1 Prohibited Use

The <Company Name Here> email system shall not to be used for the creation or distribution of any disruptive or offensive messages, including offensive comments or attachments about race, gender, hair color, disabilities, age, sexual orientation, pornography, religious beliefs and practice, political beliefs, or national origin. Employees who receive any emails with this content from any <Company Name Here> employee should report the matter to their supervisor immediately.

1.3.2 Personal Use

Using a reasonable amount of <Company Name Here> resources for personal email is acceptable, but non-work-related email should be saved in a separate folder from work-related email. Sending chain letters or joke emails from a <Company Name Here> email account is prohibited. Virus or other malware warnings and mass mailings from <Company Name Here> shall be approved by <Company Name Here> VP Operations before sending. These restrictions also apply to the forwarding of mail received by a <Company Name Here> employee.

1.3.3 Monitoring

<Company Name Here> employees shall have no expectation of privacy in anything they store, send, or receive on the company's email system. <Company Name Here> may monitor messages without prior notice. <Company Name Here> is not obligated to monitor email messages.

1.4.0 Enforcement

Any employee found to have violated this policy might be subject to disciplinary action, up to and including termination of employment.

1.5.0 Definitions

E-mail: The electronic transmission of information through a mail protocol such as SMTP or IMAP. Typical email clients include Eudora and Microsoft Outlook.

Forwarded email: Email re-sent from an internal network to an outside point.

Chain email or letter: Email sent to successive people. Typically, the body of the note has direction to send out multiple copies of the note and promises good luck or money if the direction is followed.

Sensitive information: Information that can be damaging to <Company Name Here> or its customers' reputation or market standing.

Virus warning: An email containing warnings about virus or malware. The overwhelming majority of these emails turn out to be a hoax and contain bogus information usually intent only on frightening or misleading users.

Unauthorized disclosure: The intentional or unintentional revealing of restricted information to people, both inside and outside <Company Name Here>, who do not have a need to know that information.

1.6.0 Revision History

Sample Password Policy

1.0.0 Password Policy

1.1.0 Overview

Passwords are an important aspect of computer security. They are the front line of protection for user accounts. A poorly chosen password can compromise <Company Name Here>'s entire corporate network. As such, all <Company Name Here> employees (including contractors and vendors with access to <Company Name Here> systems) are responsible for taking the appropriate steps, as outlined next, to select and secure their passwords.

1.2.0 Purpose

The purpose of this policy is to establish a standard for the creation of strong passwords, the protection of those passwords, and the frequency of change.

1.3.0 Scope

The scope of this policy includes all personnel who have or are responsible for an account (or any form of access that supports or requires a password) on any system that resides at any <Company Name Here> facility, has access to the <Company Name Here> network, or stores any nonpublic <Company Name Here> information.

1.4.0 Policy

1.4.1 General

- All system-level passwords (root, enable, NT admin, application administration accounts, and so on) must be changed on at least a quarterly basis.

- All production system-level passwords must be part of the <Company Name Here>-administered global password management database.

- All user-level passwords (email, web, desktop computer, and so on) must be changed at least every three months. The recommended change interval is every month.

- User accounts that have system-level privileges granted through group memberships must have a unique password from all other accounts held by that user.

- Passwords must not be inserted into email messages or other forms of electronic communication.

- Where SNMP is used, the community strings must be defined as something other than the standard defaults of `public`, `private`, and `system`, and must be different from the passwords used to log in interactively. A keyed hash must be used where available (for example, SNMPv2).

- All user- and system-level passwords must conform to the guidelines described next.

1.4.2 Guidelines

A. General Password Construction Guidelines

Passwords are used for various purposes at <Company Name Here>. Some of the more common uses include user-level accounts, web accounts, email accounts, screen saver protection, voicemail, and local router logins. Because very few systems have support for one-time tokens (dynamic passwords that are used only once), everyone should be aware of how to select strong passwords.

Poor, weak passwords have the following characteristics:

- The password contains fewer than eight characters.

- The password is a word found in a dictionary (English or foreign).

- The password is a common usage word, such as

    - Names of family, pets, friends, coworkers, fantasy characters, and so on

    - Computer terms and names, commands, sites, companies, hardware, and software

    - The words "<Company Name Here>" or any derivation

    - Birthdays and other personal information, such as addresses and phone number

    - Word or number patterns, such as aaabbb, qwerty, zyxwvuts, and 123321

    - Any of the previous password examples spelled backwards

    - Any of the previous password examples preceded or followed by a digit (as in `secret1` and `1secret`)

Strong passwords have the following characteristics:

- Contain both upper- and lowercase characters (a–z and A–Z).

- Have digits and punctuation characters as well as letters (0–9 or any in the set of !@#$%^&*()_+|~-=\`{}[]:";'<>?,./)

- Have a length of at least eight alphanumeric characters

- Do not consist of any words in any language, slang, dialect, jargon, and so on

- Are not based on personal information, names of family members, and so on

- Are never written down or stored online. Try to create passwords that can be easily remembered. One way to do this is create a password based on a song title, affirmation, or other phrase. For example, the phrase might be "This May Be One Way to Remember," and the password could be: "TmB1w2R!" or "Tmb1W>r~" or some other variation.

> **NOTE**
>
> Do not use either of these examples as passwords!

B. Password Protection Standards

Do not use the same password for <Company Name Here> accounts as for other non–<Company Name Here> access (personal ISP account, option trading, benefits, and so on). Where possible, don't use the same password for various <Company Name Here> access needs. For example, select one password for the Engineering systems and a separate password for IT systems. Also select a separate password to be used for an NT account and a UNIX account.

Do not share <Company Name Here> passwords with anyone, including administrative assistants or secretaries. All passwords are to be treated as sensitive, confidential <Company Name Here> information.

Consider this list of don'ts:

- Don't reveal a password over the phone to *anyone*.

- Don't reveal a password in an email message.

- Don't reveal a password to a boss.

- Don't talk about a password in front of others.

- Don't hint at the format of a password (as in "my family name").

- Don't reveal a password on questionnaires or security forms.

- Don't share a password with family members.

- Don't reveal a password to coworkers while on vacation.

- If someone demands a password, refer that person to this document or have the person call someone in the Information Security department.

- Do not use the Remember Password feature of applications (such as Eudora, Outlook, or Netscape Messenger).

- Again, do not write down passwords and store them anywhere in your office. Do not store passwords in a file on *any* computer system (including iPads, iPhones, tablet computers, or similar devices) without encryption.

- Change passwords at least once every three months (just as system-level passwords must be changed quarterly). The recommended change interval is every month.

- If you suspect that an account or password has been compromised, report the incident to someone in the Information Security department immediately and change all the passwords.

- Password cracking or guessing may be performed on a periodic or random basis. If a password is guessed or cracked during one of these scans, the user will be required to change it.

C. Application Development Standards

Application developers must ensure that their programs address the following security precautions:

- Support authentication of individual users, not groups

- Do not store passwords in clear text or in any easily reversible form

- Provide for some sort of role management so that one user can take over the functions of another without having to know the other's password

- Support TACACS+ , RADIUS, and/or X.509 with LDAP security retrieval wherever possible

D. Use of Passwords and Passphrases for Remote Access Users

Access to the <Company Name Here> networks via remote access is to be controlled using either a one-time password authentication or a public/private key system with a strong passphrase.

E. Passphrases

Passphrases are generally used for public/private key authentication. A public/private key system defines a mathematical relationship between the public key known by all and the private key known only to the user. Without the passphrase to unlock the private key, the user cannot gain access.

Passphrases are not the same as passwords. A passphrase is a longer version of a password and, therefore, is more secure. A passphrase typically consists of multiple words. Because of this, a passphrase is more secure against dictionary attacks.

A good passphrase is relatively long and contains a combination of upper- and lowercase letters and numeric and punctuation characters. Consider an example of a good passphrase: `The*?#>*@Traffic OnThe101Was*&#!#ThisMorning`.

All the previous rules for passwords also apply to passphrases.

1.5.0 Enforcement

Any employee found to have violated this policy might be subject to disciplinary action, up to and including termination of employment.

1.6.0 Definitions

The application administration account is any account for the administration of an application (Oracle database administrator, NT administrator, and so on).

1.7.0 Revision History

Sample Wireless (WiFi) Use Policy

1.0.0 Wireless Communication Policy

1.1.0 Purpose

This policy prohibits access to <Company Name Here> networks via unsecured wireless communication mechanisms. Only wireless systems that meet the criteria of this policy or that have been granted an exclusive waiver are approved for connectivity to <Company Name Here> networks.

1.2.0 Scope

This policy covers all wireless data communication devices (personal computers, cellular phones, PDAs, and so on) connected to any <Company Name Here> internal networks. This includes any form of wireless communication device capable of transmitting packet data. Wireless devices and/or networks without any connectivity to <Company Name Here> networks do not fall under the purview of this policy.

1.3.0 Policy

1.3.1 Register Access Points and Cards

All wireless access points/base stations connected to the corporate network must be registered and approved. These access points/base stations are subject to periodic penetration tests and audits. All wireless network interface cards (PC cards) used in corporate laptop or desktop computers must be registered.

1.3.2 Approved Technology

All wireless LAN access must use corporate-approved vendor products and security configurations.

1.3.3 VPN Encryption and Authentication

All computers with wireless LAN devices must utilize a corporate-approved virtual private network (VPN) configured to drop all unauthenticated and unencrypted traffic. To comply with this policy, wireless implementations must maintain point-to-point hardware encryption of at least 56 bits. All implementations must support a hardware address that can be registered and tracked (a MAC address). All implementations must support and employ strong user authentication that checks against an external database such as TACACS+ or RADIUS.

1.3.4 Setting the SSID

The SSID shall be configured so that it does not contain any identifying information about the organization, such as the company name, division title, employee name, or product identifier.

1.4.0 Enforcement

Any employee found to have violated this policy might be subject to disciplinary action, up to and including termination of employment.

1.5.0 Definitions

User authentication is a method by which the user of a wireless system can be verified as a legitimate user, independent of the computer or operating system being used.

1.6.0 Revision History

Appendix D

HIPAA Security Rule Standards

HIPAA is the Health Insurance Portability and Accountability Act (see Chapter 4, "Governance and Risk Management"). Passed in 1996, HIPAA is designed to protect confidential healthcare information through improved security standards and federal privacy legislation. It defines requirements for storing patient information before, during, and after electronic transmission. It also identifies compliance guidelines for critical business tasks such as risk analysis, awareness training, audit trail, disaster recovery plans, information access control, and encryption.

HIPAA Security Standards

The proposed HIPAA security regulations establish a minimum framework of standard procedures for ensuring the protection of all individually identifiable health information that is maintained, transmitted, or received in electronic form. These standards guard the integrity, confidentiality, and availability of electronic data. The safeguards are intended to protect data from accidental or intentional release to unauthorized persons, as well as from alteration, destruction, or loss. For more information on the proposed HIPAA security standards, visit the U.S. Department of Health and Human Services website at www.dhhs.gov.

Compliance with the HIPAA security rule involves meeting 18 information security standards in these four areas:

- **Administrative safeguards:** Documenting policies and procedures for day-to-day operations; managing the conduct of employees with electronic protected health information (EPHI); and managing the selection, development, and use of security controls.

- **Physical safeguards:** Security measures to protect an organization's electronic information systems, as well as related buildings and equipment, from natural hazards, environmental hazards, and unauthorized intrusion.

- **Technical security services for stored data:** Security measures that specify how to use technology to protect EPHI while stored.

- **Technical security mechanisms** (particularly controlling access to data and data transmissions)

The final rule adopting HIPAA standards for the security of electronic health information was published in the Federal Register on February 20, 2003. This final rule specifies a series of administrative, technical, and physical security procedures for covered entities to use to ensure the confidentiality of electronic protected health information. The standards are delineated in either required or addressable implementation specifications.

Administrative Procedures

Policies and procedures must be implemented and documented in each of these 12 areas:

- Training programs in security management and process issues
- Formal data-processing protocols
- Formal protocols for controlling access to data
- Internal audit procedures
- Certification of data systems for compliance with DHHS security standards
- Chain of trust agreements with covered entities with whom we exchange electronic information
- A contingency plan, to ensure continuity and preservation of data in the event of an emergency
- Security features for initial clearance of all personnel who have access to health information, along with ongoing supervision, training, and monitoring of this personnel
- Security configuration management procedures, such as virus checking, hardware and software systems review, and documentation
- Specific procedures when personnel terminate employment
- A security management structure that maintains continual risk assessment and sanction policies and procedures

Physical Safeguards

Data and data systems must be physically protected from intrusion and environmental hazards via seven basic elements:

- Designation of a specific person for responsibility of security
- Controlled access to and alteration of computer hardware
- Enforcement of "need to know" clearances
- Implementation of work station security activities
- Development of disaster/intrusion response and recovery plans

- Maintenance of security records

- Implementation of identity verification procedures for personnel to physically access sites

Technical Security Services

Software control and procedures regarding stored data include these requirements:

- Providing for internal audits and controls within data systems

- Controlling access by users through authentication

- Ensuring that stored data is neither altered nor inappropriately accessed or processed

- Granting data access to a particular privileged classes of personnel, including during crises

Technical Security Mechanisms

These requirements relate to accessed data and the transmission of stored data, to ensure that unauthorized third parties cannot easily access, intercept, or interpret data. These proposed procedures include:

- Validation that stored data being transmitted is accurate.

- Validation that received data is identical to sent data.

- Data transmissions either encrypted or controlled by a dedicated, secure line. If transmissions are not encrypted, DHHS also requires three elements:

  - Alarms to signal abnormal communication conditions

  - Automatic recording of audit trail information

  - A method for authenticating the entity receiving the data

Index

Symbols

3DES (Triple DES), 207

2013 Computerworld Salary Survey website, 4

A

abstraction, 84

acceptable use sample policy, 306-308

definitions, 310

email/communications, 310

enforcement, 310

general use and ownership, 307

proprietary information, 307

purpose, 307

revision history, 310

scope, 307

system and network activities, 308-309

unacceptable use, 308

access controls

access control lists, 184

administrative, 149-150

authentication, 183

fingerprint, 157-158

headers (IPSec), 250

multifactor, 188-189

networks, 231

overview, 183

passwords, 186-189

VPN, 317

biometrics, 189-190

controlled protection, 88

coordinators, 9

discretionary, 88, 184

identification, 183

information owners, 184

key areas of knowledge, 292

least privilege, 183

logs, 155

mandatory, 185

matrix model, 102

military classifications/clearances, 186

networks, 232

overview, 42

physical, 149

    alarm systems, 156

    audit trails/access logs, 155

    badging, 152

    biometrics, 156-157

    fingerprint authentication, 157-158

    intrusion detection, 155

    keys/combination locks, 152

    lighting, 153

    perimeters, 151

    security dogs, 153

    site selections, 150

    smart cards, 153-155

    visitors, 150

    work area restrictions, 150

remote, 192-193

role-based, 185

single sign-on, 190

    federated identities, 192

    Kerberos, 191

users

    access requests, 28

    provisioning, 184

account takeovers, 282

ACLs (access control lists), 184

Address Resolution Protocol (ARP), 230

administrative access controls, 149-150

administrative laws, 130

Advanced Research Projects Network (ARPANET), 229

Advanced Study of Information Warfare website, 129

AES (Advanced Encryption System), 207

agile software development, 262

alarm systems, 156

ALE (annualized loss expectancy), 70

alternate-site services providers, 116-117

Amazon.com "one click" software patent, 132

analysis

    business impact (BIA), 111, 114-115

    risks, 26, 70-72

    static, 269

annualized loss expectancy (ALE), 70

appliances (network security), 241

Application Layer (OSI), 227

application-level gateway firewalls, 239-241

    bastion hosts, 239-240

    benefits, 240

    costs, 238

    defined, 238

    limitations, 241

    proxy server characteristics, 239

architecture and design, 81

    assurance, 86

    evaluation models, 87

        Common Criteria. See CC

        Common Evaluation Methodology Editorial Board, 100-101

        CTCPEC, 93

        Federal Criteria, 93

        ITSEC, 91-93

        TCSEC. See TCSEC

key areas of knowledge, 297

overview, 40

SDLC

    deployment, 270-271

    design reviews, 267

    development, 268

    testing, 270

    threat modeling, 266-267

    training, 272

security models, 101-102

TCB

    defined, 81

    protection mechanisms, 84-86

    rings of trust, 81-84

ARP (Address Resolution Protocol), 230

ARPANET (Advanced Research Projects Network), 229

art theft, 19

asset classifications, 67-68

assurance, 86

evaluation

    classes, 97-98

    levels, 98-100

    models. *See* evaluation models

goals, 86

requirements, 24

asymmetric keys, 206-208

attackers, 27

attacks

categories, 127

computer forensics, 135-136

DDoS, 128

DoS, 128

dumpster diving, 128

emanation eavesdropping, 129

embezzlement, 129

highly publicized instances, 129

information warfare, 129

laws

    administrative, 130

    intellectual property, 131-132

    judicial, 130

    legislative, 130

    privacy, 133-135

network protection, 231-232

password cracking, 187

pedestrian methods, 129

phishing, 192

replay, 250

rogue code, 128

social engineering, 128

software piracy, 128

spoofing, 128

surfaces, 267

Verizon Data Breach, 127

victims, 127

audit trails, 155

authentication

fingerprint, 157-158

headers (IPSec), 250

multifactor, 188-189

networks, 231

overview, 183

passwords, 186

    cracking, 187

    creating, 188

    tokens, 189

VPN, 317

availability, 21

awareness, 72

B

B2B (business-to-business) processing, 3

backups, 172

badging, 152

Barquin, Dr. Ramon C., 138

baselines, 66

basic packet-filtering, 236

bastion hosts, 239-240

BCPs (business continuity plans), 111

BIA, 111, 114-115

creating, 112

defined, 111

DRP

alternate-side services providers, 116-117

cloud, 118

goals, 115

mobile units, 118

multiple centers, 117

recovery strategies, 116

service bureaus, 118

shared-site agreements, 116

testing, 118-119

importance, 112-113

key areas of knowledge, 299

overview, 40

scope, 114

threats, identifying, 113-114

Bell, David E., 101

Bell Laboratories "Conversion of Numerical Information" patent website, 132

Bell-LaPadula model, 101

BIA (business impact analysis), 111, 114-115

Biba model, 102

biometrics, 157, 189-190

convenience and security balance, 157

defined, 156

fingerprint authentication, 157-158

block ciphers, 214

B-Rate safe rating, 19

breach trends, 284-285

BS (British Standard) 7777, 65

BSIMM (Building Security in Maturity Model), 272

buffer overflow vulnerabilities, 27

business-to-business (B2B) processing, 3

businesses

attacks, 127

confidential classification, 68

continuity plans. See BCPs

impact analysis (BIA), 111, 114-115

information security career support, 9-10

organization structure, 10

sensitive classification, 68

C

CABs (change advisory boards), 271

Caesar cipher, 206

Cain and Abel password-cracking tool, 187

Canadian Trusted Computer Product Evaluation Criteria (CTCPEC), 87, 93

CANs (campus area networks), 233

carders, 282

careers

CBK

access control, 42, 292

architecture and design, 40, 297

business continuity and disaster recovery planning, 40, 299

cryptography, 42, 296-297

governance and risk management, 39, 294-295

legal regulations, investigations, and compliance, 41, 300

operations security, 42, 298

overview, 39

physical security, 41, 301

software development security, 43, 295

telecommunications and network security, 43, 293

certifications

benefits, 37-38

Certified Cyber Forensics Professional, 45

Certified Information Security Manager, 44

Certified Information Systems Auditor, 44

Certified in Risk and Information Systems Control, 44

Global Information Assurance Certifications, 44

HealthCare Information Security and Privacy Practitioner, 45

(ISC)2 specialization, 45

vendor-specific, 46

compliance/governance professionals, 10

demand, 4

education

Carnegie Mellon Master of Science in Information Security degrees, 4

Department of Homeland Security supported certificate programs, 6

multidisciplinary approaches, 7

popularity, 7

(ISC)2, 38-39

listing of, 9-10

Carnegie Mellon Master of Science in Information Security, 4

CBK (Common Body of Knowledge), 36

access control, 42, 292

architecture and design, 40, 297

business continuity and disaster recovery planning, 40, 299

cryptography, 42, 296-297

governance and risk management, 39, 294-295

legal regulations, investigations, and compliance, 41, 300

operations security, 42, 298

overview, 39

physical security, 41, 301

software development security, 43, 295

telecommunications and network security, 43, 293

CC (Common Criteria), 94

development, 94

Editorial Board (CCEB), 94

evaluation assurance

classes, 97-98

levels, 98-100

functional requirements classes, 96-97

packages, 95

Protection Profiles, 95-96

targets of evaluation, 95

website, 94

CCEB (CC Editorial Board), 94

CCFP (Certified Cyber Forensics Professional), 45

CCNP Security (Cisco Certified Network Professional Security), 46

CCSK (Certificate of Cloud Security Knowledge), 46

CEH (Certified Ethical Hacker), 46

CEM (Common Evaluation Methodology), 100

CEMEB (Common Evaluation Methodology Editorial Board), 100-101

Certificate of Cloud Security Knowledge (CCSK), 46

certificates (digital), 212-214

certifications

benefits, 37-38

CBK

access control, 42, 292

architecture and design, 40, 297

business continuity and disaster recovery planning, 40, 299

cryptography, 42, 296-297

governance and risk management, 39, 294-295

legal regulations, investigations, and compliance, 41, 300

operations security, 42, 298

overview, 39

physical security, 41, 301

software development security, 43, 295

telecommunications and network security, 43, 293

Certified Cyber Forensics Professional, 45

Certified Information Security Manager, 44

Certified Information Systems Auditor, 44

Certified in Risk and Information Systems Control, 44

Global Information Assurance Certifications, 44

HealthCare Information Security and Privacy Practitioner, 45

(ISC)2, 38-39, 45

vendor-specific, 46

Certified Cyber Forensics Professional (CCFP), 45

Certified Ethical Hacker (CEH), 46

Certified Information Security Manager (CISM), 44

Certified Information Systems Auditor (CISA), 44

Certified Information Systems Security Professional. *See* CISSPs

Certified in Risk and Information Systems Control (CRISC), 44

Certified Secure Software Lifecycle Professional (CSSLP), 45

chain emails, 311

change advisory boards (CABs), 271

change management controls, 168, 171

Chief Information Officers website, 3

Chief Information Security Officer (CISO), 73

CIA (confidentiality, integrity, availability) triad, 20-21

CIP (Critical Infrastructure Protection), 281

CISA (Certified Information Systems Auditor), 44

Cisco Certified Network Professional Security (CCNP Security), 46

CISM (Certified Information Security Manager), 44

CISO (Chief Information Security Officer), 73

CISSPs (Certified Information Systems Security Professionals), 36

Code of Ethics, 136-137

concentrations, 45

overview, 38

civil laws, 130

Clark and Wilson model, 102

classifications

assets/data, 67-68

military, 186

clearances (military), 186

closed systems, 85

cloud computing, 118, 254

Cloud Security Alliance (CSA), 46, 254

CloudArray website, 118

COBIT (Control Objectives for Information and Related Technology), 65

Code of Ethics (ISC)2, 136-137

Code of Fair Information Practices, 139

codebooks, 202

cold sites, 117

college certificate programs, 6

combination cards, 154

combination locks (physical access), 152

commercial encryption controls website, 201

Common Body of Knowledge. *See* CBK

Common Criteria. *See* CC

Common Evaluation Methodology (CEM), 100

Common Evaluation Methodology Editorial Board (CEMEB), 100-101

common laws, 130

intellectual property, 131-132

privacy, 133

FTC electronic commerce practices, 133

international, 133-134

United States, 134-135

communications

acceptable use policy example, 310

covert channels, 102-103

IPSec, 249-250
  authentication headers, 250
  Encapsulating Security Protocol, 251
  integrity value check, 250
  ISAKMP, 251-252
  key management, 253
  modes, 250
  security associations, 251
  security policies, 252
  VPNs, 253
OSI, 226
  Application Layer, 227
  Data Link Layer, 229
  Network Layer, 228
  overview, 226
  Physical Layer, 229
  Presentation Layer, 228
  protection, 231-232
  reference model, 227
  Session Layer, 228
  TCP/IP mapping, 229-231
  Transport Layer, 228
out-of-band, 252
complexity, 29
compliance, 41
  HIPAA, 320
    administrative procedures, 321
    physical safeguards, 321
    technical mechanisms/services, 322
  key areas of knowledge, 300
  professionals, 9-10
Computer and Information Systems Managers career information website, 4
computer-based covert channels, 103
computer crimes
  categories, 127
  DDoS attacks, 128
  DoS attacks, 128
  dumpster diving, 128

emanation eavesdropping, 129
embezzlement, 129
ethics
  Code of Fair Information Practices, 139
  Internet Activities Board Ethics and the Internet standard, 138
  (ISC)2 Code of Ethics, 136-137
  Ten Commandments of Computer Ethics, 138
forensics, 135-136
highly publicized instances, 129
information warfare, 129
laws
  administrative, 130
  intellectual property, 131-132
  judicial, 130
  legislative, 130
  privacy, 133-135
pedestrian methods, 129
rogue code, 128
social engineering, 128
software piracy, 128
spoofing, 128
Verizon Data Breach, 127
victims, 127
Computer Ethics Institute Ten Commandments of Computer Ethics, 138
computer forensics, 135-136
Computer Security Act, 134
Computerworld Magazine
  annual hiring forecast survey website, 10
  salary survey (2013) website, 4
confidential classification, 186
confidentiality. See also access controls
  Bell-LaPadula model, 101
  least privilege, 183
  models, 20
  synonyms, 20
confidentiality, integrity, availability (CIA) triad, 20

configuration controls, 168, 171

consequences/likelihood matrix (risks), 26

contact smart cards, 154

contactless smart cards, 154

Continuity Central website, 113

continuity. *See* **BCPs**

Control Objectives for Information and Related Technology (COBIT), 65

controls

    detection, 27

    dual, 29

    people, 29

    prevention, 27

    process, 29

    protection, 84-86

    responsive, 27

    risk analysis, 71

    technology, 29

covert channels, 102-103

cracking passwords, 187

C-Rate safe rating, 19

credit card fraud, 282

criminal laws, 131

CRISC (Certified in Risk and Information Systems Control), 44

Critical Infrastructure Protection (CIP), 281

cryptography, 201

    codebooks, 202

    digest-creation techniques, 209

    digital

       block ciphers, 214

       certificates, 212-214

       hashing functions, 214

       PPK implementation, 215-217

       signatures, 209-210

    history, 201

    key areas of knowledge, 296-297

    keys, 206

       asymmetric, 208

       Identification Friend or Foe (IFF) System, 208

       symmetric, 207

       types, 206

    NSA, 201

    overview, 42

    plain text, 202

    random number requirements, 203

    Secure Hashing Algorithm, 210

    strength, 203

    substitution ciphers, 206

    telegraphs, 202

    terminology, 201

    transposition encryption example, 203-205

cryptosystems, 203

CSA (Cloud Security Alliance), 46, 254

CSSLP (Certified Secure Software Lifecycle Professional), 45

CTCPEC (Canadian Trusted Computer Product Evaluation Criteria), 87, 93

custodians of information resources, 73

customer confidential classification, 68

cyber forensics, 45

cybercrimes

    breach trends, 284-285

    carders, 282

    definitions, 282

    phishing, 283

    spear phishing, 283

    Stuxnet worm, 284

    ZeuS Banking Trojan, 282-283

D

DAC (discretionary access control), 184

data

    backups, 172

    classifications, 67-68

confidentiality, 232

encryption standard (DES), 207

flow stack, 227-229

hiding, 84

integrity, 232

labels, 89

Data Link Layer (OSI), 229

DDoS (Distributed Denial of Service) attacks, 128

decryption keys, 206

asymmetric, 208

Identification Friend or Foe (IFF) System, 208

public-private. *See* PPK

symmetric, 207

types, 206

de facto policies, 65

defense in depth

defined, 22

dual controls, 29

networks

basic security infrastructures, 235

firewalls. *See* firewalls

IDSs, 245-248

IPSs, 248

routers, 236-237

physical access controls

badging, 152

keys/combination locks, 152

lighting, 153

perimeters, 151

security dogs, 153

process controls, 29

technology controls, 29

degaussing, 174

de jure policies, 65

demilitarized zone (DMZ) networks, 243

Denial of Service (DoS) attacks, 128

Department of Defense. *See* DOD

Department of Homeland Security supported certificate programs, 6

deployment (software), 270-271

DES (Data Encryption Standard), 207

design. *See* architecture and design

destroying media, 174

detection controls, 27

development

Common Criteria, 94

policies, 62-63

software. *See* SDLC

development phase (SDLC), 268-269

digital cryptography

block ciphers, 214

certificates, 212-214

hashing functions, 214

PPK implementation, 215

PGP, 216

SET, 217

S/MIME, 217

SSL, 215

TLS, 216

signatures, 209-210

digital signatures, 232

disaster recovery planning. *See* DRP

discretionary access control (DAC), 184

discretionary protection, 88

disposing, media, 173-174

Distributed Denial of Service (DDoS) attacks, 128

Division A (TCSEC), 90-91

Division B (TCSEC), 88-90

Division C (TCSEC), 88

Division D (TCSEC), 88

DMZ (demilitarized zone) networks, 243

documenting policies, 63

guidelines, 67

procedures, 67

regulations, 64-66

standards and baselines, 66

DOD (Department of Defense)

ARPANET, 229

security clearances, 70

TEMPEST program, 129

dogs (security), 153

domain protections, 89

DoS (Denial of Service) attacks, 128

DRP (disaster recovery planning)

alternate-site services providers, 116-117

cloud, 118

defined, 111

goals, 115

history, 111

mobile units, 118

multiple centers, 117

overview, 40

service bureaus, 118

shared-site agreements, 116

strategies, identifying, 116

testing, 118-119

dual controls, 29

duties, separating, 68-69

E

EALs (Evaluation Assurance Levels), 98-100

education. *See also* **certifications**

Carnegie Mellon Master of Science in Information Security degrees, 4

Department of Homeland Security supported certificate programs, 6

multidisciplinary approaches, 7

Electronic Communications Act, 134

email, 310-312

emanation eavesdropping, 129

embezzlement, 129

employee screenings, 69

Encapsulating Security Protocol (ESP), 251

encipherment, 232

encryption

keys, 206

asymmetric, 208

Identification Friend or Foe (IFF) System, 208

public-private. *See* PPK

symmetric, 207

types, 206

transposition example, 203-205

VPN, 317

enforcement, 310

environmental security. *See* **physical security**

ESP (Encapsulating Security Protocol), 251

ethical hackers, 46

ethics

Code of Fair Information Practices, 139

Internet Activities Board Ethics and the Internet standard, 138

(ISC)2 Code of Ethics, 136-137

Ten Commandments of Computer Ethics, 138

European Information Technology Security Evaluation Criteria. *See* **ITSEC**

evaluation models, 87

Common Criteria, 94

development, 94

Editorial Board (CCEB), 94

evaluation assurance classes, 97-98

evaluation assurance levels, 98-100

functional requirements classes, 96-97

packages, 95

Protection Profiles, 95-96

targets of evaluation, 95

website, 94

Common Evaluation Methodology Editorial Board, 100-101

CTCPEC, 93

Federal Criteria, 93

ITSEC, 91

assurance classes, 92-93

TCSEC, compared, 91

TCSEC
  Division A, 90-91
  Division B, 88-90
  Division C, 88
  Division D, 88
  European version. *See* ITSEC
  ITSEC, compared, 91
  overview, 87
  TNI, 91
exploits, 27
extranets, 234

F

facility controls
  access
    badging, 152
    keys/combination locks, 152
    lighting, 153
    perimeters, 151
    security dogs, 153
    site selections, 150
    visitors, 150
    work area restrictions, 150
  environmental/life safety, 158-159
  technical
    alarm systems, 156
    audit trails/access logs, 155
    biometrics, 156-157
    fingerprint authentication, 157-158
    intrusion detection, 155
    smart cards, 153-155
fail-secure system controls, 168
Fair Credit Reporting Act, 134
Fair Debt Collection Practices Act, 135
false negative errors (IDSs), 248
false positive errors (IDSs), 247
fastest growing occupations website, 4
FC (Federal Criteria) for Information Technology Security, 87, 93

fear, uncertainty, and doubt (FUD), 29
Federal Information Security Management Act, 135
Federal Trade Commission (FTC), 133
federated identities, 192
FFIEC (Federal Financial Institutions Examination Council), 64
File Transfer Protocol (FTP), 231
financial cybercrimes, 128
  breach trends, 284-285
  carders, 282
  definitions, 282
  phishing, 283
  spear phishing, 283
  ZeuS Banking Trojan, 282-283
Financial Services ISACs, 281
fingerprint authentication, 157-158
finite-state machines, 85
FIPS (Federal Information Processing Standard), 207
fire detection/suppression controls, 158-159
firewalls, 237
  application-level gateway, 239-241
    bastion hosts, 239-240
    benefits, 240
    costs, 238
    defined, 238
    limitations, 241
    proxy server characteristics, 239
  choosing, 245
  demilitarized zone, 243
  homing, 238
  packet-filtering, 241-242
  screened host, 242-243
  screened-subnet, 244
foreign nationals, 150
forensics, 135-136
forwarded emails, 311
FS-ISACs (Financial Services-Information Sharing and Analysis Centers), 281

FTC (Federal Trade Commission), 133
FTP (File Transfer Protocol), 231
FUD (fear, uncertainty, and doubt), 29
functional decomposition, 267
functional requirements, 24, 96-97

G

George Washington University in Washington, D.C. certificate programs, 6
GIACs (Global Information Assurance Certifications), 44
GLBA (Gramm-Leach-Bliley Act), 68
governance
  HIPAA
    administrative procedures, 321
    compliance, 320
    enforcement, 68
    overview, 65
    physical safeguards, 321
    technical mechanisms/services, 322
    WLANs, 60-61
  key areas of knowledge, 294-295
  managers, 10
  overview, 39
  policies
    de facto/de jure, 65
    documenting, 63
    effective, 55
    guidelines, 67
    implementation, 63
    issue-specific, 60
    operations, 63
    overview, 55
    procedures, 67
    programme-framework, 59
    programme-level, 57-59
    publishing, 55
    regulations, 64-66
    security objectives, 62

    standards and baselines, 66
    structure, 55
    system-specific, 61
    tools, 55
    types, 57
  responsibilities, 73
  standards
    asset and data classification, 67-68
    hiring practices, 69-70
    risk analysis, 70-72
    separation of duties, 68-69
    user education/training/awareness, 72
Gramm-Leach-Bliley Act (GLBA), 68
grudge attacks, 128

H

hardware segmentation, 84
hashing functions, 214
HCISPP (HealthCare Information Security and Privacy Practitioner), 45
healthcare
  HealthCare Information Security and Privacy Practitioner (HCISPP), 45
  HIPAA
    administrative procedures, 321
    compliance, 320
    enforcement, 68
    overview, 65
    physical safeguards, 321
    technical mechanisms/services, 322
    WLANs, 60-61
  WLAN security, 60-61
heating, ventilation, and air conditioning (HVAC) controls, 159
hiding data, 84
hierarchy, 83
HIPAA (Health Insurance Portability and Accountability Act of 1996), 65, 135
  administrative procedures, 321
  compliance, 320

enforcement, 68

overview, 65

physical safeguards, 321

technical mechanisms/services, 322

WLANs, 60-61

hiring practices, 69-70

homing, 238

hot sites, 116

human covert channels, 103

**HVAC (heating, ventilation, and air condition-
ing) controls, 159**

I

**ICMP (Internet Control Message
Protocol), 231**

identification

authentication, 183

fingerprint, 157-158

headers (IPSec), 250

multifactor, 188-189

networks, 231

overview, 183

passwords, 186-189

VPN, 317

biometrics, 189-190

credentials, 183

Friend or Foe (IFF) System, 208

identity theft, 282

IDs (users), 169

IDSs (intrusion detection systems), 245-246

false negative errors, 248

false positive errors, 247

good characteristics, 247

intrusions, defined, 246-247

subversion errors, 248

IETF (Internet Engineering Task Force), 249

IFF (Identification Friend or Foe) System, 208

incident response team members, 9

information

flow model, 102

owners, 184

resources managers, 73

storage, 84

warfare attacks, 129

**Information Sharing and Analysis Centers
(ISACs), 281**

**Information Technology Security Evaluation
Criteria (ITSEC), 87**

InfoSec

organization structure, 10

professionals future, 285

umbrella, 7

integrity. *See also* **access control**

Biba model, 102

models, 21

value check (IVC), 250

verification, 173

intellectual property law, 131-132

intelligence attacks, 127

interdependencies (operations), 175-176

internal auditors, 73

**International Information Systems Security
Certifications Consortium.** *See* **(ISC)2**

international privacy laws, 133-134

International Safe Harbor Principles, 134

Internet, 233

Activities Board Ethics and the Internet
standard, 138

Assigned Numbers Authority, 230

Control Message Protocol (ICMP), 231

Engineering Task (IETF), 249

Protocol (IP), 230

Protocol address spoofing, 128

Security Association and Key Management
Protocol (ISAKMP), 251-252

as store-and-forward network, 234

intranets, 234

intrusion detection systems. *See* IDSs

intrusions, 246-247

investigations, 41, 300

IP (Internet Protocol), 230

IP address spoofing, 128

IPSec, 249-250

   authentication headers, 250

   Encapsulating Security Protocol, 251

   integrity value check, 250

   ISAKMP, 251-252

   key management, 253

   modes, 250

   security

      associations, 251

      policies, 252

   VPNs, 253

IPSs (intrusion prevention systems), 248

ISACs (Information Sharing and Analysis Centers), 281

ISAKMP (Internet Security Association and Key Management Protocol), 251-252

(ISC)2 (International Information Systems Security Certification Consortium)

   CBK

      access control, 42, 292

      architecture and design, 40, 297

      business continuity and disaster recovery planning, 40, 299

      cryptography, 42, 296-297

      governance and risk management, 39, 294-295

      legal regulations, investigations, and compliance, 41, 300

      operations security, 42, 298

      overview, 39

      physical security, 41, 301

      software development security, 43, 295

      telecommunications and network security, 43, 293

   certification benefits, 37-38

   Code of Ethics, 136-137

   goals, 38

   primary designations, 38

   specialization certificates, 45

   website, 39

ISO/IEC, 39

ISO/IEC "Code of Practice for Information Security Management," 65, 302-304

issue-specific policies, 60

IT job demand website, 285

ITSEC (Information Technology Security Evaluation Criteria), 87

   assurance classes, 92-93

   TCSEC, compared, 91

IVC (integrity value check), 250

J

John the Ripper, 187

judicial laws. *See* common laws

K

Kennedy-Kassenbaum Health Insurance and Portability Accountability Act. *See* HIPAA

Kerberos, 191

keys, 206

   asymmetric, 208

   Identification Friend or Foe (IFF) System, 208

   IPSec management, 253

   public/private. *See* PPK

   symmetric, 207

   types, 206

keys (physical access), 152

Krebs on Security website, 285

L

labeling data/media, 89, 172

LANs (Local Area Networks), 233

LaPadula, Leonard J., 101

laws

administrative, 130

common, 130

intellectual property, 131-132

legislative, 130

privacy, 133

FTC electronic commerce practices, 133

international, 133-134

United States, 134-135

layered security. *See* defense in depth

layering, 84

least privilege, 183

legal regulations, 41, 300

legislative laws, 130

life safety controls, 158-159

lighting, 153

Local Area Networks (LANs), 233

logging

media, 172

networks, 232

M

MAC (mandatory access control), 185

maintenance, 174-175

man made disaster events, 113

mandatory protection, 88-90

MANs (metropolitan area networks), 233

mantraps, 152

marking media, 172

Mary, Queen of Scots (cryptography), 202

Master of Science in Information Security (Carnegie Mellon), 4

maturity measurement models (software), 272

media controls, 172

disposition, 173-174

environmental protection, 173

integrity verification, 173

logging, 172

marking/labeling, 172

physical access protection, 173

transmittal, 173

viability, 169

memory cards, 154

metropolitan area networks (MANs), 233

military

attacks, 127

classifications/clearances, 70, 186

minimal protection, 88

mitigation planning, 267

mobile units, 118

monitoring networks, 232

Monroe Community College in Rochester, New York degree programs, 6

motion detectors, 156

Multics (Multiplexed Information and Computing Service), 82

multidisciplinary education approaches, 7

multifactor authentication, 188-189

multihomed firewalls, 238

multiple center arrangements, 117

Multiplexed Information and Computing Service (Multics), 82

multiprogramming systems, 85

multitasking, 85

music piracy, 131

N

NAT (network address translation), 245

National Council of ISACs, 281

National Retail Security Survey (NRSS), 147

National Security Agency (NSA), 201

National Security Directive 42 (NSD-42), 135

National Training Standard for Information Systems Security Professionals, 65

natural disaster events, 113

natural justice, 130

Naval Postgraduate School for Homeland Defense and Security, 6

NDCI (National Data Conversion Institute), 136

NetIQ website, 55

network address translation (NAT), 245

Network Layer (OSI), 228

networks

  acceptable use policy example, 308-309

  access control, 232

  authentication, 231

  basic security infrastructures, 235

  cloud, 254

  data confidentiality, 232

  data integrity, 232

  extranets, 234

  firewalls, 237

    application-level gateway, 238-241

    choosing, 245

    demilitarized zone, 243

    homing, 238

    packet-filtering, 241-242

    screened host, 242-243

    screened-subnet, 244

  IDSs, 245-246

    false negative errors, 248

    false positive errors, 247

    good characteristics, 247

    intrusions, defined, 246-247

    subversion errors, 248

  Internet. *See* Internet

  intranets, 234

  IPSec, 249-250

    authentication headers, 250

    Encapsulating Security Protocol, 251

    integrity value check, 250

    ISAKMP, 251-252

    key management, 253

    modes, 250

    security associations, 251

    security policies, 252

    VPNs, 253

  IPSs, 248

  key areas of knowledge, 293

  LANs, 233

  logging/monitoring, 232

  NAT, 245

  nonrepudiation, 232

  OSI. *See* OSI

  out-of-band communications, 252

  overview, 43

  protecting from attacks, 231-232

  rings of trust, 83

  routers, 236-237

  security appliances, 241

  VPNs

    IPSec-based, 253

    overview, 249

  WANs, 233

  wireless (WiFi), 317-318

NFRs (nonfunctional requirements), 265

Nilson Report website, 284

noninterference model, 102

nonrepudiation, 232

Northeastern University in Boston degree programs, 6

notarization, 232

NRSS (National Retail Security Survey), 147

NSA (National Security Agency), 201

NSD-42 (National Security Directive 42), 135

NSTISSC (National Security Telecommunications and Information Systems Security Committee) Standard 4011, 65

O

Oakley Key Determination Protocol, 252

Ohio State University degree programs, 6

one-time passwords (OTPs), 189

Open PGP, 217

open systems, 85

Open Systems Interconnection. See OSI

Open Web Application Security Project. See OWASP

OpenSAMM (Open Software Assurance Maturity Model), 272

Operation Eligible Receiver, 281

operations

  backups, 172

  configuration and change management, 171

  documentation, 174

  interdependencies, 175-176

  key areas of knowledge, 298

  maintenance, 174-175

  media controls, 172

    disposition, 173-174

    environmental protection, 173

    integrity verification, 173

    logging, 172

    marking/labeling, 172

    physical access protection, 173

    transmittal, 173

  overview, 42

  process controls, 168-169

  separation of duties, 167-168

  software support, 171

organization structure, 10

OSI (Open Systems Interconnection), 226

  ISO security services, 231-232

  layers

    Application, 227

    Data Link, 229

    Network, 228

    Physical, 229

    Presentation, 228

    reference model, 227

    Session, 228

    Transport, 228

  overview, 226

  TCP/IP mapping, 229-231

OTPs (one-time passwords), 189

out-of-band communications, 252

overwriting, 174

OWASP (Open Web Application Security Project), 268

  OpenSAMM, 272

  Top Ten, 268

owners of information resources, 73

P

packet filtering, 236-237

  basic, 236

  benefits, 236

  firewalls, 241-242

  limitations, 237

  stateful inspection, 236

Password Safe website, 190

passwords

  cracking, 187

  creating, 188

  problems, 186

  sample policy, 312-316

    application development, 315

    creating, 313-314

    definitions, 316

    enforcement, 316

    general, 313

    passphrases, 316

    protection standards, 314-315

    purpose, 312

    remote access, 316

    scope, 312

  strong, 314

  tokens, 189

  vault, creating, 190

  weak, 314

Patent and Trademark Office (PTO), 131

patents, 131

Patriot Act HR 3162, 135

PDD (Presidential Decision Directive) 63, 281
Peeler, Julie, 285
peer reviews (software development), 269
people controls, 29
people, process, and technology triad, 29
perfect forward secrecy (PFS), 252
perimeter intrusion and detection assessment system (PIDAS), 151
perimeter security controls, 151, 156
personnel
  controls, 169
  education, 149
PFS (perfect forward secrecy), 252
PGP (Pretty Good Privacy), 216
phishing, 23, 192
  financial crimes, 283
  preventing, 23
Physical Layer (OSI), 229
physical security, 41
  access controls, 149-150
  badging, 152
  educating personnel, 149
  environmental/life safety, 158-159
  goal, 147
  key areas of knowledge, 301
  keys/combination locks, 152
  lighting, 153
  media protection, 173
  overview, 147
  perimeters, 151
  security dogs, 153
  technical
    alarm systems, 156
    audit trails/access logs, 155
    biometrics, 156-157
    fingerprint authentication, 157-158
    intrusion detection, 155
    smart cards, 153-155
  threats, 148

PIDAS (perimeter intrusion and detection assessment system), 151
PIN vaults, creating, 190
PKI (public key infrastructures), 206-208
plain text, 202
policies
  de facto/de jure, 65
  developing, 62-63
  effective, 55
  outline, 302-304
  overview, 55
  publishing, 55
  standards
    asset and data classification, 67-68
    hiring practices, 69-70
    risk analysis, 70-72
    separation of duties, 68-69
    user education/training/awareness, 72
  structure, 55
  supporting documents
    guidelines, 67
    procedures, 67
    regulations, 64-66
    standards and baselines, 66
  tools, 55
  types, 57
    issue-specific, 60
    programme-framework, 59
    programme-level, 57-59
    system-specific, 61
policymakers, 9
power controls, 158
PPs (Protection Profiles), 95-96
PPK (public-private key cryptography), 215
  digital certificates, 212-214
  digital signatures, 209-212
  implementations, 215
    PGP, 216
    SET, 217

S/MIME, 217
SSL, 215
TLS, 216
Presentation Layer (OSI), 228
President Clinton, PDD63, 281
Presidential Decision Directive (PDD) 63, 281
Pretty Good Privacy (PGP), 216
privacy laws, 133
    FTC electronic commerce practices, 133
    international, 133-134
    United States, 134-135
private keys. See PPK
privileged entity controls, 169
probability, calculating, 71
process controls, 29, 168
    backups, 172
    configuration and change management, 168, 171
    documentation, 174
    interdependencies, 175-176
    maintenance, 174-175
    media, 172
        disposition, 173-174
        environmental protection, 173
        integrity verification, 173
        logging, 172
        marking/labeling, 172
        physical access protection, 173
        transmittal, 173
    media viability, 169
    personnel, 169
    privileged entity controls, 169
    record retention, 169
    resource protection, 169
    software support, 171
    SOX, 169
    trusted recovery, 168
programme-framework policies, 59
programme-level policies, 57-59

protection
    discretionary, 88
    mandatory, 88-90
    minimal, 88
    profiles (PPs), 95-96
    structured, 89
    TCB, 84-86
    verified, 90-91
protocols
    ARP, 230
    ESP, 251
    ICMP, 231
    IP, 230
    ISAKMP, 251-252
    Kerberos, 191
    Oakley Key Determination, 252
    OSI stack
        Application Layer, 227
        Data Link Layer, 229
        Network Layer, 228
        overview, 226
        Physical Layer, 229
        Presentation Layer, 228
        reference model, 227
        Session Layer, 228
        Transport Layer, 228
    PGP, 216
    RARP, 230
    SET, 217
    SKEP, 253
    SKIP, 253
    S/MIME, 217
    SMTP, 231
    SSL, 215
    TCP, 230
    TCP/IP
        applications, 231
        OSI model, mapping, 229-231
        protocols, 230-231

TLS, 216
UDP, 230
provisioning users, 184
proxy servers, 239
PTO (Patent and Trademark Office), 131
public information classification, 68
public key infrastructures (PKI), 206-208
public-private key cryptography. *See* PPK

Q

qualitative risk analysis, 71-72
quantitative risk analysis, 70-71
Queen Elizabeth I plot (cryptography), 202

R

RADIUS (Remote Access Dial-In User Service), 193
random number requirements (cryptography), 203
RARP (Reverse Address Resolution Protocol), 230
ratings
    risks, 26
    safes, 19
RBAC (role-based access control), 185
record retention, 169
recovery planning. *See also* BCPs
    alternate-site services providers, 116-117
    cloud, 118
    defined, 111
    goals, 115
    history, 111
    identifying, 116
    key areas of knowledge, 299
    mobile units, 118
    multiple centers, 117
    service bureaus, 118
    shared-site agreements, 116
    testing, 118-119

regulatory laws, 131
remote access control, 192-193
Remote Access Dial-In User Service (RADIUS), 193
remote login (Telnet), 231
replay attacks, 250
requirements gathering and analysis phase (SDLC), 265-266
resource protection, 169
responsibilities, 73
responsive controls, 27
Reverse Address Resolution Protocol (RARP), 230
rings of trust, 81
    implementing, 84
    networks, 83
    ring hierarchy, 83
    stand-alone systems, 82
risks, 39
    analysis
        consequences/likelihood, 26
        qualitative, 71-72
        quantitative, 70-71
    attackers, 27
    exploits, 27
    key area of knowledge, 294-295
    outcomes, 25
    vulnerabilities, 27
rogue code, 128
role-based access control (RBAC), 185
ROT13 cipher, 206
routers, 236-237
routing controls, 232
RSA Security 2011 breach website, 192

S

Safe Harbor Privacy Principles, 134
safe ratings, 19

SANS Security Policy Project
acceptable use, 306-308
definitions, 310
email/communications, 310
enforcement, 310
general use and ownership, 307
proprietary information, 307
purpose, 307
revision history, 310
scope, 307
system/network activities, 308-309
unacceptable use, 308
email, 310-312
passwords, 312-316
application development, 315
creating, 313-314
definitions, 316
enforcement, 316
general, 313
passphrases, 316
protection standards, 314-315
purpose, 312
remote access, 316
scope, 312
website, 306
WiFi, 317-318
SAP (special access programs), 186
Sarbanes-Oxley Corporate Responsibility and Accountability Act (SOX), 64, 169
SAs (security associations), 251
SCI (sensitive compartmented information), 186
screened host firewalls, 242-243
screened-subnet firewalls, 244
Scrum software methodology, 262
SDLC (Software Development Life Cycle), 263
built-in security, 263-264
deployment, 270-271
design reviews, 267
development, 268-269
key areas of knowledge, 295
maturity measurement models, 272
phases, 263
requirements gathering and analysis, 265-266
security overview, 265
testing, 270
threat modeling, 266-267
training, 272
Search Security Magazine information security career popularity, 7
SEC (Securities and Exchange Commission), 64
secret classification, 186
Secure Electronic Transactions (SET), 217
Secure Hash Algorithm (SHA), 210
Secure/Multipurpose Internet Mail Extensions (S/MIME), 217
Secure Sockets Layer (SSL), 215
security
administrators, 9
architects, 9
associations (SAs), 251
consultants, 9
dogs, 153
models, 101-102
policy database (SPD), 252
policy project. *See* SANS Security Policy Project
testers, 9
through obscurity, 25
sensitive compartmented information (SCI), 186
sensitive information emails, 311
separation of duties, 29, 167
benefits, 167
importance, 167
production operations, 168
standards, 68-69
servers, 239

service bureaus, 118

Service Organization Controls, 170

Service Set Identifier (SSID), 317

session laws. *See statutory laws*

Session Layer (OSI), 228

SET (Secure Electronic Transactions), 217

SHA (Secure Hash Algorithm), 210

SHA-3 Cryptographic Hash Algorithm Competition, 210

shared-site agreements, 116

signatures (digital), 209-210

single-homed firewalls, 238

single sign-on. *See SSO*

site access controls. *See facility controls*

SKEP (Simple Key Exchange Protocol), 253

SKIP (Simple Key Interchange Protocol), 253

smart cards, 153-155

S/MIME (Secure/Multipurpose Internet Mail Extensions), 217

SMTP (Simple Mail Transfer Protocol), 231

social engineering, 128

software

    agile development, 262

    attack surfaces, 267

    backups, 172

    development life cycle (SDLC)

        built-in security, 263-264

        deployment, 270-271

        design reviews, 267

        development, 268-269

        key areas of knowledge, 295

        maturity measurement models, 272

        phases, 263

        requirements gathering and analysis, 265-266

        security overview, 265

        testing, 270

        threat modeling, 266-267

        training, 272

    maturity measurement models, 272

    piracy, 128

    quality, 261

    spaghetti code, 262

    support, 171

    writing, 261

something you have plus something you know plus something you are (SYH/SYK/SYA), 189

something you have plus something you know (SYH/SYK), 188

SOX (Sarbanes-Oxley) Act, 64, 169

spaghetti code, 262

SPD (security policy database), 252

spear phishing, 283

special access programs (SAP), 186

spoofing, 128

SSAE 16 (Statement on Standards for Attestation Engagements), 170

SSCP (Systems Security Certified Practitioner), 36-38

SSID (Service Set Identifier), 317

SSL (Secure Sockets Layer), 215

SSO (single sign-on), 190

    federated identities, 192

    Kerberos, 191

standards

    asset and data classification, 67-68

    developers, 9

    hiring practices, 69-70

    outline, 302-304

    policy support, 66

    risk analysis, 70-72

        qualitative, 71-72

        quantitative, 70-71

    separation of duties, 68-69

    user education/training/awareness, 72

state machine model, 102

stateful inspection packet-filtering, 236

Statement on Standards for Attestation Engagements (SSAE), 16, 170

static analysis, 269

statutory laws, 130

storage, 84

straight packet-filtering, 236

strong passwords, 314

structured protections, 89

Stuxnet worm, 284

substitution ciphers, 206

subversion errors (IDSs), 248

SYH/SYK (something you have plus something you know), 188

SYH/SYK/SYA (something you have plus something you know plus something you are), 189

symmetric keys, 206-207

system-specific policies, 61

Systems Security Certified Practitioner (SSCP), 36-38

T

Target Corporation breach, 284

targets of evaluation (TOE), 95

TCB (Trusted Computing Base), 81

  defined, 81

  protections

    discretionary, 88

    mandatory, 88-90

    mechanisms, 84-86

    minimal, 88

    verified, 90-91

  rings of trust, 81

    implementing, 84

    networks, 83

    ring hierarchy, 83

    stand-alone systems, 82

TCP (Transmission Control Protocol), 230

TCP/IP (Transmission Control Protocol/ Internet Protocol)

  applications, 231

  OSI model, mapping, 229-231

  protocols, 230-231

TCSEC (Trusted Computer System Evaluation Criteria)

  Division A, 90-91

  Division B, 88-90

  Division C, 88

  Division D, 88

  European version. *See* ITSEC

  ITSEC, compared, 91

  overview, 87

  TNI, 91

technical access controls

  alarm systems, 156

  audit trails/access logs, 155

  biometrics, 156-157

  fingerprint authentication, 157-158

  intrusion detection, 155

  smart cards, 153-155

technical managers, 73

technology controls, 29

telecommunications

  key areas of knowledge, 293

  overview, 43

telegraphs, 202

Telnet (remote login), 231

TEMPEST program, 129

Ten Commandments of Computer Ethics, 138

terrorist attacks, 128

testing

  DRP, 118-119

  goals, 86

  models, 91

  safe ratings, 19

  software, 270

  unit, 269

threats

breach trends, 284-285

carders, 282

categorizing, 267

disposed media, 174

identifying, 113-114

man made, 113

modeling (SDLC), 266-267

natural, 113

OWASP Top Ten, 268

password cracking, 187

phishing, 192, 283

physical security, 148

ranking, 267

risk analysis, 71

spear phishing, 283

Stuxnet worm, 284

ZeuS Banking Trojan, 282-283

three-factor authentication, 189

thrill attacks, 128

TJX Corporation breach, 284

TLS (Transport Layer Security), 216

TNI (Trusted Network Interpretation), 91

TOE (targets of evaluation), 95

tokens (passwords), 189

tools

password-cracking, 187

policies, 55

top secret classification, 186

trade secrets, 68, 132

trademarks, 132

traffic padding, 232

training

software development, 272

users/personnel, 72, 149

Transmission Control Protocol (TCP), 230

Transmission Control Protocol/Internet Protocol. See TCP/IP

transmitting media, 173

Transport Layer (OSI), 228

Transport Layer Security (TLS), 216

transposition encryption example, 203-205

Triple DES (3DES), 207

Trusted Computer System Evaluation Criteria. See TCSEC

Trusted Computing Base (TCB), 81

Trusted Network Interpretation (TNI), 91

trusted recovery controls, 168

TwinStrata CloudArray website, 118

two-factor authentication, 188

U

UDP (User Datagram Protocol), 230

UL (Underwriters Laboratory) TL-15 safe rating, 19

UL (Underwriters Laboratory) TL-30 safe rating, 20

umbrella (InfoSec), 7

unauthorized disclosure emails, 312

unit testing, 269

United States

Department of Defense

ARPANET, 229

security clearances, 70

TEMPEST program, 129

Department of Health and Human Services Code of Fair Information Practices, 139

government

classification labels, 186

information system vulnerability demonstration, 281

laws, 130

National Security Agency, 201

National Security Telecommunications and Information Systems Security Committee (NSTISSC) Standard 4011, 65

privacy laws, 134-135

University of Houston Security Manual website, 73

USA PATRIOT ACT (Uniting and Strengthening America by Providing Appropriate Tools Required to Intercept and Obstruct Terrorism), 135

User Datagram Protocol (UDP), 230

users

access control. *See* access controls

access requests, 28

authentication, 183

fingerprint, 157-158

headers (IPSec), 250

multifactor, 188-189

networks, 231

overview, 183

passwords, 186-189

VPN, 317

bad security decisions, 24

education/training/awareness, 72

IDs, 169

identification, 183

information owners, 184

least privilege, 183

provisioning, 184

responsibilities, 73

V

vendor managers, 10

vendor-specific certification programs, 46

verification

integrity, 173

protections, 90-91

Verizon Data Breach, 127

virus warning emails, 312

visitor controls, 150

VPNs (virtual private networks), 193, 249

encryption/authentication, 317

IPSec-based, 253

overview, 249

vulnerabilities

defined, 27

disclosing, 28

open disclosure, 30

Operation Eligible Receiver, 281

OWASP Top Ten, 268

risk analysis, 71

W

WANs (Wide Area Networks), 233

warm sites, 117

weak passwords, 314

websites

2013 Computerworld Salary Survey, 4

Advanced Study of Information Warfare, 129

Amazon.com book ordering patents, 132

Bell Laboratories "Conversion of Numerical Information" patent, 132

Carnegie, 4

CCNP Security certificate, 46

Certificate of Cloud Security Knowledge, 46

Chief Information Officers, 3

The Cloud Security Alliance, 254

CloudArray, 118

Code of Fair Information Practices, 139

commercial encryption controls, 201

Common Criteria, 94

Computer and Information Systems Managers career information, 4

Computerworld Magazine annual hiring forecast survey, 10

Continuity Central, 113

ethical hackers, 46

fastest growing occupations, 4

Financial Services ISACs, 281

FTC electronic commerce privacy practices, 133

GIAC certifications, 44

Identification Friend or Foe (IFF) System, 208

Internet
  Activities Board Ethics and the Internet standard, 139
  Assigned Numbers Authority, 230
(ISC)2, 39
ISO/IEC, 39
ISO/IEC 17799, "Code of Practice for Information Security Management," 65
IT job demand, 285
Krebs on Security, 285
music piracy, 131
NAT, 245
National Council of ISACs, 281
Naval Postgraduate School for Homeland Defense and Security, 6
NetIQ, 55
Nilson Report, 284
NRSS, 147
NSTISSC Number 4011, 66
OWASP Top Ten, 268
password-cracking tools, 187
password/PIN vaults, creating, 190
Password Safe, 190
Patent and Trademark Office, 131
RBAC, 185
RSA Security 2011 breach, 192
SANS Security Policy Project, 306
Scrum Alliance, 262
Search Security Magazine information security career popularity, 7
Secure Hash Standard, 210
SHA-3 Cryptographic Hash Algorithm Competition, 210
SSAE 16, 170
Stuxnet worm, 284
Ten Commandments of Computer Ethics, 138
TJX Corporation breach, 284
TNI, 91
University of Houston Security Manual, 73

U.S. government classification labels, 186
vendor-specific certification programs, 46
Verizon Data Breach, 127
ZeuS Banking Trojan, 283
Whitworth Gallery art theft, 19
Wide Area Networks (WANs), 233
WiFi (wireless networks), 317-318
  access points/cards registration, 317
  approved technology, 317
  definitions, 318
  enforcement, 318
  scope, 317
  SSID, 317
  VPN encryption/authentication, 317
WLANs, healthcare security, 60-61
work area controls, 150
writing software, 261

X – Z

X.509 digital certificate standard, 212

Zimmerman, Phil, 216

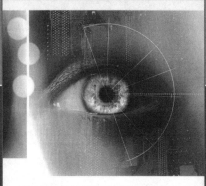

FREE
Online Edition

INFORMATION SECURITY
PRINCIPLES AND PRACTICES

SECOND EDITION

MARK S. MERKOW • JIM BREITHAUPT

Your purchase of *Information Security: Principles and Practices* includes access to a free online edition for 45 days through the **Safari Books Online** subscription service. Nearly every Pearson IT Certification book is available online through **Safari Books Online**, along with thousands of books and videos from publishers such as Addison-Wesley Professional, Cisco Press, Exam Cram, IBM Press, O'Reilly Media, Prentice Hall, Que, Sams, and VMware Press.

Safari Books Online is a digital library providing searchable, on-demand access to thousands of technology, digital media, and professional development books and videos from leading publishers. With one monthly or yearly subscription price, you get unlimited access to learning tools and information on topics including mobile app and software development, tips and tricks on using your favorite gadgets, networking, project management, graphic design, and much more.

Activate your FREE Online Edition at
informit.com/safarifree

STEP 1:   Enter the coupon code: EITWXFA.

STEP 2:   New Safari users, complete the brief registration form.
            Safari subscribers, just log in.

If you have difficulty registering on Safari or accessing the online edition,
please e-mail customer-service@safaribooksonline.com

   Addison Wesley Adobe Press   ALPHA Cisco Press  Press FINANCIAL TIMES IBM Press Microsoft Press New Riders O'REILLY Peachpit Press PRENTICE HALL que Redbooks SAMS SAS Publishing vmware PRESS WILEY wrox